On Literacy and Its Teaching

SUNY Series, Literacy, Culture, and Learning: Theory and Practice
Alan C. Purves, Editor

On Literacy and Its Teaching

Issues in English Education

Edited by

Gail E. Hawisher
&
Anna O. Soter

State University of New York Press

Published by
State University of New York Press, Albany

Printed in the United States of America

For information, address State University of New York
Press, State University Plaza, Albany, N.Y., 12246

Library of Congress Cataloging-in-Publication Data

On literacy and its teaching : issues in English education / Gail E.
Hawisher and Anna O. Soter, [editors].
p. cm.
Includes index.
ISBN 0-7914-0265-7. — ISBN 0-7914-0266-5 (pbk.)
1. English language—Study and teaching (Secondary)—United
States. 2. English teachers—Training of—United States.
I. Hawisher, Gail E. II. Soter, Anna O., 1946- .
LB1631.056 1990
428′.0071′273—dc20 89-35802
CIP

10 9 8 7 6 5 4 3 2 1

To our children—
Lance, Dayle, Benjamin—
and their many English
teachers.

Contents

Part III: Rhetoric and Composition: Designs for Integration

Part IV: The Learning of Language: Teachers and Their Students

Foreword

On Literacy and its Teaching is the inaugural volume in the series *Literacy, Culture, and Learning: Theory and Practice.* The series seeks to provide a set of volumes that encompass the range of scholarly disciplines concerned with literacy and its relation to culture and society, with particular emphasis on the learning of literature practices. The view of literacy is that it is a culturally embedded activity at once individual and social. We read and write alone, but we do so in settings and contexts that shape how we read and write.

One of these settings is the school, and this volume addresses particular issues related to the culture of the secondary school in the United States and its present and future directions. Schooling in literacy in the United States has gone through a series of shifts in emphasis over the past thirty years. The 1950s had an emphasis on social development, which was followed in the post-Sputnik era by an emphasis on the nature of the subject, English, to be learned. Such an emphasis was challenged in the 1950s by a developmental perspective that emphasized the "growth" of the child. The pragmatic need for the schools to teach basic skills came into focus in the 1970s and was followed in the 1980s by an emphasis on "excellence" and the competition of the United States with other industrialized nations as well as a realization of the importance of multilingualism and multiculturalism in an information age.

Of course, these shifts in emphasis represent less radical swings than accretions, so that the newer emphasis does not replace the prior ones but places an additional burden upon the schools and the teachers. It also places an additional burden upon those who would train teachers. Gail Hawisher and Anna Soter have brought together a volume that seeks to reflect not only the latest thinking about the teaching and learning of language, literature, and writing but also to consider that thinking within a historical and practical perspective. The volume is not a methods book but a book that is ultimately concerned with method in teaching literacy in the United States. Method is to be seen as the serious consideration of how students best learn to operate in a complex symbol system and to go about the activity of producing and comprehending texts. Method is to be seen also as the systematic way by which those formal institutions called schools using professional teachers and the best of modern technology can best abet student learning.

This volume goes further than other recent books dealing with literacy in the schools, most of which deal with a single aspect of the field. Hawisher and Soter seek, through the authors and topics they have selected, to effect a synthesis among reading, writing, language study, and literature. They also seek to bring together authors who do not subscribe to a single ideology of literacy and literacy education but who try to balance and explore the competing ideologies. Such a book addresses a need for a synthesis across perspectives and provides a preface for planning in literacy education and in the training of teachers. It becomes, I believe, a reference point for any who would write about teaching or engage in the preparation or retraining of teachers of literacy in the secondary schools of the United States.

Alan C. Purves

Preface

During the past few years the field of teacher education in general and of English education specifically has received a great deal of attention. One need only to consider the 1986 recommendations of the The Holmes Group's report, *Tomorrow's Teachers,* and the Carnegie Forum on Education and the Economy, *A Nation Prepared,* to realize the magnitude of the proposed changes for teacher education. Each, for example, advocates a plan of study leading to a bachelor's degree in arts and sciences, with teachers studying professional and pedagogical issues in education primarily at the graduate level. As we consider these reforms, we need also to probe important issues that remain unresolved for our profession. Because we know little of how teachers learn to teach, can we say, for example, that a greater number of subject matter courses or an increased number of years of schooling will result in better English teachers? Do we know how in-service training and other efforts aimed at the professional development of teachers influence the way experienced educators work with students? What does a historical perspective show us? What is new or different about reform today and are there assurances that today's efforts will be more productive than those of the past? What about teacher competency testing? Can we suggest that rigorous testing of teachers will result in improved teaching? Some would argue that instead of serving to professionalize teachers, standardized testing measures little of what is essential to instruction and may prevent an already dwindling number of teachers of color from joining our forces. These questions are among the many that need to be addressed as calls for change circulate in our journals and in the popular press. Highlighted in this book, then, are issues that must be discussed with prospective teachers, as well as with teachers in the field, because no meaningful reform of education in our society can occur without their full participation. Several of the essays included in this collection serve as a springboard for discussion surrounding educational reform.

Other developments within the field of English itself have challenged conventional thinking regarding students and the teaching of language, literature, and writing. In July 1987, at a specially convened Coalition Conference for organizations concerned with the teaching of English, sixty English educators from elementary schools, high schools, and colleges met for three weeks to discuss current practices and issues affecting English education. Because E. D. Hirsch's *Cultural Literacy: What Every American Needs to Know* had just been published and because it was invoked by the opening spokesman at this conference, some of the discussion was a necessary reaction to ideas expressed in Hirsch's book (Booth viii). (See *The English Coalition Conference: Democracy through Language,* which has appeared as this book goes to press.) Also discussed at this important gathering were recent developments in literary and rhetorical theory that seem to hold promise for English pedagogy at all levels. The recommendations from this Coalition Conference, along with the kinds of thinking that gave rise to the meeting in the first place, are all subjects of significance for teachers of English and are included in this volume.

This collection, then, grows out of a perception that English education is changing and that preservice and in-service teachers need to be participants in curricular and professional reforms that affect both them and their students. Our goal is to present English teachers with a critical view of professional concerns, with an informed perspective of new developments in research, theory, and practice, and in doing so invite them into the larger arena of educational discourse. A theme sustained throughout the book is the need to professionalize English teachers as decisionmakers in the shaping of policies and in the designing of curricula for the comprehensive field of English education.

We envision this book as integral to several courses directed at teachers and teacher educators in various stages of preparation. Faculty might select this volume as the central text for any of these courses, courses characterized by at least three different groups of students. The first group consists of preservice English teachers who are enrolled in methods courses or seminars that accompany their field experiences in the schools. Another group includes those teachers who are already employed but who often take graduate courses while teaching or during summers for professional development and for advancement in the school. Yet another group consists of graduate students from diverse backgrounds preparing to be teacher educators.

Often these groups are perceived as desiring only immediate practical applications for the classroom. We disagree with this assumption and believe that this collection—with its balanced view of educational issues as well as its reliance on theory and research to inform pedagogy—will find a ready audience among English educators.

Although some of the pedagogical issues and applications in the teaching of English are discussed in separate volumes devoted to writing, literature, or language instruction, no recent collection of which we are aware attempts to combine the whole into a single volume. That is, we have found no current anthology that addresses professional concerns as well as research and theory, along with their relation to curricula in English. Nor are the available texts commonly aimed at the secondary preservice or in-service English teacher; rather they focus on both elementary and high school teaching. We believe that many of the problems facing high school teachers are decidedly different from those in the elementary school and, as such, warrant separate treatment. As prospective teachers prepare for their careers and as experienced teachers engage in graduate work, they need, we believe, a text that presents a coherent view of both professional and curricular concerns in English education. Our volume is intended to fill this need.

Interestingly, some twenty years ago a wide range of books were aimed at the whole of a language arts curriculum. A cataloguing of texts suggests the rich resources available to English educators in the 1960s and early 1970s. Consider, for example, Herbert J. Muller's *The Uses of English* (Holt, Rinehart & Winston, 1967) and John Dixon's *Growth through English* (London: National Association for the Teaching of English), both prompted by the Anglo-American Seminar on the teaching of English held at Dartmouth College in 1966.

Also published during this time were such notable texts as J. N. Hook's *The Teaching of High School English* (Ronald Press, 1965); Walter Loban, Margaret Ryan, and James R. Squire's *Teaching Language and Literature, Grades 7–12* (Harcourt, Brace & World, 1969); James Moffett's *Teaching the Universe of Discourse* (Houghton Mifflin, 1968); and Alan C. Purves and Richard Beach's *Literature and the Reader* (NCTE, 1972).

Edited collections included Dwight L. Burton and John S. Simmons's *Teaching English in Today's High Schools: Selected Readings* (Holt, Rinehart & Winston, 1965); James Squire's *Common Purpose* (NCTE, 1966); and Charles Suhor, John S. Mayher, and Frank J. D'Angelo's *The Growing Edges of Secondary English* (NCTE, 1968).

These volumes present both practical and theoretical readings in the teaching of English that remain fascinating today. They were, however, written more than twenty years ago in another period of educational reform when proponents of the "new" English regarded the study of language as the unifying force between composition and literature. Today we have once again begun to see the importance of the study of language to literature and composition. As James Berlin has noted, "language, as we are now beginning to see, does not simply record our experience, it actually shapes it, structuring it in a way that determines what we see and do not see, what we know and do not know, and who we are and who we are not. . . . Language is determinative in the very formation of self and society (12)." We have moved away from the structuralists' view of language with its emphasis on meaning residing within the system of language and its spoken utterances to the poststructuralists' notions of the importance of the listener or reader in constructing meanings from texts. The essays in our collection reflect current theory, research, and pedagogy that continue to contribute to an accumulating knowledge base in the teaching of English. We know of no other volume in recent years that has taken on this task.

The chapters are grouped into four sections, each section directed at particular problems that face English teachers today. The first section, Teaching as a Profession:

Issues and Responsibilities, starts with a discussion by Gail Hawisher in which she argues that English education can ill afford dualistic modes of thought such as those captured in the controversy between content and procedural knowledge. It is followed with a report from the 1987 Coalition Conference in which the major issues of the profession are set forth and analyzed. All fifteen chapters in the collection relate to professional or curricular questions raised in these first two chapters.

The immediate chapters following Charles B. Harris's comprehensive analysis pertain to what it means to be a high school teacher in the late twentieth century. R. Baird Shuman traces the evolving role of English teaching in schools and ends with the observation that the structure of American education today was intended to serve a society that, in essence, no longer exists in our new age of information. The three remaining chapters in this section address some aspect of what it is like to be a teacher in this new age of information. Connie S. Zitlow discusses perceptions and expectations of preservice teachers and how they construe their roles as teachers in today's schools while Mary L. Gomez probes some findings from her research with experienced teachers participating in a national in-service program. Both these chapters highlight what teachers themselves think of English teaching in the 1980s. Then Maia Pank Mertz underscores some of the public's expectations of English teachers by discussing the use of testing as a requirement for entry into English teaching, along with its possible consequences for our profession. Each of these chapters touches upon problems surrounding reform issues—meaningful and effective instruction, the evolution of English teaching, teacher preparation, professional development, and the testing of teachers. Thus, the first section concentrates not only on problems facing English teachers but also on identifying some of the responsibilities teachers must assume if teaching is indeed to be perceived as a profession.

The next three sections shift the emphasis to curricular concerns in the teaching of English. In stressing the interconnectedness of the study of literature, composition, language, and the contexts in which students learn, each section and its essays underscore the need for a balanced curriculum that addresses the study of English in an integrated fashion.

The second section of the collection, Textual Relationships and Pedagogy: Literature and Writing, identifies the relationships that exist between our traditional notions of literature study and our emerging view of literacy in this new age of information. Each of the contributors in this section presents different perspectives on the interconnectedness of the study of literature and writing that lead to new strategies for using texts within a curriculum. Thus, the three essays in this section emphasize the way students can use their own writing to better understand literature and use literature to develop a better command of their own writing processes.

The third section of the collection, Rhetoric and Composition: Designs for Integration, turns to written composition and the various ways in which current theory and research can be translated into integrative designs for teaching. Each of the four essays in this section recognizes that in the past several years scholars and researchers have concentrated a great deal more on written composition than on the study of language or literature in a high school curriculum. The contributors of these last essays attempt to synthesize what we have learned, with each emphasizing the importance of developing a writing pedagogy that is informed by the important scholarship in composition of the past twenty-five years.

The final section, The Learning of Language: Teachers and their Students, presents two essays that relate to curricular problems of language instruction in teacher education programs and language instruction in the high school English classroom. Both Dennis E. Baron and Anna O. Soter discuss the need for the English teacher to be a language expert whether teaching in a traditional English class or in the increasingly prevalent multicultural classroom. Each of these essays, in its own way, points to problems teachers encounter in teaching literature and composition unless they are first teachers of language.

The contributors of this book address first the theory and research that lies at the heart of the described pedagogy. By envisioning preservice teachers as emerging scholars and by viewing seasoned teachers as informed professionals, this collection provides, we believe, the needed balanced perspective for teachers engaged in educational and curricular reform.

Works Cited

"A Nation Prepared: Teachers for the 21st Century" (Executive Summary). The Report of the Task Force on Teaching as a Profession of the Carnegie Forum on Education and the Economy, May 1986.

Berlin, James. "The Teacher as Researcher: Democracy, Dialogue, and Power." Unpublished manuscript, 1989.

Hirsch, Jr., E. D. *Cultural Literacy: What Every American Needs to Know.* Boston: Houghton-Mifflin, 1987.

Tomorrow's Teachers: A Report of the Holmes Group. East Lansing, Mich.: The Holmes Group, 1986.

Lloyd-Jones, Richard, and Andrea A. Lunsford, eds. *The Coalition Conference: Democracy through Language.* Urbana, Ill.: National Council of Teachers of English, 1989.

I

Teaching as a Profession: Issues and Responsibilities

Gail E. Hawisher

1. Content Knowledge versus Process Knowledge: A False Dichotomy*

Thirty-eight years before the publication of E. D. Hirsch's *Cultural Literacy: What Every American Needs to Know,* Gilbert Ryle in *The Concept of Mind* noted the false dichotomy between two kinds of knowledge—*knowing that* and *knowing how.* For Ryle, this dichotomy had to do with *possessing knowledge* in contrast to *acting intelligently* or using that capacity which enables us to perform tasks in a competent manner. The first evokes the classic figure of the book-reared scholar who knows nothing, the second, the dumb jock who also knows nothing. Ryle's purpose in examining these two aspects of knowing was to argue that knowledge and skill do not exist independently, that a competent performance comes from a considered plan, that the acquisition of knowledge is a precondition for competent action. He wanted to show that the two kinds of knowledge are inextricable and to presuppose that one exists independently of the other is erroneous. Although Ryle and his arguments receive little attention today, the debate over the primacy of content knowledge or procedural knowledge remains heated for the teaching of English in the high school and for the preparation of English teachers.

The history of teaching high school English in the United States reflects what seems to be repeated swings of the pendulum between an emphasis on teaching a subject

* I would like to thank Janet Eldred, University of Kentucky; Ron Fortune, Illinois State University; James Raths, University of Vermont; Pat Sullivan, Purdue University; and Anna Soter, Ohio State University, for the time they devoted to reading and commenting on this chapter.

matter and an emphasis on teaching the process of learning a subject. This is the debate, for example, that E. D. Hirsch calls forth when he argues against what he terms *educational formalism,* that is, "the theory that any suitable content will inculcate reading, writing, and thinking skills" (*Cultural Literacy* 21). To Hirsch and to others in our society today, the concept of teaching *any* content to encourage a process is ill-conceived. Unless members of a society can demonstrate a shared knowledge of their culture's prized artifacts, these scholars argue, that society will suffer and decline. This sort of thinking with its emphasis on the importance of reading the "classics" bears a strong resemblance to that set forth by Robert M. Hutchins (see Applebee 185–86) in the 1930s and also reflects the thinking that underlay turn-of-the-century college lists of required reading for high school students (see Applebee 35–36). Although Hirsch contends that this theory of cultural literacy is not part of the *Great Books* movement ("Cultural Literacy Doesn't Mean Core Curriculum" 47–49), he would concede, I believe, that cultural literacy emphasizes content rather than procedural knowledge.

Cultural literacy stands in contrast to recent teacher education programs in which English teachers were encouraged to formulate and to adhere to *behavioral* objectives (see, for example, discussions in Maxwell and Tovatt), statements distinguished by verbs that specified precisely the action or process required by the student to carry out a particular learning goal. For a high school English class in the 1970s, goals might be expressed in terms that directed students "*to distinguish* between words and referents"; "to *explore* the paragraph as an interrelated whole"; and "to *observe* people and situations closely." Those of us who have taught in the high school recognize such statements as typical of those appearing in school districts' curriculum guides. Thus, instead of evidencing a list of required facts, such as that which accompanies Hirsch's book, school curriculums tend to consist of lists specifying what students should be able to do as a result of their learning.

Another way to highlight this distinction finds the content and process split misplaced. Scholars advocating this view argue instead that debates over pedagogical models have tended to occur along the lines of conservative and liberal, with the conservative view stressing subject matter over process and the liberal view stressing the process of student learning over subject matter. Stephen Tchudi, for example, describes today's educational climate by stating that the times are difficult "for the teacher who is committed to a *personal growth* or *experience-centered* or *student-centered* or *process-oriented* approach to English teaching" (16). His statement encapsulates the liberal perspective whereas Hirsch's perspective is conservative. But regardless of how the split is conceived, certain language seems to characterize an emphasis on content while other language suggests an emphasis on process. Consider, for instance, the examples listed in Table 1.1.

As with many lists, this attempt to categorize falls apart in places because distinctions become blurred and the same words are used to evoke different concepts. Not only might some words be appropriately placed in both categories, but also the listed

Table 1.1

A False Dichotomy

Emphasis on Content	*Emphasis on Process*
Applied to Education in General	
liberal arts	education
conservative	liberal
traditional	progressive
"Academics"	"Educationists"
humanistic	empirical
intellectual rigor	personal growth
subject-centered	student-centered
mastery of subject	exploration of subject
content knowledge	experience
theoretical	practical
facts	skills
subject matter	pedagogy
teacher	facilitator
Applied to Composition and its Teaching	
product	process
expository writing	expressive writing
analytic	holistic
Applied to Literature and its Teaching	
"Great Books"	"Adolescent Novels"
literature	reading
objective	subjective
analysis	response
Applied to Language and its Teaching	
prescriptive	descriptive
"la langue"	"parole"
"competence"	"performance"
absolute standards	relativism
drill	application

words tend to evoke extremes. Hirsch, for example, uses the categories of "the facts people" and "the skills people" (133) to demonstrate an unreasonable polarization in education, yet few educators think of themselves in these terms. Most would argue that their position lies somewhere between and that the dualistic language fails to capture the essence of their interpretation of education. But regardless of the shortcomings of the list, the categories suggest, I believe, the inherent danger of relying on concepts associated with either content knowledge or procedural knowledge as sufficient for the education of our students. It is dichotomy that English education can ill afford.

In this chapter, I wish to examine the debate over subject-centered versus student-centered learning that has characterized English teaching in the schools be it literature, composition, or language. I discuss the way this dichotomy between an emphasis on *knowing that* or *knowing how* has manifested itself most recently in these three strands of English education. Then, relying on the work of Lee Shulman, I suggest the way this same dichotomy has affected the preparation of teachers and argue that the fusing of the two kinds of knowledge is necessary if we are to prepare prospective English teachers who are at once knowledgeable and competent. Highlighted throughout the discussion are suggestions contributors to this book have offered for integrating the *how* and *what* of English teaching.

LITERATURE AND ITS TEACHING

At the heart of the debate in literature teaching seems to be *what* should be taught, *how* this particular content should be taught, and finally *why* it should be taught—in other words, the goals we have for teaching a particular content in a particular way. Terms often encountered in discussions include *Great Books* versus *Adolescent Novels, literature* versus *reading, analysis* versus *response,* and *objective* versus *subjective. Subject-centered* versus *sutdent-centered* and *intellectual rigor* versus *personal growth* also relate to the debate in literature teaching as do *experience* and *exploration* when contrasted with terms denoting an emphasis on *content* and *mastery* of a subject. Each of the aforementioned terms suggests the debate over the what, how, and why of literature teaching.

The question as to why literature should be taught is perhaps the most important because over the years it has inevitably shaped the content of a literature curriculum and suggested the methods that might be used for the various purposes of teaching. Arthur Applebee points out that at least three traditions have informed our decisions for teaching literature (1) the ethical tradition in which students through literature should learn those values prized by our society; (2) the classical tradition in which students should develop disciplined minds through close analysis of language in texts; (3) and the nonacademic tradition in which students through reading should come to appreciate the joys of good literature. Although these are traditions inherited from other centuries, I argue that none seems remote to twentieth-century English teachers.

Hirsch's notion of cultural literary descends from the ethical and cultural heritage tradition; today's emphasis on critical thinking skills echoes some of the concerns of the classical tradition; and twentieth-century literature textbook titles such as *Adventures in Appreciation* and *Exploring Literature* evoke a subject matter to be experienced in the nonacademic tradition.

Interestingly, these traditions and their descendants at different periods in the past 100 years have been used sometimes to argue for an emphasis on content and, at other times, for an emphasis on process. Today the emphasis on content is evidenced in Hirsch's essentially ethical model; Lynne Cheney's arguments for content-oriented courses in history and literature also reflect this cultural heritage model. John Dewey and his followers of the progressive education movement of the 1930s and 1940s were also concerned with ethics, and their emphasis is process- or student-centered. In rejecting the traditional body of accepted literature for high school students, Dewey and his followers removed themselves from the cultural-heritage model but not from issues of ethical behavior. They believed that contemporary reading and direct experience with modern-day problems could engender the important values of our society. Their concern with ethical behavior is suggested by the phrase "values education or clarification," terminology that we still hear today (see Oser 920–21). Note that the language of values education or values clarification lacks the historical perspective of the phrase *cultural heritage,* putting values squarely in the present, with none of the nostalgic yearning for ideals of the past. The words *education* and *clarification* also denote a process, suggesting to some a content-less curriculum. Unsurprisingly, then, not unlike today, the cultural-heritage model for literature was invoked in the 1950s as an argument against what was perceived as the progressives' lack of academic rigor (Applebee 187). Despite progressive education's concern with moral behavior and the betterment of society through the improvement of the individual, an emphasis on classical content supplanted an emphasis on contemporary experience in literature teaching.

Methods of teaching literature have also been influenced by both literary theory and learning theory. When critical theory has shaped curriculum, it has usually been at the hands of scholars in departments of English; when learning theory has shaped curriculum, it has usually been at the hands of scholars in colleges of education. Literary theory since tha late 1930s has placed an emphasis on close attention to texts themselves whereas learning theory has tended toward the process of encouraging meaning-making in students. When reading theory has influenced literature teaching, again process has been emphasized; *reading* as a subject is housed in colleges of education.

Although their methods were not integrated into the schools until the early 1960s the New Critics have perhaps had the greatest influence on the teaching of literature during the past twenty-firve years in large part because today's high school teachers received their education from proponents of new criticism. With its emphasis on meaning residing within a text and its methods of close analysis of the language and form of a text to "find" this meaning, it supplied the rigor that academic reformers saw as lacking in high school curricula of the early 1960s. Thus, although new criticism was concerned with *how* a text means, in educational circles it marked a return to an emphasis on the importance of the subject matter of literature.

Increasingly, literary theory has moved away from this focus on the content and form of a text. For the past twenty years or so, some critics have argued that the "truth" of a text lies not so much within its pages as within the reader and have stressed the importance of the reader's prior experience and knowledge in constructing meaning from encounters with texts. Louise Rosenblatt has suggested it is not so much a question of meaning residing in text *or* reader but rather one of text *and* reader—a transaction negotiated between the two. Susan Suleiman calls this shift in focus *audience-oriented criticism,* and the group of critics associated with this orientation are usually known as proponents of subjective criticism or reader-response theory. Largely as the result of Louise Rosenblatt's pioneering work, this movement has had some effect on high school literature teaching.

Although subjective criticism emerged from literary scholarship, much of its emphasis on pedagogy is student-centered probably because it focuses on the reader's, hence the student's, response to a text. In writing of the diversity of approaches to subjective criticism, Jane Tompkins states that "reader-response criticism is not a conceptually unified critical position, but a term that has come to be associated with the work of critics who use the words *reader, the reading process,* and *response* to mark out their area of investigation" (ix). Note that these are the same phrases usually associated with process aproaches to teaching. Louise Rosenblatt is special not only because she was one of the first to set forth a transactional theory of a literary work that recognized the role of the reader but also because she applied it to teaching. And, because of Rosenblatt's work and because of the emphases Tompkins mentions above, the application of literary theory in the classroom today usually is one which seeks to integrate the *what* and *how* of literature into one pedagogical model.

Yet attempts at this integration, as George Newell points out in chapter 8, are not always easy for teachers. Literature teaching, Newell argues, has been so closely tied to teaching students to write analytical papers about literary works that many of the goals we advocate for students' engagement with texts are undermined. Even when teachers value students' personal responses, they often believe they are not adequately preparing students for college unless emphasis is placed on the close analysis and written interpretation of a text in the tradition of the New Critics. Approaching the problem of balancing content and process from another angle, Robert Probst has suggested that literature is a subject in need of a purpose and that out inability as a profession to decide why literature should be taught has led to much of the confusion surrounding literature teaching today. Probst believes that the solution lies in helping students to join in the dialogue of our culture afforded by the study of literature. He argues that "such a reconception would pay attention to the literary heritage—the great works and the great authors and the themes that they dealt with—and to the interests and abilities of the students, and to the nature of the transaction between the student and the texts" (see chapter 7). The problem then becomes one of how we go about genuinely inviting students into the important conversations that concern our society and culture.

Ron Fortune (see chapter 9) presents an interesting solution to the problem of integrating procedural and content knowledge and, in doing so, gives us one method by which to draw students into important conversations. Fortune's aim is to enhance student's learning in literature and writing by engaging students with the creative processes of great writers through studies of their manuscripts in progress. Students also use additional materials such as correspondence, journals, and perhaps some of the particular author's other published writings to give them a window on what goes into great writers' decisions. In this way, they are not only studying the content of literature but also probing the various acts comprising the activity of writing. When they move to the task of doing their own writing, they have many different resources, including their prior writing, upon which to draw for ideas. Because they have become so involved with both the author's drafts and other timely materials that seemed to influence the author's decisions, students can also become engaged in some of the important dialogues of our culture. Importantly, Fortune argues that this activity is not one that should be used to the exclusion of others for literature study and composition instruction. Fortune believes that if the various tasks that go into using manuscripts in high school classes are "routinized," so to speak, into a process, the dynamics of the learning will suffer. Just as the writing process, when misapplied, no longer calls forth the energetic mental activity that characterizes writing, so too this method for teaching can be sapped of its vigor.

Probst and Fortune both understand the dilemma of the bipolar division of content and process and seek ways to unite the two in literature teaching. Newell, in addition, through his research in the schools, explains the way this dichotomy affects teachers' methods of teaching students literature and the problems it causes. But others, instead of viewing the dichotomy itself as the problem, enlist the bipolar terms to support their position. In *American Memory,* Cheney argues that today's students lack knowledge of our cultural heritage and that "usually the culprit is 'process'—the belief that we can teach our children *how* to think without troubling them to learn anything worth thinking about, the belief that we can teach them *how* to understand the world in which they live without conveying to them the events and ideas that have brought them into existence" (5). Granted that implicit in her argument is the assumption that some procedural knowledge is important, but she lodges this complaint against *process* from the perspective that good teaching has to do with "transmitting culture" (6). Good teachers, we respond, do not *transmit* culture; rather they become learners with students, providing materials that enable students to engage our culture through a study of its artifacts in ways that simultaneously engage them. Teaching students to remember primarily the content of literature, as a part of our cultural heritage, does justice neither to students nor to the subject matter at hand.

We must be sure that today's heated debates over literature instruction do not obscure what we have learned from the past regarding teaching itself. In 1971, while assessing the impact of the 1966 Anglo-American Dartmouth Seminar on literature teaching, Alan Purves wrote:

> If the Dartmouth Seminar represents a powerful new trend in the curriculum, as I think it does, it is a trend away from the historical treatment of literature, which degenerated into biography and history, away from the "critical" analysis of literature, which degenerated into critical formalism and rigidity, toward a treatment of the student as audience and as an active participant in the literary transaction between writer and reader. It seeks to give the student confidence in his response, his judgment, and his taste. It pays attention to the affective side of the literary work and of the student. It can degenerate into a psychologism that might neglect the work of literature or into a sentimentalism about literature and about the student—whether it will or not remains to be seen. (*Handbook* 703)

If, indeed, the teaching of literature has degenerated into "psychologism" and "sentimentalism" (and I don't think it has), we must be careful not to return to older emphases that did not work with students and give them new titles in the name of reform.

COMPOSITION AND ITS TEACHING

Nowhere is the debate over process and content more evident or more heated than in discussions focusing on written composition and its teaching. Perhaps because for the past twenty-five years or so composition studies have gone through a dramatic transformation, the argument over process versus product has received more than its share of attention. During this time, the field has not only recognized its historical traditions in classical rhetoric but also has acquired an impressive research base. At the same time, scholars, drawing on the fields of rhetoric, linguistics, cognitive psychology, and anthropology among others, have constructed elaborate conceptual frameworks for what was once considered an atheoretical discipline. Indeed, twenty years ago one could scarcely label it a discipline. As it has emerged from pedagogical beginnings, however, and practice has become increasingly grounded in theory, teachers have departed from old, uniform methods of teaching—hence, today's disagreements over the *best* way to teach writing.

Interestingly, the primary question that shaped literature teaching over the century (*why* should we teach it?) has until recently been less of a force in composition teaching. Because composition has been considered a skill rather than one of the liberal arts like literature, it was assumed that members of a literate society should be able to write. There was no debate about it. In fact, so predominant was this assumption and so closely was the written word associated with Godliness that writing competence early in our history became equated with moral rectitude. Shriley Brice Heath writes that in the latter half of the nineteenth century, "the ability to write well became linked to individual identification and personal characteristics of moral and cultural value" (43). Unlike the study of literature, then, the ability to write was (and is?) associated with one's moral deportment and ethical standards. These unreasonable connections served only to stress the importance of writing as a fundamental skill that all students must acquire.

The bipolar terms in Table 1.1 that usually characterize discussions regarding composition teaching are the words *process* and *product,* with the first linked with the writing or composing process and the second associated with the current traditional pedagogical model. The term *current traditional,* coined by Daniel Fogarty in 1959 and describing a way of teaching writing that went virtually unchallenged until the 1960s, over the years came to denote an emphasis on teaching the correctness of the mechanics of language, a correctness which ultimately characterizes an error-free final product. Although the 1966 Darmouth Seminar (with important contributions from British scholar and researcher James Britton and American scholar James Moffett) emphasized self-expressive modes of writing, not until the appearance of Janet Emig's 1969 dissertation on the composing processes of twelfth graders and Donald Murray's short article, "Teach Writing as a Process, not a Product," did process approaches begin to establish themselves in writing classes. In addition, the work of composition scholars Ken Macrorie, Peter Elbow, and Donald Graves along with that of researchers Linda Flower and John Hayes influenced writing pedagogy profoundly, turning it away from product-centered approaches to today's widely accepted "process" approaches.

When we consider the distinctions made in Table 1.1, we find that not surprisingly, process approaches should also be associated with a student-centered curriculum. Process pedagogy, after all, places emphasis on what students do; that is, by learning and practicing what researchers documented expert writers do in recursive fashion—planning, drafting, reviewing, revising, editing, and sharing their writing with others—students are thought to be able to learn to compose more effectively. But this turn to a student-centered curriculum also represented, in some circles, a shift away from academic writing toward expressive writing (writing for and sometimes about the self), often to the neglect of transactional writing (writing to inform or persuade). This change in the kind of discourse thought appropriate for school writing, in part, was the result of both Murray and Macrorie using personal experience narratives to illustrate their methods and, in part, a reaction against the lack of experiential writing in the schools that was reported by both Emig and Britton. Moffett's developmental theory was also influential. In *Teaching the Universe of Discourse,* Moffett places narrative discourse in close proximity to the writer and suggests that it thus requires less abstract reasoning than expository or persuasive writing. Hence, a certain type of process-centered writing instruction begins with personal narrative and moves to other writing. Its critics argue that it seldom progresses beyond personal experience.

Along with this self-expressive teaching model and other approaches that emphasize *process* but not necessarily personal experience, recent times have witnessed the rise of additional reasons for composition teaching. Adding to the goal of literacy for all members of a democratic society, composition theorists and scholars have suggested that writing enhances learning, and thus to write is to learn. Two aspects of this concept seem especially pertinent to a discussion of procedural versus content knowledge: writing to enable self-knowledge and writing to learn a content. The first grows out of the emphasis on expressive writing while the second is most clearly demonstrated in writing-across-the-curriculum programs and relies primarily on "reading and writing connections."

In addition to valuing the student's "authentic voice" (i.e., the student's own personal writing style), expressive pedagogy often presents writing as a way of discovering truth about oneself. That is, through such methods as "free writing," students are encouraged to discover meaning; thus, when they write about themselves, composing provides a means of self-discovery. As Lester Faigley explains in his 1986 article, "Competing Theories of Process," expressive writing pedagogy implies "that writing development can aid personal development . . ." (531). This emphasis on self-discovery leads some to argue that the "psychologism" and "sentimentalism" Purves warned us of in 1971 did not show up in literature teaching; rather, they manifested themselves in composition teaching. What is important here for our purposes, however, is not so much the focus on self, but the emphasis on composing as a learning tool, a learning tool that can after all be extended beyond the self.

Concepts associated with reading and writing connections promote a write-to-learn teaching model and extend discovery of meaning to students' interaction with texts. To help students engage content, this model argues, we can teach them to read analytically, marking text as they go, and to summarize, synthesizing another writer's ideas through the process of writing. Students then can be encouraged to examine critically the ideas and structure of particular texts to discover issues that interest them for their own writing. In research exploring the reading processes and writing products of college students, Mary Lynch Kennedy found that the more able writers in her study read and reread, pencils in hand, making notes as they progressed. Furthermore, their final products showed a constructive use of these notes. These methods can encourage high school students to use reading effectively in their writing by practicing techniques that proficient readers and writers employ. Thus, pedagogical approaches to writing instruction, while advocating process, can also stress reading as a path to good products, the balance between the two resulting in improved writing and learning.

Contributors to this volume recognize the dilemma that overemphasizing either process or product creates for writing instruction. In showing us what classical rhetoric has to offer modern students and teachers of writing, Sheryl Finkle and Edward Corbett note that the expressive theorists' approach to writing instruction, with its heavy emphasis on student writing processes, probably does not help students become better writers. Finkle and Corbett recommend a program that recognizes the importance of *inventio* (the discovery of arguments), thus stressing the content and issues students must find and engage if they are to accomplish their aims in a piece of writing.

Relying on both classical and modern rhetorical theory, Andrea Lunsford and Cheryl Glenn believe that good writing instruction must demonstrate a balanced emphasis on the writer, the text, and the reader. Overemphasizing the text promotes product-centered teaching approaches that we learned were not effective; over-emphasizing the writer can result in students not progressing beyond themselves. Stressing the reader to the exclusion of text and writer can result in manipulative prose that has lost the voice and intended subject matter of its author. Lunsford and Glenn extend the application of the rhetorical triangle so that the student, in-draft texts, and teacher all receive attention. In doing so, they emphasize the social aspects of texts that can transform the writing class to one in which all participants become learners-in-progress. Martin Nystrand gives us many ideas for achieving this social milieu within a writing class. One of his suggestions introduces the notion of "authenticity" for teachers' discourse; that is, to be more than critics of student work, teachers must ask questions that have no preset answers, questions that draw them into the learning circle with their students. In addition, Cynthia Selfe shows us how the networking capabilities of technology can contribute to a cooperative and collaborative learning setting. Striking a balance, then, among the elements of the rhetorical triangle, on the one hand, and on what we might call the elements of the *pedagogical triangle,* on the other, strengthens the dynamics of the writing class.

In 1982, when Maxine Hairston wrote her important article "Winds of Change," many in the profession viewed the debate between process and product emphases as settled: process approaches to teaching writing demonstrated a clear advantage over product approaches. In schools, the task at hand became one of disseminating this new knowledge, with the National Writing Project sites providing leadership in this effort. Finding ourselves embroiled in the discussion yet another time is perhaps somewhat surprising. Stanley Fish contends that "the emergence of factions with a once interdicted activity is a sure sign of its having achieved that status of an orthodoxy" (as quoted in Clifford and Marcus 256). Thus, process approaches to writing instruction suffer from their acceptance. Yet a careful examination of the arguments against these once-new methods reveals a different dispute, a debate over what makes for worthy content in student writing. Literature? Student experience? Reading from primary sources? Ongoing dialogues in our society? Student-initiated ethnographic research? If literature is indeed a subject in search of a purpose, then composition teaching, I believe, remains a pedagogy in search of a subject. With its emphasis on using writing as a means of engaging students with a subject matter, the writing-across-the-curriculum movement may signal the way.

LANGUAGE AND ITS TEACHING

For some time now, language and its teaching seem to be in search of both a purpose and a subject matter. The belief that a philological approach to its study promotes mental discipline has been put aside, and the conviction that the study of traditional

English grammar leads to good writing has finally been rejected (if bemoaned) in our schools today. What has occurred in this process, however, is that the teaching of language has lost its traditional mission: that is, to improve students' command of the standard dialect of the community. Without this charge, another reason must be found for its teaching. This dilemma continues to plague language studies, with innovative movements at various times making some headway into school curricula, before finally being resoundingly rejected.

In 1965, *Freedom and Discipline,* a report from the Commission on English for assessing high school English teaching, gave the following reasons for teaching language studies:

1. Grammar study is necessary for, or at least helpful in, the eradication of faults, and consequently it develops the power to read and write and speak well.
2. Grammar study makes possible easier communication between teacher and student.
3. Grammar study is necessary as preparation for the study of foreign languages.
4. Grammar study is a good discipline. (26–29)

The report proceeds to debunk each of the above except for the third one. The report ends its survey with the following observation: "Since grammatical study can be both illuminating and useful, it should ordinarily be made a part of the curriculum in such a way as to exploit its potential usefulness" (30). Certainly this argument for teaching language is not very convincing. The report does go on, however, to recommend an approach that stresses the application of grammatical knowledge rather than "drill for the sake of drill" (30). But what is most remarkable about the language section of the 1965 assessment is that we seem to have made so little progress in the past twenty-five years of so of language teaching.

Those who argue for the primacy of content in language teaching are those who advocate school or "traditional" grammar. That this grammar is largely derived from Latin and has never fit English, a Germanic language, has not prevented it from being the accepted grammar of the schools. At various times, this approach has also included "parsing" (defining the relationship of each word in a sentence to every other word) and "diagraming" (illustrating these relationships). Thus, emphasis on content in language study in high schools has primarily concerned itself with inculcating in students accepted Standard English usage.

Efforts at reform in language teaching seemed to flounder throughout the history of English instruction. A research monograph that Raven McDavid edited in 1963 reported on the generally favorable attitudes of the National Council of Teachers of English (NCTE) toward language from 1911 to 1963. Articles from fifty-two years of the *English Journal* supplied the evidence for the monograph. It concluded that in 1963 no longer was there a debate over *whether* grammar should be taught; rather the debate was on *which* grammar should be taught. It went on to note that traditional grammar was "rejected as arbitrary and erroneous" and that "structural linguistics

[was] too confusing for even many teachers, let alone students, to understand" (61–62). The final chapter indicates that there was some hope in 1963 that Noam Chomsky and transformational grammar would provide an appropriate grammar for the schools. Transformational grammar, however, was also later assailed for its difficulty and, as a school subject, is probably less taught today than structural grammar.

Yet, despite these early assessments, in the late 1960s and early 1970s, linguistics revitalized language study and pedagogy in the schools, and student-centered curricula that included a rich subject matter evolved. Such study recommended *descriptive* rather then *prescriptive* grammar in which students were encouraged to carry out their own descriptions of spoken language rather than to memorize eighteenth-century prescriptive rules. Dialects and their variations also characterized language study, and slang, jargon, cant, along with variations of black and Appalachian speech communities received attention in English classes. Along with these synchronic approaches to language study were also diachronic studies, that is, historical examinations of the beginnings of our language and its forebears. Such studies allowed students to see language as constantly changing and growing, and provided them with material for hypothesizing about the future of English. Semantics (the study of meaning) also became the province of English classes, further enriching the study of language.

These curricula are not common today. In fact, sentence combining may be one of the few remaining contributions that recalls the influence of linguistics in the schools. The back-to-basics-movement of the later 1970s reemphasized what was perceived as a need for the teaching of school grammar, and descriptive grammar, along with historical studies, stopped receiving much attention. Both Dennis Baron and Anna Soter (see chapters 14 and 15) deplore the lack of attention to language study today. Baron argues that any preparation of teachers in modern studies of linguistics has little effect on school teaching because these studies are not a part of the high school's curriculum. Soter fears that the increase in multicultural classrooms will find a teaching staff totally unprepared for its challenges. Both argue for a much greater emphasis on studies that recognize the dynamics of language teaching.

Although many critics of our schools accuse process of robbing the content from literature and composition teaching, making this same argument against language instruction is difficult. What was recognized in the late 1960s as the New English no longer exists. Despite literary theory having adopted constructs from the Swiss linguist, Ferdinand de Saussure, and composition studies making use of advances in sociolinguistics and pragmatics, the study of language in high schools shows little of this linguistic influence. When language is taught today, it is through traditional grammar, and workbooks tend to look very much like the ones used by previous generations. Currently, debates over language and its teaching focus not so much on *how* or *what* should be taught but rather on *whether* it should be taught at all. Our discussions about language study, as with our workbooks, are not very different from previous generations of English teachers.

ENGLISH TEACHERS AND THEIR PREPARATION

Interestingly, this same debate over the primacy of content knowledge or process knowledge has characterized debates in teacher education programs. Shulman, in writing about this split, emphasizes that "teaching necessarily begins with a teacher's understanding of *what is to be learned and how it is to be taught*" (7). He goes on to state that "the key to distinguishing the knowledge base of teaching lies at the *intersection of content and pedagogy,* in the capacity of a teacher to transform the content knowledge he or she possesses into forms that are pedagogically powerful and yet adaptive to the variations in ability and background presented by the students" (15) (emphasis mine). In each of the above statements, Shulman, in "Knowledge and Teaching: Foundations of the New Reform," recognizes the complex knowledge that teachers of all disciplines must attain if they are to teach well. Teaching, Shulman asserts, means transforming the content of a discipline into an effective pedagogy that helps students to understand. Nowhere in the above statements, or in the entire article for that matter, does he privilege procedural knowledge or disciplinary knowledge over the other. To separate the pedagogical from the disciplinary in teacher preparation programs is to handicap prospective teachers and hence their students.

Yet the administrative organizations of colleges and universities for teacher education often contribute to the problem. Policy and administrative decisions that house the teaching of a subject in a separate college or department from the subject itself exacerbate problems caused by a division of the two. Majoring in English education or English at many universities means that students encounter different faculties and often receive different university degrees.

This is not to suggest that these administrative divisions are new. Indeed, their roots go back more than 100 years to before English was a proper subject for study and probably have their beginnings in the creation of Normal Schools, established by individual states exclusively for the preparation of school teachers. Nor am I suggesting that English education faculty in colleges of education should be incorporated into departments of English (although this is an excellent idea). Rather it is to underscore the difficulty of trying to integrate pedagogical and disciplinary knowledge for English education majors when the two are taught in different places. Indeed, scholars separate them into different research paradigms, with studies in English a part of the humanities and studies in English teaching a part of the social sciences.

Colleges and universities are aware of the problems caused by this traditional separation. *Tomorrow's Teachers,* the 1986 Holmes Group report (prepared on behalf of deans of colleges of education from throughout the country), argues for greater participation in teacher education by faculty in subject matter disciplines. In addition to making education courses primarily a part of graduate study, their plans call for collaborative efforts in teacher education between education and liberal arts faculty. The task then becomes one of developing teacher education programs that integrate both pedagogical and disciplinary knowledge through such collaborative efforts. If we as a profession accuse faculty in education of having erred in recent years years in privileging the *how* over the *what* of teaching, I believe we must also lay blame at the feet of English faculty. For too long, too many have paid too little attention to what goes on in English education. English, as a profession on the college level, often dismisses teaching. Faculty are tenured for writing about the *what;* pedagogy counts little. In isolating teaching from the subject of English, this neglect, I believe, has contributed to the anti-intellectualism that sometimes characterizes teacher education programs.

Interestingly, the emphasis on procedural knowledge in teaching has not always been the rule. In another important article, Shulman points out that tests for teachers of the last century were content-oriented; unfortunately, however, this content was often school grammar or recall of the "facts" of literature. For English teachers the questions included:

1. When should the reciprocal pronouns *one another* and *each other* be used? the correlative conjunctions *so as* and *as as?*
2. Name and illustrate five forms of conjugation.
3. Name and give four ways in which the nominative case may be used ("Those Who Understand" 4).

Note that each of the above questions asks for recall of information and would be classified at the bottom of the hierarchy of cognitive behaviors (Bloom).

Admittedly, these questions focus ostensibly on school grammar, and, as a profession, we agree that prospective teachers must understand more than the facts of literature, composition, or language studies. In this period of reform, we must be careful, once again, not to replace what we have with something we already learned was not effective in teacher preparation. As Shulman points out, "Mere content knowledge is likely to be as useless pedagogically as content-free skill. But to blend properly the two aspects of a teacher's capacities requires that we pay as much attention to the content aspects of teaching as we have recently devoted to the elements of the teaching process" ("Those Who Understand" 8). Thus, to balance the practical with the theoretical, the *doing* with the *knowing,* is as much a goal, indeed a more important goal perhaps, for preparing English teachers as it is for teaching our subject matters.

CONCLUSION

The Coalition Conference of the various members of the English profession seems to have encouraged unity and good will among scholars, researchers, and teachers alike. Charles Harris (see chapter 2) writes that he retains his optimism about the future of English studies because of the consensus that was "earned" at the conference. He writes that "the best of current theory and research in the areas of learning and cognition, language and composition, reading and literature, as well as from classroom experiences of sixty dedicated teachers" guided the meeting, helping participants to understand the full spectrum of knowledge teachers must know. Harris also notes that consensus was not reached outside the conference with those who support the kind of teaching that promotes the surface knowledge contained in E. D. Hirsch's dictionary. Yet Hirsch himself writes, "There is no insurmountable reason why those who advocate the teaching of higher order skills and those who advocate the teaching of common traditional content should not join forces. No philosophical or practical barrier prevents them from doing so, and all who consider mature literacy to be a paramount aim of education will wish them to do so" (*Cultural Literacy* 133).

Admittedly, although considerable, the philosophical and practical differences do not plague our profession as much as the bipolar extremes evoked by the language itself. The dualistic modes of thought we use to categorize our discipline and its pedagogical approaches divide us. The seeming opposites, which cannot occur independently without the other, allow one group to assume power over the other. Hence, the argument over *process* and *content* becomes a debate over *good* and *evil,* with adherents of one group periodically achieving influence in our society. Members of this group have, after all, through this manipulation of language, become the bearers of *truth.*

Debates over pedagogical models will continue. As they rage, however, remembering what Purves reminded us of some years ago in arguing for the importance of historical perspective in language research might be useful. He writes, "The verbal sniping . . . shows up in language education as a matter of research and curricular evidence. One often hears the dichotomy of process and product to describe this difference of approach, or rather this distinction among approaches since I believe it is a distinction without a difference. Processes produce products, and one has the liberty to focus on either aspect, but one may not assert the superiority of either to the other, just as one cannot separate the 'dancer from the dance'" ("Paradox" 4). Our task as teachers and teacher educators, then, becomes one of promoting an integrated approach to the study of English and the preparation of English teachers. Ryle's ridicule of the distinction between *knowing that* and *knowing how* is useful because it sheds light on our reform efforts of the 1990s. Reform in English education must demonstrate a balanced perspective, a perspective that seeks not only to unite binary oppositions into productive syntheses but also seeks to preserve the rich diversity of knowledge among us.

Works Cited

Applebee, Arthur N. *Tradition and Reform in the Teaching of English: A History.* Urbana, Ill.: National Council of Teachers of English, 1974.

Britton, James, et al. *The Development of Writing Abilities (11–18).* London: Macmillan, 1975.

Cheney, Lynne. *American Memory: A Report on the Humanities in the Nation's Public Schools.* Washington, D.C.: National Endowment for the Humanities, 1987.

Clifford, James, and George E. Marcus, eds. *Writing Culture: The Poetics and Politics of Ethnography.* Berkeley: University of California Press, 1986.

Elbow, Peter. *Writing Without Teachers.* New York: Oxford University Press, 1973.

Emig, Janet. *The Composing Processes of Twelfth Graders.* Urbana, Ill.: National Council of Teachers of English, 1971.

Faigley, Lester. "Competing Theories of Process: A Critique and Proposal." *College English* 48 (1986): 527–42.

Flower, Linda, and John R. Hayes. A Cognitive Process Theory of Writing. *College Composition and Communication 32 (1981): 356–86.*

Fogarty, Daniel. *Roots for a New Rhetoric.* New York: Russell and Russell, 1968.

Freedom and Discipline in English: Report of the Commission on English. New York: College Entrance Examination Board, 1965.

Guidelines for the Preparation of Teachers of English Language Arts. Urbana, Ill.: National Council of Teachers of English, 1986.

Hairston, Maxine. "The Winds of Change: Thomas Kuhn and the Revolution in the Teaching of Writing." *College Composition and Communication* 33 (1982): 76–88.

Heath, Shirley Brice. "Toward an Ethnohistory of Writing in American Education." *Writing: The Nature Development and Teaching of Written Communication,* Marcia Farr Whiteman, ed. 2 vols. Hillside, N.J.: Lawrence Earlbaun, 1981. 25–45.

Hirsch, Jr., E. D. '"Cultural Literacy' Doesn't Mean 'Core Curriculum.'" *English Journal* 74 (1985): 47–49.

________. *Cultural Literacy: What Every American Needs to Know.* Boston: Houghton-Mifflin, 1987.

Kennedy, Mary Lynch. "The Composing Process of College Students Writing from Sources." *Written Communication* 2 (1985): 434–56.

Macrorie, Ken. *Telling Writing.* Rochelle Park, N.J.: Hayden, 1970.

Maxwell, John, and Anthony Tovatt, eds. *On Writing Behavioral Objectives for English.* Champaign, Ill.: National Council of Teachers of English, 1970.

McDavid, Jr. Raven I., ed. *An Examination of the Attitudes of the NCTE toward Language.* Champaign, Ill.: National Council of Teachers of English, 1965.

Murray, Donald. "Teach Writing as Process not Product." *The Leaflet* November (1972): 11–14.

Moffett, James. *Teaching the Universe of Discourse.* Boston: Houghton Mifflin, 1965.

Oser, Fritz K. "Morals Education and Values Education: The Discourse Perspective." *Handbook of Research on Teaching.* Merlin C. Wittrock, ed. New York: Macmillan, 1986. 917–41.

Purves, Alan C. "Evaluation of Learning in Literature." *Handbook of Formative and Summative Evaluation of Student Learning.* Benjamin S. Bloom, J. Thomas Hastings, and George F. Madaus, eds. New York: McGraw-Hill, 1971. 699–766.

———. "Paradox of Research." *English Education* 16 (1984): 3–13.

Rosenblatt, Louise. *Literature as Exploration.* 4th. ed. New York: Modern Language Association, 1983.

Ryle, Gilbert. *The Concept of Mind.* New York: Barnes and Noble, 1949.

Shulman, Lee S. "Those Who Understand: Knowledge Growth in Teaching." *Educational Researcher* 15 (1986): 4–14.

———. "Knowledge and Teaching: Foundations of the New Reform." *Harvard Educational Review* 57 (1987): 1–22.

Suleiman, Susan R. "Introduction: Varieties of Audience-Oriented Criticism." *The Reader in the Text: Essays on Audience and Interpretation.* Susan R. Suleiman and Inge Crosman, eds. Princeton, N.J.: Princeton University Press, 1980. 3–45.

Tchudi, Stephen N., ed. *English Teachers at Work: Ideas and Strategies from Five Countries.* Upper Montclair, N.J.: Boynton/Cook, 1986.

Tompkins, Jane P. "An Introduction to Reader-Response Criticism." *Reader-Response Criticism: From Formalism to Post-Structuralism.* Jane P. Tompkins, ed. Baltimore, Md. The Johns Hopkins University Press, 1980. ix–xxvi.

Tomorrow's Teachers: A Report of the Holmes Group. East Lansing, Mich.: The Holmes Group, 1986.

Charles B. Harris

2. *Report from the Eastern Shore: The English Coalition Conference*

In the summer of 1987, sixty English teachers met for three weeks at the Aspen Institute for Humanistic Studies on Maryland's Eastern Shore to talk about the teaching of English.[1] Conference planners chose this heavily wooded former plantation on the picturesque Wye River because it affords an appropriate mix of seclusion and (from an English teacher's perspective) near Lucullan amenities. What we could not have anticipated was the almost metaphorical relationship between the region's topography and what Phyllis Franklin describes as the "single coherent consensus about the teaching of English at all levels" (4) that emerged from the meeting.

John Barth, native to the Eastern Shore marshes that figure so prominently in his fiction, describes the suggestive richness of the region as follows:

> In Civil War times Maryland was a Border State. Mason's and Dixon's Line runs east-west across the top and then, appropriately, north-south down the Eastern shore, which was heavily loyalist in the Revolution and Confederate in the War Between the States. Marsh country is a border state, too, between land and sea, and tide-marsh doubly so, its twin diurnal ebbs and floods continuously reorchestrating the geography. No clear demarcations here between fresh and salt, wet and dry: Many many square miles of Delaware happen to be Delaware instead of Maryland owing to a seventeenth-century surveyors' dispute about the mid-point of a line whose eastern terminus is the sharp Atlantic coast but whose western peters out in the Dorchester County marshes, where the "shoreline" at high tide may be a mile east from where it was at low, when reedy islets muddily join the main.... Your webfoot... marsh-nurtured writer will likely by mere reflex regard many conventional boundaries and distinctions as arbitrary, fluid, negotiable.... (5)

The distinctions Barth wishes to negotiate are aesthetic: "form versus content, realism versus irrealism, fact versus fiction, life versus art" (5). But the contraries threatening to divide the participants at Wye Woods were more varied. Most prominent, perhaps, were the binary oppositions informing recent debates in the profession. True consensus would require skillful navigation between the Scylla and Charybdis of process and product, skills and content, theory and practice. Less obvious but as potentially disruptive were our competing organizational loyalties. Many of the eight national English associations comprising the Coalition had once been factions within the National Council of Teachers of English (NCTE) or Modern Language Association (MLA) that had splintered off out of dissatisfaction with the aims and priorities of the parent organization.[2] As the three-week conference wore on and the inevitable fatigue set in, would old wounds, long thought healed, begin to ache and throb, would political monsters, long dormant in the recesses of organizational memories, begin to stir and move their slow thighs?

And what of the seemingly endemic suspicion, condescension, and misunderstanding that bedevils relations between teachers at the three levels of schooling represented at the conference, the elementary, the secondary, and the collegiate (or, as one conference wag put it, the primary, the secondary, and the tertiary)? While we all teach the same language, we soon came to realize that we do not necessarily speak it, at least not in our professional lives. For the first few days of the conference, jargon abounded. College teachers, who baffled their colleagues from the schools with specialized usages of terms such as *situatedness, contextualization, paradigm shift,* and *text,* were befuddled in turn by schoolteachers' references to *scope and sequence, basal readers,* and *language arts.*[3] The intellectual heroes of the collegiate group bore such names as Derrida, Foucault, Eagleton, and Kristeva; the schoolteachers arrived talking of Piaget, Vygotsky, Bruner, and Dewey. Even the ways we habitually describe our academic roles differed markedly. "I teach nineteenth-century fiction," one college teacher said to Fred Burton, an elementary school teacher from Columbus, Ohio. "That's interesting," responded Fred. "I teach twentieth-century children."

Acutely mindful of what Wayne Booth calls "the common aims that divide us," conference planners remained apprehensive throughout the four years preceding the event that we might end up a coalition in name only. We persisted, despite our doubts and disagreements, because we believed that recent reports critical of American education, which were already beginning to influence policymakers and the public, sometimes betrayed a limited understanding of English as a field. In particular, we feared that publications by William Bennett, E. D. Hirsch, and Allan Bloom and forthcoming reports by Lynne Cheney and Chester E. Finn and Dianne Ravitch threatened to return English to a pedagogical model that decades of our best research had demonstrated was ineffectual and unreliable. To counter these threats and correct these misunderstandings, it seemed both appropriate and necessary that a coalition of English teachers representing various perspectives and levels of schooling yet who potentially could speak with a unified voice should meet to establish directions for the study and teaching of English into the twenty-first century.

In organizing the Coalition Conference, we had in mind two earlier conferences that significantly influenced the discipline, the Basic Issues Conference (1958) and the Dartmouth Seminar (1966). As the result of major changes in the discipline and in the culture, that influence had become greatly extenuated in the intervening decades. On the one hand, virtually every assumption about the teaching of English accepted in the 1950s and early 1960s has been called into radical question. In the areas of writing, reading, and language acquisition, for instance, the focus of scholarly attention has shifted from product to process. Similarly, definitions of literature have been generally broadened, the canon as well as the idea of canonicity itself have been challenged, and the notion of the self-contained, autonomous text has, at least in some camps, been replaced by the more encompassing concept of textuality.

On the other hand, societal changes have resulted in a vastly altered student population. Increasing numbers of today's students are nonnative speakers, many of whom spent their early years in war-torn communities. Compared to school-age children of twenty-years ago, a greater percentage of today's children are likely to abuse drugs and alcohol, to engage in sexual activity at an early age, to live below the poverty line, to come from one-parent or two-earner families, to have an after-school job. More immersed in media and technology than their counterparts of twenty years ago, today's school children have grown up with and have been influenced in largely unidentified ways by television and computers. In general, English today is taught in a culture that is more pluralistic, more technologically influenced, more open, and therefore more complicated than the days of the Basic Issues Conference and the Dartmouth Seminar.

Accordingly, we determined that the group assembled in Maryland would have to be a heterogeneous mix, drawn from various racial, ethnic, geographic, and economic groups as well as from public and private schools at all levels. We came from twenty-three states and the District of Columbia. Eleven of us, almost 20 percent, are minorities; thirty-four of us, nearly 60 percent, women. (Only four of the twenty-eight participants at the Basic Issues Conference and only five of the forty-six conferees at Dartmouth had been women.) While the Dartmouth Seminar had billed itself as representing "all levels of education," only four of its participants held primary assignments in the schools. Similarly, only four classroom teachers participated in the Basic Issues Conference. By contrast, twenty-one participants in the Coalition Conference, more than one third of our membership, teach in elementary and secondary schools; another five, whose appointments are in colleges or divisions of education, specialize in teacher education. Twenty-nine of us teach in English departments at the postsecondary level—in community colleges, B.A./M.A. institutions, or, in a few cases, major research universities. The remaining five held administrative positions at the headquarters of NCTE, Association of Departments of English (ADE), or MLA.

A motley company we were, assembled there on the Eastern Shore to seek consensus despite our divergent backgrounds and experiences, our multiple priorities and agendas. Concordance seemed so unlikely that, as Phyllis Franklin recalls, "we opened the conference with accounts of why we thought it would not come about" (4). In Wye Woods, the July heat was already beginning to filter through the loblolly pines. Beyond the woods lay the Chesapeake Bay, with its tidal marshes and semisaline rivers, its Maryland blue crabs and Medusa jellyfish. Out there, air, water, land, and Earth's living matter, although teeming with variety, formed a complex ecosystem that functioned as a single organism. Could our own diversity be resolved into a similar ecology of purpose?

That consensus emerged is clear; why it emerged is difficult to specify. The fact that we met for three weeks, long enough to air our differences and to change our minds, was a crucial factor. Serendipity doubtlessly played a role, but so did the conference's formal organization. We met daily in two strands, one arranged according to level of schooling, the other, reconstituted each week, comprised of a systematic mix of teachers from the three levels. At plenary sessions, we heard progress reports from the strands and presentations from visiting speakers and selected conferees.[4] During the course of the conference, special interest groups formed and found time to meet outside of scheduled activities. Supplementing the productive talk and attentive listening were hundreds of pages of written material, including a list of books and articles each of us was asked to read before the conference, position papers written by each participant, and numerous essays containing thoughts, proposals, and disagreements that were generated "spontaneously" by participants during the conference. By the end of the meeting, all three of the Aspen Institute's photocopying machines and a fourth in a neighboring town had to be repaired. Such an intense communication exchange ensured that the full range of personalities and intellectual commitments gathered at Aspen Institute was expressed.

Consensus began to emerge early in the second week, impelled, I believe, by our responses to three speakers, two of whom had been scheduled to speak and a third who decided to drop in. Chester E. Finn, Assistant Secretary of Research and Improvement, U.S. Department of Education, was invited to address the group because we knew he endorsed Hirsch's recommendations and Hirsch himself had declined our invitation to participate. As expected, Finn extolled the putative virtues of the Hirschean program, then almost gleefully recounted a catalogue of facts that, according to a 1986 assessment of high school juniors, seventeen-year-olds do not know (e.g., that Columbus reached the New World before 1750, that Washington commanded the American Revolutionary forces, that Toronto is not in Italy). Because students do not know these facts, Finn deduced, they must never have encountered them in school. The reason for this omission, he continued, is that educators have "abdicated" their responsibility to impart knowledge and content, focusing instead on "skills." Citing the commercial success of Hirsch's *Cultural Literacy* and Bloom's *The Closing of the American Mind,* Finn concluded by entreating the conference participants to "catch up" with the American public.

Not surprisingly, Finn's condescending manner raised our collective hackles. Our internal differences appeared paltry when compared to the conceptual gulf separating Finn's idea of sound educational practices and our own. The group's reaction was so adverse, that Jane Christensen, NCTE's Deputy Executive Director and one of the conference planners, called Hirsch and asked him to reconsider his decision not to join us. Hirsch graciously agreed to fly in aboard a chartered plane and, while his pilot waited, to explain his program of cultural literacy to the conference. Whereas Finn had assumed an adversarial stance, Hirsch approached us as his colleagues, not as "part of the problem."[5] He attempted to explain that his brand of cultural conservatism actually serves progressive ends, because people lacking the circumscribed body of information that constitutes "cultural literacy" are disadvantaged. The following exchange, as reported by Elbow, ensued:

> Marie Buncombe (a black faculty member at Brooklyn College) asked, "Can't I be literate and not like you?" Remarkably, Hirsch didn't say, "But of course!" and go to talk about the senses in which we can have common culture and still diversity. Instead he talked about the sadness—the "down side of cultural literacy" (his phrase)—that cultural literacy and multiculturalism are in fact at odds. As in Richard Rodriguez (*The Hunger of Memory*), one must choose between them. (6)

At this point, we began to realize the necessity of transcending the kind of binary thinking underlying Finn's and Hirsch's argument. One of the "spontaneous" essays written during the conference is entitled "Either/Or Distinctions: The Flight from Complexity." In it, Robert Denham eloquently expresses the dangers of oppositional thinking:

> Both the language and the mode of some of our recent discussion, it seems to me, have tended toward rejecting rather than reshaping... opposing categories and so have reduced the rich complexity of language and learning to something less than it is. In one of the recent documents about goals, for example, we find these oppositions: constructing meaning vs. memorizing facts, making-meaning vs. mastering a predetermined body of knowledge, goals defined as experiences students should have vs. goals defined as peices of information. "Memorizing," "predetermined," and "pieces" load the case a bit against the other set of items in this series of oppositions: we naturally draw back from things that are routine, permanently fixed, and disparate or unconnected. My point, however, is that such dichotomies are false. It's difficult to see how either meaning or experience can be dissociated from facts, information, or knowledge.... Any adequate theory of language and learning must, it seems to me, get beyond a model of dialectical opposition to something more inclusive, holistic, and... interactive.

Similarly, Janet Emig reminded us in another "spontaneous" essay that at least three kinds of learning exist: learning that, learning how, and learning why. Emig continued, some "of the schemes we are considering—Hirsch on cultural literacy, for example—focus upon the first form of knowing exclusively; espouse a transmission model of culture, a model, incidentally, I thought the profession abandoned at Dartmouth." The ideal classroom should incorporate all three modes of learning. To recoil too drastically from the Hirschean valorization of content risked tilting the scales in the opposite direction, toward the knowing how or skills camp Assistant Secretary Finn had accused us of occupying. Balance was all. Similar to Barth's "webfoot, . . . marsh-nurtured writer," we, too, sought synthesis, coalescence of the various boundaries and distinctions, demarcations and bifurcations, that characterized the recent debates over educational reform and, at times, the discipline of English itself.

On the conference's eighth day, Shirley Brice Heath, Professor of English and Linguistics at Stanford University, coaxed us out of our reactive mode and set us on the road to consensus. Rooted in recent research in learning theory, the model Heath presented and the pedagogical implications of that model may be summarized as follows.[6] Learning is based on making connections between what we already know and new information we encounter. Indeed, without prior knowledge, new knowledge probably cannot be attained in any meaningful sense at all, a point Hirsch competently addresses in chapter 2 of *Cultural Literacy.*[7] While all learners come to school equipped with an extensive range of background knowledge, the information possessed may vary widely from student to student and may not, indeed, as Finn's study demonstrates, usually does not, comport with narrow definitions of *cultural literacy.* But if learning begins with the knowledge students bring to the classroom, it does not remain there, a point critics—and, alas, a few practitioners—of "expressive" writing or "affective" reading frequently misunderstand. Writer-based prose, whether in the form of free-writing activities or journals, helps students tap into their prior knowledge, ensuring a degree of intellectual involvement with a concept. So does classroom discussion in which students are encouraged to develop hypotheses and to test them on their own. Such activities focus on what students already know in order to help them build on it. The goal is a constant expansion of the student's store of personal knowledge, an ongoing conversion of secondary knowledge into primary knowledge throughout the years of formal education and beyond.

In the classroom we envision, students engage in extended acts of writing, reading, speaking, and listening "in such a way as they experience it as making a difference" (Elbow 66). These practices are then followed by extensive reflection, an important element in Heath's model. "At all levels of schooling," Franklin reports, "the group concluded [that] students need to get above and outside their own practices and understand how language works. In this way, they can become sufficiently self-critical to improve their work and adapt what they know to a variety of situations" (5).[8] The activities of engaged reading, writing, speaking, and listening followed by opportunities to reflect on these practices should result in an active learner who theorizes about his or her own learning and whose command of the language arts is exemplary.

An impressive body of research indicates that the setting most conducive to effective learning and retention is interactive, which is the classroom mode endorsed by the conference. George Hillocks contrasts this approach, which he calls the *environmental mode,* with the *presentational mode* characteristic of the conventional, performance-based classroom. "Teachers in [the environmental] mode . . . are likely to minimize lecture and teacher-led discussion. Rather, they structure activities so that, while teachers may provide brief introductory lectures, students work on particular tasks in small groups before proceeding to similar tasks independently. Although principles are taught, they are not simply announced and illustrated as in the presentational mode. Rather, they are approached through concrete materials and problems, the working through of which not only illustrates the principle but engages students in its use" (122). Language itself is an inescapably interactive activity, which assumes an audience (real or imagined) and some kind of response. At its most effective, the interactive English classroom functions as a community, providing not only frequent opportunities for language use (reading, listening, writing, speaking) but support and reactions from the class and the teacher. In Richard Lloyd-Jones's elegant phrase, it becomes a "goodly fellowship of writers and readers."

The subject of the interactive classroom is language, broadly defined, and the set of practices associated with language. How to use writing and talk as ways of knowing. How to write effectively to a variety of audiences and for a variety of purposes and occasions. How to read, interpret, and evaluate increasingly difficult and syntactically more complex texts. How to recognize the historical and cultural influences on language and its users. How to recognize when others use language to manipulate or influence us. These practices are inextricably bound to course content, including a broad variety of texts, both print and visual, literary and otherwise, representing a range of cultures and historical periods. All modes of textuality, including the electronic, should be examined, and student writing should itself provide material for close analysis. Because literature usually presents the greatest test of our interpretive and evaluative abilities, it should constitute a significant portion of the texts assigned. In addition to those works often described as "classics," students should be invited to read from the full panoply of our literary traditions, including works representing their own cultures and regions, the pluralistic American experience (including works by women and by racial and ethnic minorities), and the world at large.[9] While language study, particularly theories of language and systems of describing language, should be included in the English curriculum, rote exercise as a pedagogical mode should be avoided. In the interactive/integrative classroom we propose, examples of language used for systematic grammatical analysis and description as well as for vocabulary study should be selected from what the students regularly read, hear, speak, and write.

While our definitions of useful knowledge may be more inclusive than Hirsch's and our notion of significant literature more democratic than Bennett's, we do not disparage content. If we refuse to engage in list making, it is not because we respect knowledge less than they, but because we view such lists as reductive and usually in the service of a particular political or social agenda. Yet it must be understood that our differences with the adherents of Hirsch and Finn are paradigmatic rather than methodological. From our perspective, the argument as they formulate it, that it is better to teach content than to teach skills, is, at best, a red herring, at worst, meaningless.

Our appreciation and understanding of a Flannery O'Connor short story, for example, will be enhanced if we know certain facts about O'Connor's life and aesthetic: that she was a Roma Catholic living in the Protestant South, that she suffered from a debilitating disease that forced her to live most of her brief life as a semi-invalid, that she considered herself to be a religious writer. ("[M]y subject in fiction," she wrote, "is the action of grace in territory held largely by the devil" [118].) However interesting these facts may be, they are, in themselves, inadequate substitutes for the experience of reading O'Connor's fiction. Yet if the facts are made available to students in an effective manner, as the result, say, of having students read and discuss and write about pertinent selections from O'Connor's letters and essays, the information becomes incorporated into the student's store of prior knowledge. Thus integrated, knowledge about O'Connor does not merely contribute to but becomes an active ingredient in the student's reading experience.

This sense of integration is what the critic Louise Rosenblatt has in mind, I believe, when she describes the reading experience as a "richly fused cognitive-affective matrix" (40). At these moments, students do not respond separately to what they know about a text and their immediate experience of that text. Rather, the cognitive and the affective responses become fused, or, "perhaps more accurately," are apprehended "as facets of the same lived-through experience..." (46). At these moments, perceived dichotomies between skills and content dissolve into a seamless, integrated practice.

Mihaly Czikszentmihalyi describes this "deep, spontaneous involvement with the task at hand" as a state of "flow" (22). Such states do not themselves constitute learning experiences so much as they signify that learning has occurred. They are the payoff, the enjoyment that makes the hard work involved in learning worthwhile. Flow occurs when we experience a balance between a specific intellectual challenge—a poem to be understood, a math problem to be solved, a concept that needs to be worked through and formulated in writing—and our ability to meet that challenge. The dialectic of flow is both external, partly an objective feature of the situation, and internal, "partly... the result of one's subjective attitude" (22–23). When the challenge overwhelms a student's capacity to act, when, for example, a student lacks sufficient prior knowledge to work a particular math problem or understand a particular short story or write a particular kind of essay, flow is inhibited. It is similarly inhibited when the challenge is incommensurate to the student's abilities. On the one hand, students become frustrated and anxious; on the other hand, they become bored. In both instances, the intrinsic value of the experience becomes diminished to the point that meaningful learning does not take place.

Even when attained, states of flow are by nature transitory. "An essential feature of this structure of challenges and skills," explains Czikszentmihalyi, "is that their balance is not static. If the complexity of challenges one faces does not increase with time, flow gives way to boredom. As we practice an activity, our skills in it increase until they outweigh the challenges" (23). Accordingly, teachers must try to calibrate classroom activities in such a way that the complexity of challenges may be intensified or reduced in accordance with the students' abilities to meet those challenges. Because students at different ages and stages of development learn in different ways, and because these variations are likely to be more pronounced among children and adolescents, effective calibration in the secondary classroom is difficult, to say the least. While individualized programs of study are probably the most efficacious approach, practical considerations such as class size and time restrictions limit the feasibility of this instructional mode. But the integrative/interactive classroom as outlined above, which incorporates the principles of individualized learning into a community of learners, is both feasible and effective.

Such a classroom is, properly speaking, neither teacher- nor student-centered so much as it is learning-centered. It is based on the assumptions that the language arts are social and interactive, that meaning is negotiated and constructed, and that learning is active and relational. As Booth writes, "our conceptual worlds are not given but taken, not poured in but sucked in. Each mind actively constitutes its world . . ." (17). A large part of that world comprises information, including the information that Finn values and the terms on Hirsch's list. But that information is "sucked in" only when "charged by some motivated experience." What "sticks," Booth argues, 'is what we can construct into a context, one that provides a reason for attending to it" (17). The classroom we envision establishes a climate conducive to active inquiry and the practice of various means of inquiry, encourages reflection, in oral and written language, on these means of inquiry, and integrates all the language arts. It seeks to produce intrinsically motivated learners, who are both skillful practitioners and sophisticated theorists of the language arts.

While the teachers' function in an interactive classroom may appear to be deemphasized, nothing could be further from the case. Teachers determine classroom objectives, articulate these objectives clearly and specifically, set clear criteria for performance, and select the materials and problems designed to engage students with one another and with the teacher. They determine tasks, comment on performances, provide encouragement, serve as resources, and, as skilled practitioners of the language arts the students need to acquire, set an example. If these multiple roles are to be performed effectively, teachers in the interactive classroom must command a considerable range of knowledge. They should be conversant with contemporary learning theory, especially as it relates to language acquisition and cognitive development. They should have read widely in the literature of various cultures and time periods and should be thoroughly grounded in recent literary and reading theory as well as recent writing theory and practice. Given current projections that by the year 2000 a majority or near majority of students will be nonnative speakers, all English teachers, not just a few specialists, should be familiar with language structures, particularly as they relate to American dialects, English as a second language (ESL), and English as a foreign language (EFL), and they should be sufficiently aware of our diverse national culture to recognize the assumptions of students from many backgrounds. Most important, they should know that the various subjects within this field we call English—reading, composition, literature, language, and so on—are conceptually and practically interconnected and that no defensible hierarchy exists among them, that, indeed, the best approach to the teaching of English is integrative and ecological.

Throughout my discussion of the 1987 English Coalition Conference, I have relied on a metaphor of ecology, relating the sense of community shared by the sixty participants, the consensus that community fashioned, and the ecological and holistic nature of the classroom we envision to the natural setting we enjoyed for three weeks. Yet, even as we collaborated, the delicate balance of that magnificent ecosystem was threatened, the Chesapeake itself not immune to impurities and pollutants wafting in on air currents from industrial areas on all sides. Scattered about us, in the trees and on the islands (including Wye Island, around which some of us sailed on a rare free afternoon), were reminders of a grander pollution: to the north, the National Security Agency's (NSA) Espionage City at Fort George G. Meade and the U.S. Army's Edgewood Arsenal for Chemical and Biological Weapons Development' to the south, the Wallops Island Rocket Research and Test Firing Center and the Bloodsworth Island Naval Bombing Target; to the west, the Naval Surface Weapons Center and the headquarters of the Central Intelligence Agency (CIA). In Washington, D.C., only ninety minutes away, the Iran Contra hearings gripped a nation, proving once again that language itself is vulnerable to pollution by those who would use it to conceal, obfuscate, and control.

Democracies, like ecosystems, are fragile things, dependent on conditions that permit the balance of rights and relationships necessary to their preservation. A theme of patriotism, even jingoism, had characterized many of the educational reform documents, with their ominous references to national risk and legacies lost. On the conerence's last day, we realized that we, too, had been talking about America, although not in a narrowly nationalistic or chauvinistic sense. "Where language is corrupted or bastardized," writes George Steiner, "there will be a corresponding decline in the character and fortunes of the body politic" (78). That was our theme, the relationship between democracy and language. "Democracy through language" was not a "public-relations hook," as the *Chronicle of Higher Education* alleged ("English Teachers" 9), but an article of faith, an affirmation of our belief that effective self-government in a democracy depends upon a sophisticated understanding of language, that language has the power to empower.

If, as H. G. Wells observed, civilization is a race between education and catastrophe, our civilization's responsibility to establish the best educational system possible becomes, in our parlous age, fraught with urgency. The educational goal of the Hirscheans is "shared literate culture," the knowledge of a circumscribed and specific set of informational items. Knowing these items, they believe, will open doors to "independent thought and economic success" (Hirsch, "Postscript," 26). In a notorious passage, Hirsch writes, "It should energize people to learn that only a few hundred pages of information stand between the illiterate, between dependence and autonomy" (143). But the Coalition remains skeptical that memorizing bits of information, even 5,000 bits of information, will lead to independence of any kind, especially independence of thought. The Coalition believes that democracy is better served and catastrophe best kept at bay by a nation of learners, "a nation in which teachers, students, parents, and the great public would all be engaged in self-education—all eagerly reading and talking together about matters that matter" (Booth 21). These learners might not all know the same facts—in an age approaching information overload, the idea of such uniformity seems almost quaint—but the knowledge they have will be deep, and they will have acquired a lifetime habit of reflection. They will be "scrupulous to understand, alert to probe for blind spots and hidden agendas, and, finally, critical, questioning, skeptical," possessing what conferee Robert Scholes calls "textual power" (16). In short, they will have acquired the independence of thought politicians publicly praise but often privately fear.

Implementing the educational model we propose will not be easy. Hirsch's proposal, around which the "shared content" advocates have rallied, enjoys enormous popular appeal, having brought him fame and fortune virtually unprecedented among English professors. (If he sometimes behaves like a man merchandising an idea rather than professing one, it is easy to understand why.) Although touted as a "new idea" ("Postscript" 26), the notion of cultural literacy is quite traditional, with its conceptual ties to the prescriptive tradition of the nineteenth century, the Great Books tradition of the 1930s and 1940s, and the Basic Issues Conference of the late 1950s[10]—which explains its attraction to the political right. Unlike the Coalition model, which grows out of research in the areas of learning theory, language theory, rhetorical/writing theory, reading theory, and literary theory and at whose complexity and power I have only been able to hint, the Hirschean model is rather easily grasped, easily reduced to slogans and catch phrases.[11] The equation of intelligence with erudition has a certain no-nonsense quality that appeals to the same conventional wisdom which insists that formal grammar instruction is the best way to teach writing, despite twenty years of research findings to the contrary. (I yield to no one in my respect for good old American horse-sense, but in this instance it is simply misguided.)

Unlike our recommendations, which stipulate changes in the English curriculum, teacher education programs, and the environment in which many teachers are forced to work,[12] the shared-content model is easily adaptable to current conditions. Whereas the interactive model requires small classes that meet for extended periods of time and that include healthy amounts of writing and discussion, the teacher-centered, knowledge-transmission model can be easily implemented in large classes, which is the norm in most secondary schools today. Although Hirsch nods briefly at the integrative, intensive curriculum that the Coalition believes is essential to meaningful learning, the "curriculum reform" he develops at length in *Cultural Literacy* invloves a "return" to the extensive curriculum. "We should teach more surveys that cover large movements of human thought and experience" (132), he writes, ignoring recent evidence that surveys have remained a staple in undergraduate literature curricula for forty years and are, indeed, required in the English major at 70 percent of the nation's institutions (Harris 61). At the secondry level, too, the pattern of requiring an American literature survey in the junior year and a British literature survey in the senior year continues to predominate. The Hirschean "curriculum reforms" require few changes. To the contrary, they perpetuate the coverage model, which has come under increasing attack from the profession at large in recent years.[13]

Moreover, intense focus on content tends to sustain the current organization of the field of English, with its range of often tenuously related subdivisions and specializations. There is something faintly undemocratic about this arrangement, which resembles a mosaic rather than a melting pot. The Coalition model does not subvert the necessity of specialization. As Gerald Graff has observed, "Anyone seriously committed to the idea of democratic mass education has to acknowledge the obvious necessity for some form of bureaucratic departmental organization and the specialized division of labor that entails" ("Taking Cover" 42). But, in the Coalition model, the demarcations separating our various areas of specialization become more fluid, and the invidious distinctions among them disappear altogether. Similarly, the often hostile relationships between English departments and schools or colleges of education will have to be repaired because the integrative/interactive English classroom requires a teacher as thoroughly grounded in learning theory as in the so-called content areas of English studies.

The shared-content approach further preserves the status quo by feeding into the current mass assessment mania, which tends to equate effective teaching with the amount of information transmitted to the student. Obviously, measuring information is easier and far less expensive. But the results of these tests are often compared on a school-by-school or state-by-state basis, which exerts unhealthy influences on the curriculum, as teachers are exhorted by principals eager for public relations gains to "teach to the test." As Czikszentmihalyi notes, measuring how many correct answers students have marked on a standardized test "is not terribly useful unless one knows whether the students want to retain, use, and increase the information learned. Knowledge that is not intrinsically motivated is not much good to anybody" (18). In a statement endorsed by the whole group, the Coalition calls for assessment instruments that measure more than mere information retrieval and affirms that the most trustworthy assessment is usually conducted by individual teachers in their own classrooms as an integral part of the teaching process.

So the Coalition model, with its revisionary implications, will not be easily implemented. Yet, after two year's reflection on the consensus of Wye Woods, I remain optimistic. Our consensus was not self-fulfilling, the predictable accord of a group selected because they shared a predetermined set of assumptions. Indeed, most of us were meeting personally for the first time. Concurrence was earned. Yet, because it was derived from the best of current theory and research in the areas of learning and cognition, language and composition, reading and literature, as well as from the classroom experiences of sixty dedicated teachers, the consensus that emerged in Wye Woods was guided by a certain inevitability. This is why I have retained my optimism. The relatively brief history of English as a school subject, although diverted by periodic attempts to "return to basics," has never really reverted. Rather, the field has continued to evolve through a series of accommodations, assimilations, and redefinitions, in the direction of greater comprehensiveness and inclusiveness, its scope "too broad, its influence on those who teach it too consuming, for it to long remain confined within a narrow framework" (Applebee 255). The consensus of Wye Woods continues this tradition, forging our profession's variegated commitments, concerns, and priorities into an ecological project that will lead us boldly into the twenty-first century.

Notes

1. Funds for the conference were provided by the Rockefeller Foundation, the Mellon Foundation, the Exxon Foundation, and the National Endowment for the Humanities.

2. These associations are the Association of Departments of English, the College English Association, the College Language Association, the Conference for Secondary School English Department Chairpersons, the Conference on College Composition and Comunication, the Conference on English Education, the Modern Language Association, and the National Council of Teachers of English. Joe D. Thomas provides an interesting account of the College English Association's "secession" from the NCTE (1–8).

3. By the end of the conference, we were able to poke affectionate fun at our jargonistic tendencies. A delightful example was "The Coalition Country Blues," written and performed by Jim Bob Jumpback (a.k.a., Joe Lostracco, a community college teacher from Austin, Texas) and his group, The Dips (comprised of five teachers from the three school levels), the chorus of which goes:

   I've been so situated
   That I'm constipated
   And I'm sure that
   Elbow gets my drift.

Though the canon exploded
And lit'racy eroded
I don't give a paradigm shift!

The Elbow of the fourth line is, of course, Peter, a participant in the conference.

4. The visiting speakers were Chester E. Finn; E. D. Hirsch, Jr.; Shirley Brice Heath; Gerald Graff; and Jerome Singer. Conferees who presented talks or led demonstrations were Wayne Booth, Janet Emig, Richard Lloyd-Jones, Nellie McKay, Robert Scholes, William Teale, and Brooke Workman.

5. Shortly after his visit to Wye Woods, Finn told the *Chronicle of Higher Education,* "They are part of the problem, the people who met there. I had hoped they would be part of the solution. What's worse is they're influential in the field, so the solutions to the problems they have caused will have to be made not with them, but in spite of them" ("In Box," 9). In a recent essay, Hirsch similarly misrepresents our intentions, contending that we "would trivialize the teaching of shared content if presented the opportunity of doing so" (22). Hirsch, who, as does Finn, attended the conference for less than half a day, dismisses the Coalition consensus thusly: "... a group-think conference is not itself the place to encourage independent thought" (23).

6. In constructing this summary, I have relied heavily on the report of the 1987 English Coalition Conference. Entitled *Democracy Through Language* and edited by Richard Lloyd-Jones and Andrea A. Lunsford, the report has just been published jointly by NCTE and MLA as this present volume goes to press. At times, I have silently incorporated into my essay the actual language of the report, which is itself a paraphrase and consolidation of various resolutions and positions adopted in principle by the entire group.

7. Without prior knowledge, according to Adams and Bruce, "a complex subject, such as a text, is not just difficult to interpret; strictly speaking, it is meaningless" (20).

8. And we do mean at all levels. Even grammar, the study of which some surveys indicate should be a postponed until the twelfth grade, could, if approached interactively, be taught to the youngest of our students. "It's not a question of whether or when to teach grammar but how. The content of grammar isn't the issue [Heath] said, but how it's taught. Teaching grammar is perfectly appropriate, even in kindergarten—she wants to see it in kindergarten—but it must be by means of an active, empirical, inductive process. Students, even kindergarteners, need to be asked to use and find language and then ... examine it, discuss the usages, and work out hypotheses about how it is used. In effect—and she acknowledges this and has tried it out extensively—she is saying we can make students into little participant-observer anthropologists: hypothesis makers" (Elbow 7).

9. See "Some Plain Truths about Teaching English," point three ("A Coalition of English Associations" 14).

10. As Arthur Applebee points out, the "most important assertion" of the Basic Issues Conference" was that English must be regarded as a 'fundamental liberal discipline,' a body of specific knowledge to be preserved and transmitted rather than a set of skills or an oppor-

tunity for guidance and individual adjustment" (193). Applebee also provides information about the prescriptive tradition (6–8) and the Great Books movement (185–88).

11. Sometimes, Hirsch seems to sense the reductive nature of his argument. At one point in *Cultural Literacy,* he describes the intensive curriculum as "essential" (128) and even declares that facts and skills are "inseparable" (133). Yet the major thrust of his argument provides those who insist upon the primacy of content all the ammunition they need. As Booth writes in his open letter to Hirsch, "Your alphabetized list and your emphases are certain to provide many educationists with just one more way of avoiding a solid education in literature, rhetoric, history, language, math, and science. Again, I know that you don't want that. But just watch what happens" (21). While the Hirscheans rather than Hirsch himself will cause most of the mischief, he must share part of the responsibility for their excessess.

12. These conditions are frequently intolerable. In an essay circulated at the conference, Brooke Workman, an Iowa high school teacher, writes: "When the American high school English teacher arrives at school on a hot, humid Monday morning, he or she knows that the institutional environment will work against the best of her lessons. The teacher knows that the world—as well as the world of the students—had realities and rhythms that counter what is wanted most of all: learning." Recommended changes in teaching and learning conditions are contained in a document entitled "Rights and Responsibilities for Students and Teachers," included in the Lloyd-Jones and Lunsford report. Among these is the Coalition recommendation that secondary teachers be assigned no more than four classes per day and a maximum of 100 students, that classroom be free or virtually free of interruptions (from intercom announcements, for example), and that class periods be sufficiently long for the achievement of educational objectives.

13. A large majority at the April 1987 Minnesota Conference on the Future of Doctoral Study in English, attended by representatives from eighty-two institutions, agreed that "the principle of coverage of a select canon of British and American authors had collapsed as an effective organizational tool for the discipline at large" and "that an effective curricular and disciplinary organization ought to embody an integration of reading and writing at all levels of theory and practice" (Denham 37). Graff presents a convincing argument for the abandonment of this outmoded curricular model in *Professing Literature.*

Works Cited

"A Coalition of English Associations Responds to Education Reformers." *MLA Newsletter* 16.3 (1984):14–15.

Adams, Marilyn, and Bertram Bruce. *Background Knowledge and Reading Comprehension.* ERIC, 1980 ED 520 346.

Applebee, Arthur N. *Tradition and Reform in the Teaching of English.* Urbana, Ill.: National Council of Teachers of English, 1974.

Barth, John. *The Friday Book: Essays and Other Nonfiction.* New York: Putnam's, 1984.

Bennett, William. "'To Reclaim a Legacy': Text of Report on Humanities in Education." *Chronicle of Higher Education* 28 November 1984:16–21.

Bloom, Allan. *The Closing of the American Mind: How Higher Education Has Failed Democracy and Impoverished the Souls of Today's Students.* New York: Simon and Schuster, 1987.

Booth, Wayne. "Cultural Literacy and Liberal Learning: An Open Letter to E. D. Hirsch, Jr." *Change* 20.4 (1988), 11–21.

Cheney, Lynne E. *American Memory: A Report on the Humanities in the Nation's Public Schools.* Washington, D.C. National Endowment for the Humanities Office of Publications, 1987.

Czikszentmihalyi, Mihaly. "Intrinsic Motivation and Effective Teaching: A Flow Analysis." *New Directions for Teaching and Learning: Motivating Professors to Teach Effectively,* J. Bess, ed. San Francisco: Jossey-Bass, 1982: 15–26.

Denham, Robert D. "Response to the Minnesota Conference on the Future of Doctoral Study in English." *ADE Bulletin* 89 (Spring) 1988:37.

Elbow, Peter. "A Remarkable Consensus." *Massachusetts English Teacher.* March 1968: 1, 6–7.

Finn, Chester E., and Diane Ravitch. *What Do Our 17-Year-Olds Know?* New York: Harper and Row, 1987.

Franklin, Phyllis. "From the Editor." *MLA Newsletter* 19.3 (1987): 4–5.

Graff, Gerald. *Professing Literature: An Institutional History.* Chicago: University of Chicago Press, 1987.

________. "Taking Cover in Coverage." *Profession 86.* New York: Modern Language Association, 1986. 41–45.

Harris, Charles B. "The ADE Ad Hoc Committee on the English Curriculum: A Progress Report." *Profession 87.* New York: Modern Language Association, 1987. 60–65.

Heller, Scott. "English Teachers Favor Emphasis on How to Read, Write, Think, Rather than on Becoming Familiar with Specific Literary Works." *Chronicle of Higher Education* 5 August 1987: 9–10.

Hillocks, George, Jr. *Research on Written Composition: New Directions for Teaching.* Urbana, Ill.: ERIC Clearinghouse on Reading and Communication Skills and the National Conference on Research in English, 1986.

Hirsch, Jr., E. D. *Cultural Literacy: What Every American Needs to Know.* Boston: Houghton-Mifflin, 1987.

________. "A Postscript by E. D. Hirsch, Jr." *Change* 20.4 (1988): 22–26.

"In Box." *Chronicle of Higher Education,* 12 August 1987:9.

O'Connor, Flannery. *Mystery and Manners,* Sally and Robert Fitzgerald, eds. New York: Farrar, Straus, and Giroux, 1961.

Rosenblatt, Louise M. *The Reader, The Text, The Poem: The Transactional Theory of the Literary Work.* Carbondale: Southern Illinois University Press, 1978.

Scholes, Robert. *Textual Power: Literary Theory and the Teaching of English.* New Haven, Conn.: Yale University Press, 1985.

Steiner, George. *After Bable: Aspects of Language and Translation.* New York: Oxford University Press, 1975.

Thomas, Joe D. *Sansculotte: A Nonknickerbocker History of the College English Association (1938–1975).* Lewisburg, Penn.: College English Association Foundation, 1987.

R. Baird Shuman

3. *Secondary School English Teachers: Past, Present, Future*

In order to understand the role of English teachers in today's schools, one must know how English evolved as a school subject and how, through the years, both the definition and training of high school English teachers have changed. One must also know some of the structural and curricular changes that have taken place in the secondary schools of the United States from the nation's inception to the present day.

High school English teachers and secondary school English teachers were one and the same in the United States until the twentieth century. In a society that was largely agricultural, American education was organized on the 8-4 plan. The first eight years of school were considered the elementary years. They concentrated on those areas of learning that today are considered the basics: reading, writing, and arithmetic.

The secondary years, which encompased the four years of high school, grades nine through twelve, had a set, college-preparatory curriculum. Until the early 1900s, high school graduation requirements and college entrance requirements were identical because it was assumed that anyone who attended school beyond the elementary level did so in order to prepare for college. Through the years, however, as the organization of public schools has changed, the junior high school and the middle school, as well as the senior high school, have generally come to be considered secondary. In some communities, students' secondary educations technically begin as early as the fifth or sixth grades.

Middle schools are not high schools, but they are considered secondary schools. Secondary school teacher certification in English in many states still enables people to teach in middle schools, junior high schools, and senior high schools, even though it is becoming increasingly common for states to issue separate certificates for the various levels of secondary education and for college and universities to offer course work specifically in middle-level education.

THE NINETEENTH-CENTURY SECONDARY SCHOOL

From the founding of the United States until shortly after 1900, fewer than 10 percent of all teenagers continued their educations beyond the eighth grade. The work from which most people derived their livelihoods did not require a high school education, so secondary and postsecondary education were reserved for the small and select group of students who planned to go into the professions—law, medicine, the clergy, or teaching. Most students, except for some of those who planned careers in teaching, were male.

People who contend that high school graduates at the turn of the century were more literate than their present-day counterparts are correct. These critics, however, usually omit one crucial detail from their assessments—whereas 10 percent of the nation's youth attended secondary school at the turn of the century, nearly 100 percent of today's youth stay in school until age sixteen, and a large percentage of these students eventually obtain high school diplomas.

Despite the vehement outcries of people who accuse our schools of not educating young people effectively, the United States has in its population today the largest percentage of competent readers and writers it has ever had. Because such a large percentage of the school-age population is in school, admittedly not all high school graduates are functionally literate, although the recent widespread use of competency tests to ensure that students have mastery of basic minimal skills has made it more difficult for one to be graduated from high school without mastery of the rudiments of reading, writing, and mathematics. High schools, which once were highly selective, are now open to everyone. Today's deficient readers and writers might well have been totally illiterate had they lived two or three generations earlier.

The spread of free, public education and the nationwide enactment of compulsory attendance laws have changed the educational landscape dramatically since 1900 and in so doing have changed as well the definition of secondary education. Given these changes, the roles of secondary school English teachers have also changed considerably as schools have sought to address the needs of their increasingly diverse student bodies.

THE BEGINNINGS OF CHANGE

In 1892, the National Education Association's (NEA) Committee of Ten, an outgrowth of the educational reform movement of the 1890s, gave its support to the 8-4 configuration upon which most precollegiate education in the United States was based. The committee recommended that four curricula be available to students for the four high school years.

The classical curriculum was modeled after the curriculum of the German *Gymnasium,* which prepared students to enter training for law or the clergy. It had long been in place in American education and was to be retained, as was the

Latin-scientific curriculum, roughly akin to the curriculum of the German *Realgymnasium,* whose aim was to prepare students to pursue scientific studies or medicine at the university.

Also recommended were a modern language curriculum appropriate to those interested in teaching foreign languages or in entering the diplomatic service, and an English curriculum, aimed at preparing the university students who would pursue studies roughly equivalent today to the liberal arts curriculum (*Report of the Committee of Ten* 17).

The committee called for longer and more intensive study of fewer subjects than high school students were typically exposed to at that time. In an effort to move toward equality of educational standards across the country, the committee suggested greater uniformity of approach and methodology, largely so that students continuing to colleges and universities would have similar background knowledge, something that was not ensured by the broad range of secondary school offerings up to that time. Because each of the four curricula was college-preparatory, secondary education clearly was still synonymous with college-preparatory education.

Less than a decade after the Committee of Ten deliberated, however, the NEA's influential Committee on College Entrance Requirements issued a report that called for substantial changes in the definition of secondary education and for significant curricular changes as well. This committee, appointed in 1895, recommended that secondary education commence at grade seven rather than at grade nine, that science courses be sequential, and that students be permitted to pursue some electives.

It called for provisions that would allow gifted students to enroll in accelerated programs and, perhaps more important than any of its other recommendations, it stipulated that academic studies in secondary schools be described in terms of units, each unit representing the study of a substantive secondary school subject for four or five hours a week over an entire school year (*Report on the Committee on College Entrance* 670–72).

Until this time, secondary schools had various emphases, often dictated by the interests and training of those teaching in them. Courses of study were not defined by such standard measures as the Carnegie unit, which is widely used today. When the concept of a standard unit of study was devised, higher institutions were assured that students from New York State or Virginia who had credit for three or four units of mathematics or foreign language had training at least roughly equivalent to that given their counterparts in Ohio, Massachusetts, or Rhode Island.

This report first pointed toward the development of junior high schools, whose establishment was much supported by the fledgling labor unions that were beginning to come into prominence early in the twentieth century. The unions, eager to keep unskilled and semiskilled teenagers out of the labor force for as long as they could, supported the idea of having elementary school end with grade six and having adolescent students attend a transitional institution that would educate them through grade nine.

Union leaders reasoned that under the new organization, noncollege-bound students, who would normally have left school at the end of the eighth grade, would probably stay in school another year in order to complete junior high school. In earlier generations, the prevailing agrarian economy could absorb unskilled and semiskilled people into its work force more readily than the new industrial society.

The 6-3-3 configuration offered hope that students who had no thought of going to college would be kept out of the labor market for an additional year, thereby reducing the numbers of unskilled or semiskilled people who entered the industrial work force every year. Before long, the conventional 8-4 pattern in public education was replaced in many urban and suburban school districts by a 6-3-3 pattern, in which junior and senior high schools were both regarded as secondary institutions.

THE EMERGING SECONDARY SCHOOL ENGLISH TEACHER

The offerings in the earliest American secondary schools were extremely limited and were packed into a school year that sometimes ran for only two or three months. Besides the classical languages, students studied religion, history, sometimes astronomy, and English, both language and literature. This humanistic emphasis prepared the few students who passed through such schools to enter universities that offered a liberal arts education to small groups of students taught a standard curriculum by one or two masters. It was not unusual for graduating classes of universities such as Yale to have in them fewer than twelve men who had all pursued an identical curriculum.

As time passed, more science and mathematics were incorporated into the curricula of universities, some of whose graduates inevitably became secondary school teachers. These teachers initially had no specific training in pedagogy and, in most cases, taught essentially as they themselves had been taught. Because they were reasonably well-grounded in the limited range of subjects that constituted their university course work and because secondary schools were small and informal, often staffed by only one or two teachers, university graduates were considered capable of teaching every course offered at the secondary school level.

As a result of university graduates not pursuing academic majors as university students do today, most of them had had as much emphasis during their university years on Latin and Greek as they had had on English literature or on history or on mathematics and science. Those graduates who ultimately became secondary school teachers were generalists rather than specialists and taught what needed to be taught. If they served in a school that employed several teachers, they might then be permitted to teach what they personally preferred, subjects that interested them rather than subjects in which they had had the kind of emphasis that an academic major in a modern college or university presently provides (Stiles 184).

Secondary schools in the second half of the nineteenth century were somewhat stronger than most such institutions had been earlier, largely because teachers were beginning to be better trained and some were beginning to specialize. In the late eighteenth and early nineteenth centuries, not all secondary school teachers were university graduates, and few elementary school teachers had completed more than elementary school themselves.

Until the current century, teacher certification requirements were largely nonexistent. People learned how to teach by teaching. In the early days, a teacher might teach grammar, foreign languages, history, mathematics, science, and religion. Specialization was not practical or possible in most of the small secondary schools that dotted the young nation.

Even with the growth in the late nineteenth and early twentieth centuries of normal schools, institutions designed specifically to train teachers, students preparing to be high school teachers essentially finished their university programs and plunged directly into teaching in which, during their initial year, they often survived by their wits rather than because they had been prepared in any organized way to be teachers. The normal schools were designed primarily to train elementary school teachers, and the prevailing attitude was that anyone who had finished a university program knew how to teach in the college-preparatory programs that comprised secondary education.

Vestiges of this attitude have recently surfaced in states such as Virginia and New Jersey, both of which currently grant initial teacher certification in their major fields to college graduates whose majors are in subjects offered in the secondary school curriculum. The major difference between such new certification requirements and the former standards for employing secondary school teachers is that the provisional certification granted to such people nowadays can be made permanent only after they have taught satisfactorily for a given length of time, during which they have been supervised regularly in the classroom. They must also complete some approved professional training in order to receive permanent certification.

TWO HARVARD UNIVERSITY PRESIDENTS AND PUBLIC EDUCATION

Two presidents of Harvard University, living more than a generation apart, Charles W. Eliot and James Bryant Conant, have had a profound effect upon secondary school teaching generally and upon the teaching of English specifically. Significantly these two heads of the oldest and most prestigious university in the United States felt that secondary education and the training of teachers were matters of sufficient importance that they spent considerable time investigating such topics as secondary school curriculum and the training of teachers for secondary schools. Both men persevered in gathering data that suggested new directions for both precollegiate and teacher education.

Charles W. Eliot, a mathematician and chemist, served as Harvard's president from 1869 until 1909, and in 1892 was appointed chair of the NEA's Committee of Ten. Although Eliot was strenuously opposed to lock-step university education, he advocated the kind of uniformity in secondary education that would permit colleges and universities to assume that their entering students had certain minimal backgrounds and abilities on which the higher institution could build. Under Eliot's presidency, Harvard moved to a highly controversial program of electives that eliminated the stereotyped curriculum that then characterized most higher education in the United States.

Eliot envisioned a reorganization of public education, favoring a 6-4-4 configuration in which the first two years of college, those in which general education is emphasized, would be added to the secondary school curriculum. He thought that such a change, clearly a precursor of the community college movement, would make higher education more readily available to the nation's youth. In this way, many young people could go to college without leaving home (Krug 49), thereby extending the base of higher education and putting it within the financial reach of more students than had previously been able to benefit from it.

Eliot's attempts to liberate university students from a set curriculum was not lost on secondary school teachers and administrators. The secondary school population changed drastically during the first two decades of the twentieth century as compulsory attendance laws were enacted in most states and as sweeping curricular changes were mandated by legislation such as the Smith-Hughes Act of 1917, which encouraged vocational education at the secondary school level and provided federal funds for its implementation.

The traditional college-preparatory education of the past offered little promise for secondary schools that were now admitting hordes of students who had no thought of continuing to college and who, in many cases, had significant problems in such basic areas as reading, writing, speaking, and simple arithmetic, problems that still beset education today.

In time, Eliot's idea of elective courses pervaded the secondary schools of the nation, an outcome that Eliot had not foreseen. This meant that by the 1950s and 1960s, English teachers had great motivation to teach in their own fields and to sharpen and extend their skills within the field of their academic training, to specialize in specific areas of the curriculum. The range of courses available for them to teach broadened to include not only grammar and traditional literature but also such elective courses as genre studies, writing, journalism, oral English, and theme courses, such as "Death and Dying," "War Literature," and "The Young Adult Novel." English became an entrenched requirement in secondary school curricula, nearly all of which demanded three years of English for all students between grades nine and twelve.

James Bryant Conant, president of Harvard University from 1933 until 1953, was, like President Eliot, a scientist. He has been a professor of chemistry before his appointment to the presidency of the university. He admitted to having had negative feelings about courses in pedagogy and about colleges of education. As he came, however, to adopt the broad view that university presidents must necessarily develop if they are to succeed, Conant became increasingly concerned with teacher training and with the schools. He spent the early years of his retirement examining secondary schools and exploring the ways in which higher institutions train teachers.

Conant called for comprehensive high schools (*American High School* 11–40) that would replace small secondary schools with severely limited offerings, and his recommendations were heeded as consolidation of small schools took place across the country during the 1960s and early 1970s. Conant advocated that secondary school programs be individualized to suit the particular needs and abilities of each student and by the 1970s, some schools, through computerized scheduling, were able to provide all students with programs unique to them every week or every month. Conant also called for ability grouping on the secondary school level. He specifically recommended that slow readers be given special consideration and that developmental reading programs be instituted.

Conant suggested specific curricular requirements for high school graduation, and many states adopted his recommendations with dispatch. He recommended four years of English rather than the three that many states required at that time. Conant gave teeth to his recommendation by specifying that "Each student should be required to write an average of one theme a week. Themes should be corrected by the teacher. In order that teachers of English have adequate time for handling these themes, no English teacher should be responsible for more than 100 pupils" (50–51).

At the time Conant did his research, English teachers typically taught about 140 students a day in five periods. Although few districts have achieved Conant's ideal of having English teachers responsible for a maximum of 100 students, his recommendation resulted in some reduction in student load for English teachers and heightened administrative awareness of the unique demands English teachers face in grading written work. The NCTE has provided school administrators and boards of education with constant reminders of Conant's proposal and has recently upgraded its recommendations to reflect the suggestions of the 1987 Coalition Conference (see chapter 2).

Conant's investigation of teacher education led him to conclusions that have broad implications for secondary school English teachers. Convinced that American public education could prosper only if substantial changes took place in the way teachers are prepared, Conant advocated that prospective secondary school teachers be recruited from among college students in the upper one third of their classes academically (*American Teachers* 81). He contended that college students should not have to sit through classes that are boring and repetitious to them but that they should be encouraged to meet some course requirements by taking proficiency examinations.

In order to ensure the most comprehensive possible preparation for teachers in the fields in which they teach, Conant contended that teachers in grades seven through twelve should be certified in one subject area only, a recommendation that repudiated the routine practice of certifying all secondary school teachers in a major field and in one or more minor fields.

Addressing the training of English teachers specifically, Conant suggested that it was not sufficient for those preparing to teach merely to have completed the English major offered by most colleges and universities. This major, usually weighted heavily in favor of traditional literary offerings, might provide adequate background for the prospective graduate student in English or American literature but would not serve the secondary school teacher well.

Conant said that in addition to the English major, secondary school certification in English should be based upon satisfactory completion of courses in the structure of the English language and in modern grammar, in adolescent literature as well as in the traditional offerings in British and American literature, in the teaching of reading, in speech and drama, and in advanced-level composition. Conant's recommendations were accepted by most states virtually as he presented them, and certification requirements have increasingly come to reflect these recommendations.

It is heartening that two presidents of one of the country's most prestigious private institutions should have become concerned as fully as Eliot and Conant did with matters of public secondary education. These two men, whose academic training was essentially scientific, became champions for a liberal, humanistic teacher education. Their recommendations, widely heeded by the educational community, led the way to stronger teacher training programs, brought about more uniform secondary school requirements, and gave credence to the notion that teachers should be given every encouragement to specialize.

WHAT ARE THE BOUNDARIES OF THE ENGLISH TEACHER'S JOB?

By the 1920s, it was difficult to say what English was because English teachers were beginning to teach a broad array of courses in literature, in such social skills as etiquette, in language, and in writing, a condition that persists in some degree to the present. Many English teachers had received no formal training for the teaching they were being called upon to do.

In his presidential address to the NCTE in 1920, James F. Hosic emphasized the need for the profession to define what it was about, to make a clear statement stipulating the boundaries within which it was working. A few years later, Hosic's colleague, Dudley Miles, wrote that "as a professional group we [English teachers] do not know what we are trying to do" (Miles 1). This need for definition and direction has persisted even to the present.

The dichotomy that exists between the college and university definition of English and that of both elementary and secondary schools has long been evident. In most higher institutions today, particularly in the more prestigious ones, English is defined as the study and criticism of literature. Courses in film have sprung up, but literature is still at the heart of most college English programs. Although writing courses are offered, in most schools they are second to literature, as are courses in the history and structure of the English language and in modern grammar.

Beginning English teachers have regularly expressed dismay at discovering that literature constitutes a small corner of the secondary school English program, where the emphasis usually is more on grammar and writing than on literature. Given the diverse student bodies found in today's schools, many secondary school students have not developed reading skills sufficient to allow them to read the literature traditionally found in the British/American canon. Schools have placed increased emphasis on minority literature as well as on adolescent literature, yet many English programs in colleges and universities require little emphasis in such areas. The one course in adolescent literature mandated by most states for teacher certification in English is not enough to make teachers feel competent in a field that is rapidly changing and expanding.

The rush to programs with multiple electives in the secondary schools of the 1960s and 1970s has slowed in recent years as many schools move toward more standardized curricula, and this is probably desirable. In the period when multiple electives were in vogue, many an English teacher had to plan courses in sports literature, animal literature, death and dying, vocational literature, and all manner of other specialties, often with only a few days' warning.

Although the multiple electives idea is a philosophically sound one because it seemed designed to make the greatest use of each teacher's specific talents, it became a travesty in many school districts as English teachers were assigned to teach courses for which they had little preparation and in which they sometimes had little interest. A ten -or twelve-week course conceived over a weekend is not likely to benefit many of the people taking it. Also, unless such courses are carefully planned and monitored in terms of a school's overall English program, many students may take the requisite number of courses for graduation credit without having studied the areas of English they need in a balanced and coherent English program.

School administrators found that the electives approach to education sometimes caused serious disbalances in class size and that they often had to compromise the ideals of such programs by insisting that students take electives they did not wish to take in order to distribute teaching loads fairly. Faced with recent stringent budgets and motivated by the back-to-basics philosophy that has been popular, most school administrators have moved back to having English teachers teach overall semester-long or year-long courses, identified by grade level, that include a combination of literature, language, writing, oral English, and listening skills.

WHO TEACHES ENGLISH TODAY

Today's English teachers, particularly if they are graduates of the teacher training programs of accredited higher institutions, will generally have had the sort of background in English that Conant recommended. They will also have had both general and special methods courses, a course in educational psychology, a course in educational foundations, and a supervised teaching internship in a secondary school.

A national accrediting agency, the National Council for the Accreditation of Teacher Education (NCATE), has done a great deal since the 1960s to bring about uniform standards of teacher preparation throughout the United States and has also moved toward allowing certified teachers to be granted reciprocal certification when they move from one state to another.

Surveys by Elizabeth Cowan and Jeannie Oakes present information that suggests what the typical English teacher in the United States of the 1980s is like. Holly O'Donnell's overview of these surveys reveals a great deal about who goes into the secondary school teaching of English as a career and about how these teachers perceive themselves.

First, the reports reveal that the average secondary school English teacher in the United States in the 1980s was a white female between thirty and thirty-nine years old. Most of them had been teaching from eight to fifteen years and earned an average annual salary of $20,106.97. The majority taught either in a suburb of a large city or in a small town or rural setting. Most entered teaching because they like to work with people and because they love their subjects and want to share their academic enthusiasms with others. As a group, they felt that their hopes for a satisfying career had been fulfilled reasonably well.

Most of them had had college or university majors or minors in English, and most had taken additional course work in either English or education after they had been certified. They had also attended in-service training programs in English that focused on the secondary school teaching of the subject.

Most of those surveyed said that they would become English teachers again if they had it to do over, although they felt that they did not have enough help in doing their jobs, which require an average of 12.47 hours of work each week outside the twenty-five or more hours they spend in actual classroom teaching. Although most belonged to three or more professional organizations, they did not usually attend the national or state meetings of those organizations. They do, however, read their publications at the rate of about nine per year and consider their professional journals valuable to them as teachers. They say that if they were to leave teaching, it would be because of personal frustration or lack of satisfaction with their own job performances. As a group, they complain that they have little influence over school issues.

Most of the teachers surveyed do not support the recent emphasis on teaching basic skills to the exclusion of more intellectually challenging materials. They resist such quick-fix suggestions as those contained in E. D. Hirsch's recent *Cultural Literacy* (Heller 10). They think that students should be permitted to leave school at age fourteen if they can pass a standard exit examination. At the top of their list of matters with which they think professional organizations should concern themselves is the quality of teachers.

They find that lack of student interest is one of their greatest frustrations, and this concern, of course, is related to the fact that today's teachers, who cannot always employ dramatic methods of teaching, are dealing constantly with students who were brought up with television and whose attention spans are as short as their expectations of being entertained are long.

The teachers surveyed considered themselves to be politically moderate, but they also saw themselves as more politically liberal than their colleagues in other subjects. English has more teachers older than fifty than other subject areas do, indicating perhaps that English teachers do not have as many opportunities for outside employment as teachers in such areas as mathematics and science. Most said, however, that they would not quit their jobs for higher status positions or for higher paying ones. Most think they should have a greater influence over school policies relating to discipline, curriculum, and instructional methods.

WHAT THE SCHOOLS OF TOMORROW MIGHT OFFER

In 1970, Neil Postman envisioned many more drastic changes in the emphasis of English teaching than are evident in contemporary schools in the United States. Postman went so far as to question whether English as we know it will continue as a part of the curriculum of the future (160). He points out that there is no guaranteed way of predicting "what subjects the future will require" (160). He asserts that what students learn in school must have survival value and that students who are forced to study primarily such old media as novels, poems, essays—the fare in most English classes—are not being taught something that has survival value.

Postman goes on to propose a reshaping of the traditional English curriculum into a McLuhan-like program in media ecology, one that would study media as ever-present environments. In small ways, many schools are already moving in the direction Postman suggests, but they are doing so tentatively and, in most cases, they are also clinging to their traditional orientations even as they move toward the development of a new orientation.

The three-week meeting of sixty teachers of English, curriculum experts, and English professors was convened as the Coalition Conference at Wye Plantation in Maryland in the summer of 1987, and their meeting and recommendations Charles Harris has discussed in detail in chapter 2, so they are not discussed here except to say that they would alter considerably the range of materials that are used in teaching English. They encourage an approach that leads students to solve problems and to reach independent conculsions. They urge that English teachers, whose paper-reading load is greater than that of teachers in other fields, teach no more than eighty students per day in no more than four classes and that they be given ample time to attend professional meetings (Heller 10) so that they can keep abreast of recent developments in their field.

The Coalition Conference was modeled after the Anglo-American Seminar on the Teaching of English held at Dartmouth College over a period of several weeks in 1966. Two significant books, Herbert J. Muller's *The Uses of English* and John

Dixon's *Growth through English,* grew out of this conference and presented the group's recommendations, which essentially called for an entirely new approach to English, one that was student-centered and response-oriented.

The recommendations of the Dartmouth Seminar were widely disseminated to English teachers across the country not only through the books that grew out of the conference but also through the government-sponsored Project English Curriculum Centers that sprang up across the country to point teachers in the direction of the New English. Despite these efforts, however, and despite many programs for teachers sponsored by the National Defense Education Act (NDEA) at that time, changing popular and political attitudes toward education have negated many of the gains made immediately after the Dartmouth Seminar.

Today, the public and the U.S. Office of Education are calling for an increased emphasis on content in all teaching areas. Significantly Hirsch's *Cultural Literacy,* with its list of 4,400 names, dates, and phrases that every American needs to know, and Allan Bloom's *The Closing of the American Mind,* which calls for schools to return to the educational ideals expressed by Plato in *The Republic,* have been near the top of the nonfiction best seller list since their publication and are having a profound effect upon educational policy at local, state, and national levels.

A public largely innocent of such movements as transformational/generative grammar, deconstructionism, and process-oriented writing wants to return to the methods and materials of its own school days, not realizing that the virtues of the past can insidiously become the liabilities of the future. Schools designed to educate the masses in England during the Industrial Revolution quite understandably emphasized such virtues as obedience, punctuality, and conformity. These virtues were appropriate to first generation students who were living through the transition from individual cottage industries to an industrialized society. In order to survive in the work force, they had to be punctual and obedient. They had to conform.

Society today is training people to enter a work force that demands problem-solving, that values initiative, that in many cases thrives on divergent thinking. Schools with a narrow back-to-basics approach are preparing students for a society that no longer exists. Even though still demanding and assuming such skills as basic literacy, tomorrow's industrialized, computerized society will require members of its work force to reason, to reach conclusions, and to make decisions independently.

Today's teachers have no greater challenge than to take leadership positions in helping a public, whose educational vision can be myopic at best and nationally catastrophic when carried to extremes, to see that education is the cutting edge of the future and that it can afford to be neither static nor regressive.

Works Cited

Bloom, Allan. *The Closing of the American Mind: How Higher Education Has Failed Democacy and Impoverished the Souls of Today's Students.* New York: Simon and Schuster, 1987.

Conant, James Bryant. *The American High School Today.* New York: McGraw-Hill, 1959.

________. *The Education of American Teachers.* New York: McGraw-Hill, 1963.

Cowan, Elizabeth. *How English Teachers See the Profession.* ERIC, 1983. ED 240 757.

Dixon, John. *Growth through English.* Reading, U. K.: National Association for the Teaching of English, 1967.

Heller, Scott. "English Teachers Favor Emphasis on How to Read, Write, Think, Rather than on Becoming Familiar with Specific Literary Works," *Chronicle of Higher Education,* 33 (5 August 1987): 9–10.

Hirsch, Jr., E. D. *Cultural Literacy: What Every American Needs to Know.* Boston: Houghton-Mifflin, 1987.

Hosic, James F. "The National Council of Teachers of English," *English Journal* 10 (January 1921):1–10.

Krug, Edward A. *The Shaping of the American High School.* 2 vols. Madison: University of Wisconsin Press, 1972.

Miles, Dudley. "The Council and the Classroom Teacher," *English Journal* 17 (January 1928):1–8.

Muller, Herbert J. *The Uses of English.* New York: Holt, Rinehart and Winston, 1967.

Oakes, Jeannie. *208 English Teachers. A Study of Schooling in the United States.* Technical Report Series, No. 11. Los Angeles: California State University, 1980. [ED 214 881]

O'Donnell, Holly. "ERIC/RCS Report: A Profile of an English Teacher," *English Education* 17 (December 1985):235–37.

Postman, Neil. "The Reformed English Curriculum." *High School 1980: The Shape of the Future in American Secondary Education,* Alvin C. Eurich, et al., eds. New York: Pitman Publishing Corporation, 1970. 160–68.

Report of the Committee of Ten on Secondary School Studies. Washington, D.C.: 1893, Bulletin 205.

Report on the Committee on College Entrance Requirements. Washington, D.C.: Proceedings of the National Education Association, 1899.

Stiles, Lindley J., A. S. Barr, Harl R. Douglass, and Herbert H. Mills. *Teacher Education in the United States.* New York: Ronald Press, 1960.

Connie Swartz Zitlow

4. "To Think About What I Think": Inquiry and Involvement

> Teachers who themselves are submerged, who feel in some sense "finished," like the desks before them or the chalkboard behind, can hardly move students to critical questioning or to learning how to learn.... [Teachers] play roles in many ways defined by others, although their interpretations of these roles must, in some manner, be grounded in an understanding of themselves.... Boredom, lassitude, automation... erode self-awareness and the desire to make sense. It ought to be possible to bring teachers in touch with their own landscapes. Then learning may become a process of the "I" meeting the "I."
>
> —Maxine Green, *Landscapes of Learning*

How involved are preservice English teachers as learners? In the process of preparing to teach, have they been encouraged to think about their own classroom experiences? Are they aware of the ideas, values, assumptions, and projections that will ground their teaching practices in secondary English classrooms?

This chapter stresses the need for preservice teachers (1) to involve themselves as learners; (2) to probe as well as to articulate their beliefs about teaching in the English language arts classroom. Exploring the images that emerge in the language of preservice teachers is a way to look at those beliefs.

IMAGES AND TEACHERS' DECISIONS

An image is an idea or mental picture expressed as a statement, sometimes metaphorically. Jean Clandinin defined images as both the coalescence of past experiences and the perspective from which new experience is taken (173). She found that a teacher's image of the "classroom as home" or of "language as the key" revealed what was important as experience and practice came together (149). As a result of perception or imagination, images represent a general class of entities and make stored information easier to manipulate. Through language, one is capable of having an image of the world and also talking about it. Images are, therefore, specific views of individual's mental models that can be set up for inspection.

Teachers' decisions grow out of personal practical knowledge, a body of knowledge held in a unique way because it is derived from one's lived experiences. This knowledge, as explained by Freema Elbaz, consists of rules of practice, practical principles, and images. Knowledge becomes available for practice through the medium of images (132). Images are more inclusive than rules of practice or practical principles. Elbaz suggests that beginning teachers would have fairly clear images but few rules of practice and inadequate practical principles to guide their work (135).

Shaped by theoretical knowledge, school folklore, and current school context, images are more than a picture of what has been experienced (Clandinin). They function in a dynamic process of ordering and condensing various aspects of one's knowledge and guide decisionmaking (George Lakoff and Mark Johnson). Meaning, motive, feeling, beliefs, intentions, values, and assumptions are all part of the mental picture or image. Images thus encompass, and give insight into, teacher-candidates' conceptual frameworks—their ideas and projections about curricular approaches, learning priorities, the teacher's role, the school's function, and their various career concerns. Images and concerns reveal what prospective teachers recollect of past experiences and what they might use to shape future teaching events.

GOALS FOR TEACHER EDUCATION

The argument for exploring preservice teachers' conceptual frameworks stems from the belief that teachers' backgrounds, interests, and experiences influence what is taught and what is attended to in the classroom. Dan Lortie has asserted that instructional methods are wasted unless teachers-to-be are aware of their preconceptions and internalizations (231). The awareness begins with thinking about one's response to an idea or situation and with critical exploration of what solution seems preferable when various approaches to classroom teaching are observed or discussed. Goals promoted in teacher education should include active thinking about beliefs and teaching preferences, the ability to synthesize past and current practices in terms of values and understandings, and a developing knowledge of connections between theoretical frameworks and practice situations. New teachers, in this way, might learn to articulate and inspect their imagery and challenge it in light of new knowledge and understanding.

Preservice teachers' espoused ideas will not, of course, solely determine classroom practices. Constraining factors and consequences in various contexts will differ as an array of problems contribute to the complexity and uncertainty of given school situations (Schön 17). However, barriers or obstacles to teaching, often attributed to outside factors such as curricular documents or community expectations, may be the result of teachers' own perceived fears. Before preservice teachers enter classrooms as new teachers, they may be unaware of the discrepancy between their ideas about instruction and what would be necessary to carry out their stated curricular priorities. What goes on in teachers' heads and their commitment to stated constructs precedes the reality in school and class contexts (Diamond 32). Certain instructional practices must take place for curricular approaches to be implemented. For example, when direct presentation is predominant and the amount of student participation is low, classroom conditions at any educational level do not fit a growth construct (38).

Teachers must determine what is most important—mental discipline, relevance, measurement, basics, knowledge of a selected heritage, the developmental efforts of the students. Within the constraints of the school structure, choices are made by each classroom teacher. Diamond found that obstructions to the act of teaching—cited by teachers to explain their traditional, didactic teaching—cannot always be attributed to school administrators. Therefore, teacher educators must ask if preservice teachers' core and central beliefs have been altered (41). Are they able to forge a personally effective approach to action that will help them inform and explain what they, as decisionmakers, do in the secondary English classrooms?

The value of preservice teacher's expression and subsequent reflection on teaching and learning is that such probing can help make becoming a teacher a more conscious effort and lead to habits of ongoing, self-directed inquiry and growth. As a profession, then, it behooves us to ask certain questions:

1. Are preservice teachers able to stand back from and discuss their notions of school, life; and in so doing, are they aware of the values and beliefs they will take into the classroom as teachers?
2. Are there predominant metaphors in preservice teachers' expressions about schools, teachers, and students? Are there patterns that can be attributed to different educational backgrounds and experiences?
3. Do preservice teachers' various images concerning learners, the subject matter of English, and future teaching roles conflict with their statements about learning priorities?
4. When images and concerns are probed, what information can be gained by teacher educators and by preservice teachers?

Following a discussion of the varied content that can be considered the teaching of English, this chapter explores the role of the teacher in determining what happens in the classroom. Data from a study with preservice English teachers is summarized to show what can emerge when prospective teachers are encouraged to probe, articulate, and "think about what they think." The preservice teachers' images of past school experiences, English classrooms, teachers, college-supervised field work, and education courses are described as the background for their ideas about the teacher's and learners' roles, instructional and curricular priorities, and career concerns. The chapter concludes with recommendations for teacher education.

TEACHING ENGLISH

English teachers will not be capable of finding cracks in their cosmic egg—the forces and counterforces that act upon the teaching of English—until they have developed a personally articulated set of principles and theories to justify, explain, and inform what they do (Boomer 135). Educational changes recommended in various reform proposals are part of English teachers' cosmic egg. The changes must be considered by teachers who are aware of recent developments in the field of English and who are capable of being decisionmakers.

The content of the English curriculum has been many things: word recognition and spelling, identification of parts of speech and parsing sentence patterns, written composition as the study of various forms, literature study as exposure to British and American classics, reading to prepare for life, oral and written skill competency, or students' growth in language use. George Henry points out some of the curricular considerations: "English education is sorely burdened by the stress of dissension over what to select from the amorphous field of English—whether current adolescent literature or *Antigone,* . . . as for education—whether to cast its fortunes with behavioural objectives or transactionalism, whether to go in for close reading or for English as therapy" (112). A confusing and complex situation exists for preservice English teachers.

In current English education courses, preservice teachers read and hear ideas about encouraging students to respond as they read literature, engage in discussions, and compose thoughts in oral or written forms (Moffett; Petrosky; Rosenblatt). However, in secondary English classrooms, they often see a heavy emphasis on mechanics and rote answers (Goodlad; Squire and Applebee). As Garth Boomer has pointed out, polarities exist between professional habit, such as correcting every error in student work and using only "good" literature, and the possibility of other approaches, replacing teacher correction with student editing and including young adult fiction and nonprint media as literature (137–38).

WHAT? AND WHAT FOR?

When we ask preservice teachers what comes to mind when they think about teaching English or what they think should be encompassed by the teaching of English, they begin to examine their beliefs about the content and purpose of an English curriculum. They need to be aware of their own curriculum construct system, which comprises their understandings about materials, activities, students, classroom settings, and the school context (Bussis, Chittenden, and Amarel 49). This construct encompasses both the surface content or classroom activities (the "what") and the organizing content or learning priorities of the curriculum (the "what for"). If teachers understand the connections between the "what" and "what for," we assume that they will be better able to transform intentions for learning into practices. As previously noted, the "what" and "what for" of the curriculum can be very troublesome for preservice

English teachers because, according to Henry, a distinct structure for English as a subject has not been clearly formulated.

LEARNING AND TEACHING PRIORITIES: A CONTINUUM

Teachers must be involved in active theorizing about the goals for the study of English and how those are shaped by prior assumptions about the nature and purpose of education. When curricular and instructional topics are discussed by teachers, some noticeable concerns or principles can be identified that will influence priorities attended to in practice (Oberg13–15). Bussis, et al. placed teachers' learning and teaching priorities on a continuum ranging from narrow to comprehensive concerns. Their definitions are rephrased below. The priorities are then explained with examples of various approaches applicable to English teaching.

The classroom goals for those having *narrow* priorities are centered around a limited range of behaviors and a concern with grade-level facts and skills. Literature is then taught as a body of information to be acquired from the teacher/authority and remembered by the student/receiver. Composition means the product that results from following set formulae when writing; language is drill in correct usage and identification; and reading is skill in decoding. In a narrow approach, successful teaching and learning activities are defined as those leading to acquisition of behaviors that are segmented, measured, and tested in unchanging patterns. The frequently used image of a *conduit* or *pipeline* characterizes a narrow approach.

Middle-range priorities are associated with concern that students show some internal quality such as initiative and independence in discovering the right answer. A teacher's responsibility is to set up problems and meaningful activities to help students learn how to make decisions and to find the predetermined answers. The value of literature and written expression can be hidden behind lists of what is needed to promote basic socialization. A good teacher chooses the right materials according to established standards and strives to "get students interested." The worthy students, in turn, demonstrate effort in learning what is useful. Education is often viewed as a *tool* for the future.

Comprehensive priorities, by way of contrast, are expressed by teachers concerned with more synthesized and integrated internal resources. Bussis, et al. describe comprehensive priorities as those most evident in effective teaching. Ideas of awareness, purpose, understanding, reflection, sensitivity, and reciprocity appear in teacher's thinking. They tend to stress the essential integrity of mental life—cognition is not separated from emotion, nor intellectual growth from personal growth. Comprehensiveness also refers to the subsuming power of priorities (55). When learning priorities are comprehensive, acquiring facts and skills is not seen as an end in itself but important in the service of a learner's developing sense of purpose.

In the English classroom, students' experiences as they read, write, listen, speak, and think are important to a teacher who holds comprehensive priorities. Students' personal and cognitive development are of concern because they are encouraged to generate insights and judgments about connections (or gaps) between their ideas and those of others. This approach can make use of content of various kinds as a medium of expression to encourage thinking and the building of knowledge. Within a rigorous structure, student choice—ownership—is both possible and vital. The image of such an educational approach is that of a *window* into the world and self (Elbaz). Teachers are learners, resources, mentors, coworkers. Students are not seen as boxes to be filled, but as active, involved participants who are capable of learning.

A teacher's personal attention to students and interest in their involvement as learners is a crucial component if education at all levels is to be more than an assembly line or holding place. That personal attention is shaped by life experiences including the way teaching and learning occur in formal education settings. Because certain dispositions toward teaching develop over time and are carried into the teaching role (Goodlad 125), what happens in classrooms must be an object of study in teacher education along with the acquired pedagogical skills and content knowledge. In English education classes, the elements of good teaching must be modeled and experienced, as well as discussed. Faculty members must not only show an interest in how the students and subjects come together but also promote a reflective stance toward their own teaching and continued learning. The question asked by Christopher Clark is crucial: "Do the teachers of teachers have the courage to think aloud as they themselves wrestle with troubling dilemmas . . . ?" (10). Preservice English teachers need to see in their own college courses models of the attitudes, abilities, and knowledge required of effective teachers and need help learning what to look for, what it may mean, and what then to do. Too often, immersion in the school classroom tends to preclude teachers' inquiry, particularly if the habit of reflective thinking has not been experienced in teacher education. A part of such inquiry is to explore the conceptual frameworks of preservice teachers.

A BACKGROUND STUDY

Data from a study conducted with twenty preservice English teachers showed that participants' images about their classroom experiences and fieldwork provided the background for their thinking about teaching (Zitlow). This inquiry, which explored the conceptual frameworks of eight graduate and twelve undergraduate students seeking secondary English certification, revealed that prospective teachers' involvement in their own learning determined whether they held more comprehensive or more narrow images about what the teaching of English can be. The study relied on the intensive interview and case study methodology of naturalistic inquiry. Qualitative data were collected from individual, one-hour, semistructured interview sessions, written questionnaires, and appropriate documents and records.

Many of the twenty preservice English teachers believed that they should have a theory of education; however, they were not aware that they already possessed developing theories that could serve as guiding frameworks when they taught. Their images of schools as hostile places—the control and competition "out there"—contributed to repeated fears about not succeeding when "on stage." Many of them did not seem to hold strong enough beliefs to withstand the perceived pressure.

IMAGES OF SCHOOL

The preservice teachers' personal lives and previous school experiences served as the sources for their imaginative rehearsals as they anticipated their future conduct as teachers in secondary English classrooms. As Maxine Greene pointed out in "How Do We Think about Our Craft," their new understandings and new knowledge seemed to interact with what they understood and knew before (61). As one preservice English teacher said, "past teachers, past educational experiences . . . a lot of the ideas that I have now come directly from things that I experienced." The following themes emerged from the study as the predominant images—about schools, English classrooms, and teachers—that the respondents took to their university classrooms and school field experiences.

The School. The perceived positive or negative effects of the preservice teachers' past education were intertwined with feelings about school. The description of their high schools—as a nuturing place where they were challenged and encouraged to learn, a playground where no one guided the choices made, as a factory or prison where control and rigidity prevailed, as a war-like zone where competition was the primary emphasis—revealed the individual's school landscape. The size or setting of the schools varied, but when the landscape was described as an "outrageous" place where students "put in their time" enduring a "hostile" atmosphere, the image was that of a factory or prison. Pressure to excel in sports and academics was equated with the competition of a sporting event or game to those who felt they had succeeded. However, when the image was of sides against each other (sometimes in war-like combat), not everyone could be a winner. Those who felt "lost in the crowd" in very large schools did not view themselves as part of the select few who won. Feelings about competition with other students, about perceived combat against distant managers, and about the control of "narrow-minded and negative teachers" were part of the school images of many of the preservice teachers.

The English Classroom. Grammar drills with an emphasis on isolated skills and recall was the activity that had taken place most often in the secondary English classrooms of the twenty preservice teachers. Remembering lectures about content and instructions to "read this and we'll take a test," they realized how their secondary experiences contrasted with ideas about teaching English that were discussed in English education courses. The preservice teachers reflected upon and judged what had happened in their secondary classes:

> "We did very little writing. We read quite a bit, but we didn't have to write about it."
> "I'm scared to write because of my experiences in school."
> "I never read until I came to college."

> "I couldn't stand reading when I was in high school . . . I think it stems from being made to read and I couldn't read aloud very well."
> [When thinking about English, what comes to mind?] "As a student—grammar. I always hated English, and I never thought I would end up being in English education."
> "All I could think of was grammar and what I suffered through in high school . . . they [English education classes] showed me a lot of different things. English isn't all grammar. It isn't all nose-to-the-grindstone."

Against such reflections about the past, preservice teachers often wanted their future students to have a different experience in secondary English classes from what they "suffered through."

The Outstanding Teachers. Regardless of the school setting or the unpleasant memories of some English classes, preservice teachers recalled outstanding and influential teachers. These exceptional teachers were intelligent, caring, demanding, and often described with humorous stories. Because their enthusiasm for bringing the subject matter and learners together was both contagious and challenging, they contrasted vividly with other teachers in their schools. Neither age, subject matter, appearance, grade level, nor kind of school determined whether a teacher was considered to be outstanding. Energy and honesty were the most admired characteristics even when the approaches to teaching were diverse. Responsibility for choices with "weird projects" was prevalent in the recollections. What was most meaningful to the preservice teachers was the way their involvement in learning the subject had mattered to the outstanding teachers.

Field Experiences. Prior to student teaching, these preservice teachers participated in field experiences in various settings. Personal images of high school classrooms were augmented as school landscapes became broader. These field experiences often took place concurrently with English education courses. The following section shows the way prospective teachers reacted to and interpreted their field work in conjunction with ideas they encountered in university classrooms.

The preservice teachers entered the school classrooms with great apprehension—"I was frightened for awhile"; "I hoped it wouldn't blow my whole scheme of things"; "I thought it was going to be the most horrendous experience in my life." The "real eye openers" seen in university-sponsored field experiences contributed to their fears about constraints and their concern about survival in school settings. Their interpretations are important to consider because teachers, as conscious beings, constitute the world they inhabit through the interpretations they adopt or make for themsevles.

The dominant images from the preservice teachers' field experiences were not of enthusiastic, satisfied teachers, nor of interested, participating students who felt that their teachers cared about whether they learned. Their descriptions of negative teacher attitudes toward both students and job, routine instruction of outdated content, and student passivity paralleled much of the data reported by John Goodlad. One preservice teacher was very disturbed about a cooperating teacher saying, "We are not supposed to teach grammar and spelling, but we do, because that is what we like to do."

According to these preservice teachers, little discussion occurred in most classrooms, but animated talk occurred in the lounge as teachers wondered how they would "make it through the year." Students were expected to work alone with worksheets and textbooks, often writing answers to simple recall questions. In one class "all they did was read from the anthology. They did nothing else." In another class, students read aloud every day from a high school version of the *Weekly Reader.* The response of the secondary students to the negative teacher attitude and routine instruction was apathy. One preservice teacher observed that students "acted like drones; they were dying to get out of school." As Goodlad stated, "Students may not simply get up and leave. For many, there is no viable alternative.... One learns passivity. Students in schools are socialized into it virtually from the beginning" (233).

Such descriptions of apathetic, sleeping students "putting in their time" suggests a factory, or even a prison, image. However, the atmosphere is not repressive in all secondary English classrooms, nor are all teachers so cynical and disillusioned as the one who suggested that it would be a good idea to "get out of education." Student passivity is not part of the school picture when individual teachers show enthusiasm and concern about learners and the subject matter. The centrality of the teacher's role in determining classroom activities and tone was apparent to one preservice teacher who spent time observing a classroom that was "the most fabulous thing" she had seen. She watched a teacher move around the room, joke with students, learn with students, and noted that students were eager to learn in the atmosphere created by this exceptional teacher. The contrast between what she saw in the class when both the teacher and students were "highly motivated to learn" and her own experience caused the preservice teacher to wonder why she had "missed out on this" when she was in high school.

Education Courses. How did the preservice teachers respond to education courses, specifically the English education methods and materials courses? What was viewed as reinforcement and expansion of ideas to some—"the icing on the cake" where one finds out that ideas "are not out in the frosty cold all by themselves"—was viewed as "idealism put into you" by others. The latter were disturbed by the contrast they perceived between the university and the reality in the field. One preservice teacher commented, "It's not bad, but it is just a letdown when you go out there and you find out that things aren't like what they said in the methods courses." As a profession, we must be concerned about whether preservice teachers will reject new ideas as unworkable if they see the university and school as two separate worlds (Feiman-Nemser and Buchmann).

Some preservice teachers found that methods courses and field experiences could be complementary where the field work helped to balance and clarify ideas: Field experiences "made me pull my clouds a little closer to the ground, and I think that's beneficial.... You have to have your feet on the ground. Your head might be in the clouds, but you've got to be planted, at least one foot!"

The attitudes brought to the university classroom by the preservice teachers affected their reactions to, and evaluations of, what they heard. One preservice teacher expressed impatience with others who blindly followed the way they were taught and rejected new ways of thinking about teaching and learning:

> I see that there are so many options, and I become frustrated when I hear people in my methods classes talking—they are given a chance to read all these different theories and ideas that educators have about the field and yet they cling to the ideas, the way that they were taught.... People have tunnel vision and they just keep repeating.... They may have hated the way they were taught, but for some reason they feel they have to perpetuate it.

As Boomer has pointed out, ideas read about or discussed will not catch on because they are true but rather because they vibrate positively and sympathetically with the growing intuitions and beliefs of the preservice teachers. Students involved in their learning, who see themselves as capable of shaping, controlling, or rejecting ideas are also those who see themselves as more than recipients of "stuff."

English Curriculum. The majority of the twenty preservice teachers' responses about teaching English showed growth-centered ideas, such as a concern with the students' experiences as they explored language and related materials to their lives. However, statements by some of the respondents, which revealed that they believed literature means only "good works" or that students should read to receive a specific message, were reminiscent of traditional ideas about teaching English. Statements about reading to attain the "knowledge and attitudes needed to be responsible citizens and earn a living" or to improve vocabulary for standardized test scores revealed an emphasis on skill acquisition instead of on understanding. The influence of each respondent's past and present school landscape was evident in what many thought that English, and all of education, should be. Often the preservice teachers could not see beyond what they perceived as lacking in their own secondary and college preparation.

The responses of the preservice teachers concerning English—its components, purposes, and emphases—showed that they would not want to teach English as broken into distinct parts, or isolated from other subjects. They felt that knowing grammar, meaning the identification of parts of speech or proper usage, did not guarantee that one could write. However, their responses to many questions showed more concern with "how to teach grammar" than with how to encourage students in their development and understanding of writing as a cognitive activity involving many processes. Their anxiety about grammar reflected what they remembered from past experiences which included an emphasis on grammar drills that did not lead to understanding and their view of field experiences where bored students did grammar worksheets yet could not write. We might ask if they had really understood alternative ways to approach language. In English education classes, had they been encouraged to examine what they knew about teaching writing or to experience writing workshops? They would benefit from guidance in ways to carry out in practice an emphasis on writing as a way to learn, using language to discover meaning and to express and communicate thoughts.

THE RANGE OF PRIORITIES

When we recall what the preservice teachers perceived about their schools, classrooms, and teachers, we can connect their images with the range of priorities for learning and teaching. With narrow priorities, teachers and students must know the right answers to be judged as competent in a school that is a place of control. A climate of competition often permeates a classroom or school where middle priorities inform practice. Teachers must be productive and interesting. When priorities are more comprehensive, integrating various areas of knowledge is important, and learners are challenged and nurtured. Teachers become autonomous practitioners who are responsible for their continued professional and personal learning.

As preservice teachers think about what will happen in secondary English classrooms, the educational elements of learner and learning, teacher and teaching, subject matter and schooling are all intertwined. However, some understanding about the range of priorities that are held concerning these components of education can be gained by looking at ideas expressed by the twenty preservice teachers.

Learners: Robots Acquiring Facts, Students Discovering Answers, or Learners Initiating Ideas. The images the preservice teachers held of the ideal student ranged from a well-behaved robot to an imaginative, questioning learner. The most frequently expressed views revealed middle-range ideas that students should "try hard" by showing interest in what is presented in class and assume some responsibility for their behavior and learning. To the preservice teacher who sees the ideal student as one who keeps an open mind and actively thinks about ideas, the process of learning would not be primarily the memorization of facts. Conversely, if the students' classroom behavior is of primary concern, encouraging learners to challenge the content of the subject matter with new insights and ideas would not be a priority.

Learning and Teaching Connections. Can we understand the differences revealed in various preservice teachers' beliefs about learning and teaching if we probe what they meant by "growth?" Some respondents were primarily concerned with students' growth in acquiring certain subject matter content as stated in the curriculum. Growth would be demonstrated by the well-behaved student restating the information labeled as important by the "knowledgeable" teacher. However, to most of the preservice teachers, growth would be shown by students' desire and ability to solve problems and find answers to teacher-determined questions. The enthusiastic, creative teacher would succeed as a communicator who guided the students to be answer-getters without being spoon-fed.

A more comprehensive view of learning emerged from the statements made by several of the preservice teachers who were concerned about students' growth in understanding themselves and in acquiring diverse ways of knowing. Students' skill acquisition and ability to solve problems would be subsumed by this broader view in which learners' involvement in the learning was of primary concern. The perspectives and experiences of the students were important to these preservice teachers who said they would welcome the challenge of active thinkers in their classrooms. The teacher-centered images of molding, shaping, or directing students that seemed to dominate the thinking of most of the respondents did not emerge from the expressions of those preservice teachers who held more comprehensive views of teaching and learning.

The Teacher's Role: Knower, Doer, Resource. Preservice teachers thought differently about what a teacher can do to shape, control, or reject influences of others. For most of the respondents, the idea of the teacher as transmitter of a rigid curriculum through routine instructional means was rejected as too narrow. They were discovering more desirable ways of promoting learning and more expanded images of the teacher's role. They believed that successful teachers would be caring, energetic, and knowledgeable. Teachers should be flexible—which would be defined as taking an extra day, if students needed it, to understand the material.

Many preservice teachers had talked about the importance of relating material to students' lives and encouraging their self-expression; yet they talked about how they would "teach the students how to learn" and "get them to think." However, when a preservice teacher feels that teachers should be learners with and resources to students, and viewed as capable individuals who do not need to be directed to "think," they reveal more comprehensive views of the teacher's role. Many preservice teachers have not yet come to see their own potential for determining how to use their past and present experiences and those of the students as resources for learning and teaching.

PROSPECTIVE TEACHERS' CONCERNS

Preservice teachers' thinking about the curricular, instructional, and professional aspects of teaching English is reflected in their career concerns. They may say that they would like to supplement outdated textbooks with more relevant materials including nonprint media, but they are worried about administrative control and community objections. The image of schools as hostile, besieged places leads to concerns with survival. From the position as "the new kid on the block" and "the low man on the totem pole," preservice teachers wonder if surviving the repressiveness of routine, controlled curricular demands, student passivity or aggression, and other teachers' cynicism without becoming discouraged is possible. Yet the examples of outstanding teachers from the past have shown how powerful the influence can be of survivors that manage to "weather the realities of it all and still stay excited," as one preservice teacher hoped to do.

The image of "being on stage" often encompasses the concerns of those who anticipate teaching. They hope to know how to act, that is, how to "go through the daily moves," how to be in control and to reach the audience while avoiding criticism. Many wonder if they will "know the proper lines." The traditional image of the teacher as the authority who must know all the answers causes this concern. Preservice teachers who are not as concerned with specifics they think they need to know and who are more interested in being a resource to active students are the ones with less anxiety about obstructions and battles. Confidence about the ability to continue learning accompanies an openness to various approaches—not just wanting simple "how to" answers. The belief that teachers must help students acquire the right tools to be adequately prepared for life is replaced by the belief that there is value in helping them increase their own understanding and sense of purpose.

EMERGENT PATTERNS

The findings from the study with the twenty preservice teachers resulted in the following patterns:

1. Those with narrow learning priorities had few concrete images to support their ideas.
2. No one who expressed narrow or narrow-middle concerns for learning and teaching came from a school considered a place of nurture or had been a "winner" in a competitive high school.
3. Most respondents held middle learning priorities and came from schools of control/competition.
4. When there was a concern with subject matter adequacy, it was accompanied with worry about discipline and a desire for directions of how to make lessons interesting.
5. Those with more comprehensive learning priorities had less fear of constraints and were more open to continued learning.

For all the respondents, the chance to explore their own assumptions and projections—"to think about what I think"—seemed valuable as they expressed their appreciation for being able to talk about English teaching. The need to support preservice teachers as they develop a theoretical base for their teaching is apparent if these new teachers are to move beyond their primary concern, that is, as one respondent stated, "the problems all English teachers face, such as how to teach grammar."

There must be something in the preparation of teachers to break the image of the teacher as information-disseminator to students who are answer-getters. The university faculty that teach the courses taken by preservice teachers and the classroom teachers that serve as cooperating teachers during field experiences must be themselves students of teaching and learning. How many secondary and university teachers help students build knowledge from experience and personally generated syntheses instead of treating truth as given by authority, approaching teaching as if knowledge is a commodity sold in standard-sized boxes? Such a question is not posed as a critique of specific courses taken by preservice English teachers, but as a way of acknowledging the complex factors that shape their thinking about subject matter, learning, and teaching. The critical conditions for effective learning—student involvement, high expectations, assessment and feedback—must exist at all levels of education.

RECOMMENDATIONS FOR TEACHER EDUCATION

Overlapping recommendations for English educators and for preservice English teachers emerge from the questions and interpretations which have guided this discussion:

1. A Climate For Theorizing Must Be Promoted In Which Participants Take The View Of The Homecomer. When teacher educators, cooperating teachers, and preservice teachers enter classrooms, they must be similar to the homecomer who creates a new perspective by looking with different eyes at what has been considered familiar. As Greene explained in *Teacher as Stranger,* the homecomer becomes self-conscious about what choices are made. If teachers are immersed and impermeable, they can hardly stir others to define themselves. Teachers, taking the view of the homecomer who returns home from a long stay in some other place, must interpret and reorder what is seen in the light of a changed experience. Then, in wonder and questioning, the learning begins.

This climate for theorizing is created when preservice teachers are exposed to a repertoire of approaches and encouraged to analyze teaching actions in each practice context. Unless they are encouraged to be informed decisionmakers who take initiative rather than use information mechanically, they will readily succumb to their fear of perceived obstructions and control. The role of the teacher educator, according to Greene in *Landscapes of Learning,* must be "to work to combat the sense of ineffectuality and powerlessness that comes when persons feel themselves to be the victims of forces wholly beyond their control . . ." (64).

2. Student Teachers Must Begin Their Teaching In A Supportive, Professional Environment. The quality—not the quantity—of a variety of field placements must be of concern. As they learn more about teaching, preservice teachers want assistance, direction, and feedback from cooperating teachers. However, they often observe teaching that is antithetic to their developing beliefs about teaching English. They see teachers using methods and following routines that preservice teachers know will not promote learning. They observe situations where a concern with how to make it through the day replaces a concern with what the students are experiencing. Simply increasing the amount of such field experiences will not guarantee preservice teachers' readiness to teach.

Preservice English teachers need to observe in classrooms where students are encouraged to respond to literature in a variety of formats. They need practice in ways to evaluate written work and ways to encourage increased communication and expression in writing. What do preservice teachers learn—beyond how not to teach—if they observe in classrooms where students struggle with isolated drills on mimeographed papers and wonder what they should remember for tests? Certainly preservice teachers who come from high schools of control, who are worried about their own adequacy, who fear "being on stage," will not be strong enough to continue to question and to learn without some support.

Student teachers hope for constructive suggestions from their cooperating teachers and a supportive collegial environment when they teach. They need support, not to follow the orders of one practitioner, but to make decisions with regard to their own education and that of the learners in that classroom. Too often initiative and critical thought are discouraged. Student teaching experiences must be viewed as a time to continue learning and as a chance to establish habits of self-directed growth, rather than as a time to imitate one teacher or to merely demonstrate previously acquired knowledge and skills (Zeichner and Liston). Student teachers, as other teachers, must have some measure of professional autonomy—not the autonomy of isolation—but one enriched by professional dialogue.

The following examples illustrate the need for support of various kinds and a developmental approach to supervision:

> A preservice teacher has come from a high school dominated by control; she is disturbed by the routine instruction observed in field experiences; she can talk about growth-centered ideas in the English classroom; she views the students' role as that of showing interest in content, the teacher's role as that of communicator, and the purpose of education as preparation for life; she is very concerned about surviving her debut on stage and properly playing the role that she thinks will be defined by the school district; she hopes to learn from her cooperating teacher how to develop "grace under pressure."
>
> Another preservice teacher feels she was a winner in a very competitive high school; she is disturbed by student apathy observed in field experiences; she wants students to learn more about themselves and life, with literature as a catalyst; she hopes students will see writing as an ongoing activity but evaluation is a "stumbling block" for her; she would like students to be active thinkers who challenge ideas; as the teacher she would set up guidelines for their exploration and learning; the "big menace of administration" does not concern her, but she feels as a new teacher she will have doubts and fears; she hopes for feedback and advice from a cooperating teacher who will act as her mentor.

As these examples illustrate, changes in teacher education must include a close look at teacher education classes and field placement. The NCTE publication, *Guidelines for Preparation of Teachers of English Language Arts,* addresses this issue:

> To be successful, a preparation program must (a) provide prospective teachers with models of effective teaching by means of the instruction they receive, (b) encourage

> prospective teachers to analyze the nature of effective teaching, and (c) place prospective teachers in schools where they can observe and practice various aspects of effective teaching (17).

We must, therefore, ask what is needed to further the development of each student teacher and what both the cooperating teacher and English educator can do to promote that development.

3. At all levels of education, the focus must be on the student's experience in learning. The focus for teacher educators must be on preservice teachers' experiences in learning if we expect the focus of new teachers in the classroom to be on what the secondary students are learning. In the study with the twenty preservice English teachers, the one with the most comprehensive learning priorities talked about being an involved student in high school and college. In contrast, the one whose priorities were the most narrow said her imagination did not grow until she came to college because her school curriculum was so restricted. Her lack of success and involvement as a student contributed to confused statements about what she had not learned instead of what she might promote. The degree of involvement in learning more than any other factor determined whether preservice teachers held more comprehensive images about what the teaching of English can be.

When preservice teachers focus exclusively on learning *the* method or activity to use in the classroom, the student is moved out of the picture. More appropriate learning can occur when the students' involvement with a variety of activities is the focus. The attitude of teaching as focusing on the students' experience in learning must occur in teacher education if the cycle of teaching as telling, bound by constraints, is to be broken. When the purposes for learning are understood, concern for the individuals involved, and continuing, reflective inquiry about what approaches to use will follow. Thus preservice teachers' guiding frameworks should be of more concern to teacher educators than an emphasis on training them as technicians. Encouraging preservice teachers to acquire a sound theoretical base, something that can only occur when active thinking and questioning are supported, begins with an interest in their involvement as learners.

CONCLUSION

A focus on student involvement in teaching English does not mean passing information about literature through the pipeline to passive students. The goal, instead, should be reading and responding to a variety of literature—actively discussing, thinking, and writing about ideas. A concern with student involvement in learning would replace teaching English as isolated grammar drills with that of encouraging students to write in many formats, exploring ways to communicate and express ideas in language that are meaningful to other readers. Preservice English teachers need to understand the importance of the teacher's role in promoting a climate of active involvement in the process of using language in various ways.

The approach to teaching that is concerned with student involvement is essential in the English classroom where teacher and students interactively use language. The transaction that occurs between reader and text and between composer and ideas is paradigmatic of how learning and teaching occur best. If preservice teachers are aware of their own images about learners, teachers, subject matter, and schools and if they enter classrooms as informed decisionmakers, they can become reflective practitioners who study the interactive components of students, self, and instructional experience.

Works Cited

Boomer, Garth. "The English Teacher, Research and Change (1966-1980)." *English in the Eighties.* Robert Eagleson, ed. Sydney, Aust.: Australian Association for the Teaching of English, 1982. 134–35.

Boulding, Kenneth E. *The Image: Knowledge in Life and Society.* Ann Arbor: University of Michigan Press, 1956.

Bussis, Anne, Edward Chittenden, and Marianne Amarel. *Beyond Surface Curriculum.* Boulder, Colo.: Westvies, 1976.

Clandinin, D. Jean. *Classroom Practice: Teacher Images in Action.* London: Falmer, 1986.

Clark, Christopher M. "Asking the Right Questions about Teacher Preparation: Contributions of Research on Teacher Thinking." *Educational Researcher* 17 (1988):5–12.

Diamond, C. T. Patrick. " 'You Always End up with Conflict': An Account of Constraints in Teaching Written Composition." *English in the Eighties.* Robert Eagleson, ed. Sydney, Aust.: Australian Association for the Teaching of English, 1982. 31–42.

Elbaz, Freeman. *Teacher Thinking: A Study of Practial Knowledge.* London: Croom Helm, 1983.

Feiman-Nemser, Sharon and Margaret Buchmann. "Pitfalls of Experience in Teacher Preparation"(Occasional Paper No. 65). East Lansing, Mich.: Institute for Research on Teaching, Michigan State University, 1983.

Goodlad, John. *A Place Called School.* New York: McGraw-Hill, 1984.

Greene, Maxine. *Teacher as Stranger.* Belmont: Wadsworth, 1973.

———. *Landscapes of Learning.* New York: Teachers College Press, 1978.

———. "How Do We Think about Our Craft?" *Teachers College Record* 86 (1984):55–67.

Henry, George, "What is the Nature of English Education?" *English Education* 18 (1986):4–42.

Lakoff, George, and Mark Johnson. *Metaphors We Live By.* Chicago: University of Chicago Press, 1980.

Lortie, Dan. *Schoolteacher: A Sociological Study.* Chicago: University of Chicago Press, 1975.

Moffett, James. *Coming on Center: English Education in Evolution.* Montclair, N.J.: Boynton Cook, 1981.

Oberg, Antoinette. "Construct Theory as a Framework for Research." Annual Meeting of the Educational Research Association. New Orleans, April 1984.

Petrosky, Anthony. "From Story to Essay: Reading and Writing." *College Composition and Communication* 33 (1982):19–37.

Rosenblatt, Louise. *Literature as Exploration.* New York: Barnes and Noble, 1965.

———. *The Reader, the Text, the Poem: The Transactional Theory of the Literary Work.* Carbondale: Southern Illinois University Press, 1978.

Schön, Donald A. *The Reflective Practitioner: How Professionals Think in Action.* New York: Basic Books, 1983.

Squire, James, and Roger K. Applebee. *High School English Today.* New York: Appleton-Century-Crofts, 1968.

Zeichner, Kenneth, and Daniel Liston. "Teaching Student Teachers to Reflect." *Harvard Educational Review 57* (1978):1–22.

Zitlow, Connie Swartz. *A Search for Images: Inquiry with Preservice English Teachers.* Ann Arbor, Mich.: University of Michigan 8793957, Ohio State University Ph.D. dissertation, 1986.

Mary Louise Gomez

5. *The National Writing Project: Staff Development in the Teaching of Composition*

The purpose of this chapter is fourfold: (1) to describe the organization and purposes of the National Writing Project (NWP), (2) to analyze the reasons teachers find affiliation with the project so appealing, (3) to share the experiences of four secondary teachers attempting to implement the process model following participation in a NWP summer institute, and (4) to suggest modifications to the organization and focus of the summer institutes that will better serve local teacher and school district needs.

MODEL

The NWP is a network of 166 sites located in forty-six of the United States and six foreign nations. Teachers affiliated with this project offer staff development in teaching composition to approximately 85,000 teachers of all grades and subject areas each year (Smith). Begun in 1974 by James Gray of the University of California-Berkeley and his friend and teacher Cap Lavin as the Bay Area Writing Project (BAWP), this staff development model relies on eleven key assumptions concerning teachers, teaching, and writing:

1. Schools and universities must work as partners to solve the "writing problem." New, collegial, nonhierarchical relationships between university and school staffs must be developed. The traditional top-down

program dissemination for planning school change is no longer acceptable as a staff development model.

2. Although most teachers are not adequately trained as teachers of writing, effective teachers of writing are found at all levels of school instruction.
3. These teachers can be brought together in summer institutes and trained to teach other teachers of writing in workshops held throughout the school year.
4. The best teachers of teachers are other teachers.
5. Teachers of writing must write themselves.
6. Effective programs must involve teachers from all grade levels and content fields.
7. Writing is a skill developed over time and requires constant practice.
8. Writing is a powerful tool to facilitate thinking, learning, and understanding.
9. True change in classroom practices occurs over time.
10. Effective staff development programs are ongoing and systematic.
11. That which is known about the teaching of writing comes from both research and the practice of those who teach writing (NWP Evaluation Portfolio 4).

Gray explains that his earlier involvement in three staff development projects contributed to the development of these assumptions and the formation of the BAWP. These projects included the National Defense Education Act Institute (NDEA), the Area Three English Project in California, and the English Teacher Specialist Program in California.

Although each of these programs was valuable, Gray sought to avoid weaknesses he perceived as he began the BAWP. Among these were top-down dissemination of information to teachers, lack of school/university collaboration, and unwieldy management.

Gray also cites his experiences as a classroom teacher in the 1950s and his early faculty years at the University of California-Berkeley as crucial to the development of the BAWP model. He recalls the anger he felt as a classroom teacher when university professors made negative statements regarding classroom practice while lacking information regarding existing excellence in the schools. He terms this "the arrogance of academics," and states "that in [his] gut was planted the seed to recognize teacher expertise, that special kind of knowledge which comes out of practice, that is more important than research, the kind of knowledge teachers get from practice. . . ." (Interview).

Lessons Gray learned from these experiences led, over time, to the development of a series of staff development activities in the teaching of writing in the Bay Area and to the development of a network of affiliate sites (known as the NWP) around the United States. Each NWP affiliate site bases its organization and activity upon the BAWP model.

In this model, school districts contract with each affiliate site for a series of lecture/workshops concerning the nature and teaching of writing. Teachers who have successfully completed the multiweek summer institute at each site are then paid (from funds charged to the school district) to offer presentations to a district's staff. NWP affiliate sites conduct varying approximations of this model at each location.

The BAWP has developed a hierarchy of activities through which teachers pass en route to becoming teacher-consultants (teacher-presenters) for the project. Teachers may attend one or a series of sessions offered by the BAWP. Later, they may choose to attend a five-week summer institute concerning the teaching of composing. This experience may lead to a fellow teacher or administrator nominating them for the invitational BAWP summer institute. Additional procedures preceding enrollment in the invitational institute include a formal letter of application by the nominated teacher, and a one-hour interview with Gray, BAWP Director Mary Ann Smith, and BAWP Codirector Rebekah Caplan. The BAWP staff report that between 100 and 120 teachers are nominated annually for the invitational institute. Forty-four are interviewed and twenty selected for participation each summer. The project staff attempts to create a group representative of the primary grades through college teachers, inclusive of minority teachers as well as those nonminority teachers who work with minority students and youths from low socioeconomic status families. Participating teachers at the secondary and college level are not necessarily instructors of English. Thus, the organizational model of the BAWP specifically and the NWP overall serves a large cross-section of teachers throughout the country and attempts to help them introduce to their schools various approaches to writing instruction.

TEACHING AS A PROFESSION

Reactions of teachers affiliated with the NWP point to the larger issues of the professionalization of educators. Recent work regarding teaching as a profession contains two major foci: (1) concern with increasing the rigor of the training and credentialing of teachers as a means of raising professional standards and, with these, the status of the profession, (2) concern with the deprofessionalization of educators. The Holmes Group and the Carnegie Task Force on Teaching as a Profession call for a variety of reforms, including increased liberal arts' studies for preservice teachers, tiers of licensure for practitioners, and various tests of subject matter and pedagogy, as a means of increasing teachers' professional status. Whether professionalization can be constructed in such a fashion or whether these efforts will serve their purposes is as yet unknown. While those involved with the Holmes and Carnegie efforts aim to create structures of reform, other scholars focus on teacher deprofessionalization, the increasing parallel between teaching and working-class employment. Gary Griffin, for example, refers to this phenomenon as the "paraprofessionalization" of teaching, the process by which teaching activity is reduced to that which is easily taught, easily observed, and mechanistically remediated (112).

English teachers have not been immune to a loss of control over their workplace. The continued descent of the value of the practitioner's lore to its nadir in the 1980s has been attributed to various phenomena occurring in the history of English education. Anne Ruggles Gere, for example, locates a significant moment in Charles Eliot's inaugural address as the president of Harvard (in 1860) when he "lamented the prevailing neglect of the systematic study of the English language" and "sought every opportunity to redress this neglect" (34). Thus, English teachers and their teaching have long been objects of concern for college faculty and public alike.

As federal funds were approved for NDEA summer institutes, Project English training, and the development of curriculum study centers, English scholars again began to call for research in the teaching of composition. The National Council of Teachers of English (NCTE) in 1962 formed a committee to examine the state of knowledge in composition. In the resulting publication, *Research in Written Composition,* Richard Braddock and his colleagues decry the state of knowledge concerning composition teaching. Stephen North summarizes this era, the role of Braddock's work, and the resulting twenty-five-year rush for a scientific and "sound" canon of research:

> It would be no great exaggeration to call *Research in Written Composition* the charter of modern composition. With the image it fosters—of a sort of ur-discipline blindly groping its way out of the darkness toward the bright light of a scientific certainty—it sets the stage for what I have already characterized as the field's methodological land rush. Composition is declared to be essentially virgin territory; little is known, and even that little is of questionable value, the result of blundering or careless work. If old composition is to become new composition; if the "profession," as its membership seemed ready to call it, is to take its rightful place in the academy, the dominance of practice and sloppy research would have to end. This was to be a new era, and it would demand new kinds of knowledge produced by new kinds of inquiry. (17)

Research in Written Composition sounded the contemporary call for the supplanting of the practitioner as knowledge-maker by the academician-scholar.

Where, then, do teachers locate the autonomy, collegial relationships, and validation of their worth? Mary Jalongo has suggested that four routes remain open to teachers as ways of developing dimensions of professional life—those of curriculum expert, colleague, mentor, and scholar researcher (351). Whether these are tenable alternatives is not the province of this discussion, but affiliation with the NWP seems to offer some teachers the role of expert and knowledge-maker.

THE TEACHERS: BECOMING EXPERTS

Teachers report varying reasons for participating in NWP summer institutes. When interviewed at the 1987 four-week institute of the Wisconsin Writing Project (WWP), teachers cited the following reasons for attendance: "A professor friend recommended the experience"; "I wanted to become better educated in the teaching of writing"; and "I'd heard great things about the experience." BAWP teacher consultants interviewed in 1986 offered these reasons for their initial involvement in the project:

- "A BAWP in-service was held in my district and my principal suggested I go; afterwards I went to the open, then invitational institutes."
- "Two friends were teacher consultants and they urged me to attend."
- "I go back [with Jim Gray] to the English Teacher Specialist program in California. Jim asked me to be a part of the first summer group. We were already colleagues, and he's given me many opportunities for professional advancement."

Thus, teachers seem to participate in NWP workshops as a result of the influence of college faculty, their own school administrators and friends, or colleagues with whom they work.

Affiliation with the NWP appears to respond to teachers' unmet needs regarding creativity, autonomy, and recognition, that constellation of factors in daily work sought by those who call themselves professionals. These qualities signify both control over the content of one's work and the value accorded that work by others. While opportunities to be honored as knowledge-makers are rare in the lives of most teachers, the value of their contributions to teaching strategies that can be shared with other professionals is predominant in the talk of NWP teachers. The voices of NWP teachers also reflect the concerns of their peers regarding their occupational low status, limited opportunities for career change or advancement, lack of encouragement, low public regard, the increasing mechanization of their work, and a lack of autonomy. Overall, NWP teacher consultants' talk reflects the honor and regard for their work that they find in the NWP setting.

THE COMMUNITY

Allied to the validation of the classroom teacher's lore is the creation of a community of like-minded individuals within which teachers can feel supported and nurtured. One Bay Area teacher reflects on this aspect of the experience: "It's the only thing in teaching I've ever found that never let me down, the people never let me down, the ideas continued to be valid and are even more so, it's just something you can grow with and I didn't experience that professional growth just within my district until I connected with the writing project."

This teacher's words are reminiscent of the language of other teachers interviewed who talked of isolation, disillusionment, and lack of stimulation prior to their participation in an NWP summer institute. Community, for these teachers, is partially composed of the opportunity to interact with others, people with similar interests and commitments. Both WWP and NWP teachers felt that the common focus of their attention, a commitment to becoming better at the teaching of composing, enhanced their professional lives. This supportive context continues after the summer institute for many when teachers meet monthly on Saturday mornings to present staff development sessions concerning the teaching of writing. While nominally offering inservice to any teacher and serving as a forum for presenters to "try out" their talks and workshops, these Saturday sessions reinforce ties to the "NWP community."

The opportunity to meet regularly is important for the groups' members. Also significant are individuals' perceptions of the quality of mind and characteristics of those who compose the peer group. Teachers talk about their project peers as having particular qualities of character and mind which set them apart from others. One Bay Area teacher remembered her colleagues as "impressive; they are writers and editors, not only impressive, but a kind of frightening group of people." She reflects, as do others, on the special, powerful aura of the people selected for the summer institute. Thus, the teacher participants of the institutes define their group by its common focus and by enumerating the special qualities of the membership.

Other ways exist, however, for defining the community in which these teachers participate. Marcia Effrat distinguishes three differing notions of community common to Americans and Britons: (1) as institutions or domains of society which function to produce unity, for example, families, voluntary organizations, residential groups; (2) as interaction based in face-to-face informal relationships; and (3) as distinct groups of people who interact in "overlapping friendship networks," for example, the "Jet Set." The NWP appears to serve functions for teachers common to all of the above-described conceptions of community.

First, the project provides a sense of unity or solidarity in a way similar to fraternal organizations like the Elks, Eagles, or campus fraternities and sororities. Membership in such a group readily identifies the individual as having particular allegiances, qualities of mind and behaviors, or as adhering to certain creeds or rituals. Coupled with the selection procedures are other ceremonies and rituals designed to develop fraternal bonds between teachers. For example, the BAWP staff invite the teachers chosen for that summer's institute to a springtime luncheon during which the summer program is described. This takes place in a carefully chosen context, the University of California-Berkeley Faculty Club. The location is designed to communicate to the teachers the venerable traditions of the campus and the honor bestowed upon them as NWP participants. Other participants in NWP sites also foster particular ceremonies and rituals designed to build community. These include volunteers writing and presenting a daily log of events to peers, sharing meals prepared by participants, designing t-shirt logos for the group, and end-of-institute awards ceremonies.

While the particular character of each NWP-affiliated site may differ, each project is launched by Gray with an on-site visit. Common characteristics of sites have also been compiled into a sort of "do-it-yourself" guide by Harvey Daniels and Steven Zemelman. While not endorsed by Gray, the program as described by Daniels and

Zemelman carefully details the patterns of practice of writing projects in the United States. The work of persons affiliated with the project clearly reflects a process approach to composition instruction that its adherents have found useful in a wide variety of school settings.

THE AUTHENTICATION OF TEACHER LORE

In the previous section of this chapter, I argued that the NWP creates a community for teachers by providing a common focus of concern and that this community is sustained through rituals of selection and training. The next part of the chapter explores the power of the NWP model as it validates teachers' daily experiences and concomitant wisdom.

North defines lore as "the accumulated body of traditions, practices, and beliefs in terms of which practitioners understand how writing is done, learned, and taught" (22). The lore of the practitioner is built upon a series of experiences or stories of what "works" with students. It is these stories and the accumulation of a body of such stories that the NWP seeks and shares with others.

Rebekah Caplan describes BAWP's purpose in the following passage:

> [We want to] tap teacher knowledge, to tap the expertise happening out in the schools which might be shared across a larger audience of teachers. Kids have always had problems with writing in schools. However, there are some teachers who've made a difference as we look back over the years. In 1973 Jim [Gray] set out to find those teachers who made a difference and have them share with others what they know. It is important to have someone with chalk dust still on their hands to share with others.

Teacher consultants of the project also believe the NWP is designed to seek, honor, and share practice. A Bay Area teacher regarded this function as an "empowering" process. She stated that the writing project "empowers teachers as consultants and they transmit that to teachers they are in-servicing. The number one purpose is to identify teachers and say 'you're doing a good job' and 'your influence needs to go beyond that.'" Lore at its best, in action, captured, shared with others who try to recreate one's success, is a key to the success of the BAWP. It validates and applauds the successful daily experiences of teachers and asks that they share those success stories with others. The BAWP honors teachers not as technicians, but as knowledge-makers.

The next question concerns what teachers attending summer institutes learn and how they implement the model in the classroom. The following section of this chapter describes the experiences of four secondary teachers as they returned to their classrooms in the fall of 1983 after participating in the WWP summer institute. An analysis of these experiences is also offered and culminates in nine suggested modifications to the NWP summer institute staff development.

DAILEY HIGH SCHOOL: FOUR TEACHERS IMPLEMENTED THE NWP MODEL

In an effort to understand the NWP model and its implementation in the school setting, I attended the 1983 WWP summer institute and followed four secondary teachers back to their classrooms in the autumn. The teachers permitted observation of one of their courses three times per week over the four months of the first semester of the 1983–84 school year. In addition to being observed, the teachers were also interviewed concerning their beliefs about composing, their classroom practices related to writing, and their reflections concerning the WWP summer institute and its impact, if any, on their teaching practices.

These four teachers, Patricia Garvey, Norman Holloway, Ted Lowell, and Madeleine Scott, returned to their classrooms in the fall of 1983 after participating in a four-week summer institute.[1] They also returned to the common experience of teaching in Dailey, to a school and community culture, to a set of procedures, routines, and assumptions about the conduct of classroom life. They attempted the implementation of new procedures and practices in their teaching of "U. S. History," "Metalworking," "Intermediate Foods," and ninth grade "English." The teachers differed in both their *desire* to implement the process model as presented in the summer institute and in their *ability* to implement it. The teachers' *desires* to implement these practices were conditioned by their beliefs about composing, secondary school students, schools and schooling, and their particular subject matter teaching assignments. Their *ability* to implement the model was influenced by their prior experiences in teaching, their understanding of the process model, the organization and activities of the summer institute, and the institutional constraints of the school setting.

The four Dailey teachers were all experienced in terms of classroom tenure, yet they differed in their preparation for teaching and in their particular experiences in the classroom. The subject matter specialty and prior experiences affected the amount and quality of process-oriented instruction. That is, the summer institute had different classroom outcomes for teachers who came with different background and experiences. For example, Madeleine Scott, the home economics teacher, had always wished to become an English teacher, but because she received a college home economics scholarship she changed her career plans. Her interest in English and in writing persisted; she enrolled in many English courses while in college and continued to write for personal enjoyment. Scott worked diligently throughout the semester to incorporate the process model into her "Intermediate Foods" course. Her personal enjoyment of writing and the opportunity to fulfill her early career dreams of teaching English fueled her desire for writing in the home economics curriculum. While this enthusiasm resulted in her use of activities designed to support "prewriting" and "rewriting," Scott's beliefs about her students' skills in mechanics and spelling prevented her from implementing the peer editing which the institute had emphasized. She feared that few students would be able to provide the rigorous checking of their peers' spelling and mechanics that she herself provided.

Unlike Scott, Norman Holloway had no particular interest and little prior coursework in English before enrolling in the summer institute. Holloway taught metalworking for a class of junior and senior male students, most of whom were enrolled in the industrial arts track in the high school. He was excited about the opportunity to teach what he termed "practical communication skills" to his students. His enthusiasm was tempered, however, as the semester progressed, and many of his students failed to submit the writing activities he had assigned. While not particularly skillful at implementing the process model, he worried about doing a good job at introducing the assignments and giving students "the right comments" as feedback. Key to Holloway's problems of implementation were his incomplete understanding of how to proceed with the new ideas to which he had been introduced. Furthermore, his belief that his students should not be graded on the individual assignments or that the writing should be included in the grade for the course prevented the students from thinking seriously about the work assigned. To them, ungraded work was unimportant work that should not receive a lot of attention.

These teachers' varying personal preparation in English and writing equipped them in different ways to internalize, question, or modify the model presented in the institute. While Scott had extensively practiced the craft of writing, related the information she heard to past enjoyable experiences, and transferred that understanding to classroom practices, Holloway had written little and was uncertain of his own skills. He was wary of offering feedback to his students and uncertain of the sequence of activities he should conduct in teaching writing in his class. His personal uncertainties were translated into messages of uncertainty to his students. Furthermore, these teachers' beliefs about their students' ability and the role of writing in their courses affected their assignments and the "parts of the writing process" that they emphasized.

Holloway believed his "work track" students would benefit from what he called "practical" writing. He told his metalworking class that writing always has a purpose and that while writing is conducted in school to pass a course, it has other purposes in the work world. While Holloway emphasized the practical, work-oriented job requirements of writing when he spoke with his students, he had difficulty offering them examples of on-the-job writing activities.

Holloway gave three writing assignments in the fall semester of 1983, none of which was work-related or a problem realistically solved by eleventh or twelfth grade students. These assignments included a humorous paper students were to model on an article (about how to operate a machine) published in *Reader's Digest;* a letter to a world political figure protesting the use of nuclear weapons; and a reaction to a film concerning the machine tool industry. In each assignment, Holloway ignored his own concerns for the work world of writing and the cautions of the summer institute leaders about making writing relevant for students. The assumptions Holloway makes for work-track students are not unusual; teacher assumptions about children from working class families have been documented by many scholars. Regardless of the merit of such assumptions, this teacher was unable to carry out assignments related to his beliefs about the writing needed by his students. He also failed to implement the ideals of writing as presented in the WWP summer institute; that is, all students can and should write for multiple purposes.

Another differing set of beliefs about the purposes of composing, the merit of the ideals presented in the summer institute, and students in general surfaced in Ted Lowell's ninth grade English class. Although Lowell was an English teacher, he had little background and few experiences in teaching composing. His undergraduate studies had focused on literature. He had little training in the teaching of composing and believed that the study of grammar merited significant attention by teachers and students. Lowell was unhappy with his 1983 teaching assignment of lower-level English classes because he most enjoyed teaching literature courses.

Lowell offered a diverse program of grammar study, the analysis of short stories, and occasions for writing to his first-year students. His concern for the students' achievement on future standardized English tests was expressed on a number of occasions and was reflected in his curriculum. He was also aware that district Director of Instruction, Margaret Malone, did not favor his approach. On one occasion, Lowell remarked, "Today I'm going to do grammar in isolation. Margaret doesn't like that." He also recognized that his approach was not supported by the summer institute staff.

Lowell's attitudes toward the teaching of composing skills were parallel to beliefs he held concerning the teaching of English grammar and the methods used to analyze short stories. All activities were conducted with a focus on the memorization and recall of pieces of information. Whether Lowell taught students about how to think about a short story (identify the protagonist, antagonist, setting, foreshadowing, characterization, rising action, and conflicts) or taught composition skills (identify a thesis or topic statement, add supporting details, write a conclusion), a formula formed the core of instruction. His strong beliefs about the merits of this approach and its success in aiding students to pass standardized tests rendered him unable to incorporate into his class peer editing or other practices strongly advocated by the summer institute staff.

When Lowell recognized that his beliefs about composing and about the way students learn were not supported by the NWP staff, he began to stress the weaknesses of the summer institute. His discussions of the institute with the district director of curriculum focused on his perceptions of a lack of attention to secondary school teaching in the curriculum of the institute. Here is what he stated:

> Well, one of the things about the writing project was it seemed to be geared to elementary teachers rather than secondary education. There was very little time spent in discussing writing for high school age [students]. A lot of . . . the time was spent on finding, getting money, and finding things to use, getting paper, and the utensils and getting things run off. A lot of time was spent on that. Some of the things that

> were . . . nice, but, I'm not into having my children, my students laminate their pictures, and make sure that their crayons don't run in the process and to me that just wasn't important.

Lowell's talk diffused conflicts between his viewpoint and the beliefs of others. The issue became for him a lack of attention to his concerns because the staff had a differing "focus or slant" rather than a different basis, or theory undergirding their beliefs. Lowell's viewpoint lay not in opposition to that of others, but outside the focus of their immediate concern. He justified practice in the classroom, in this way, as reasonable behavior.

Unlike Lowell, Patricia Garvey, the fourth Dailey High teacher observed, delighted in implementing the process model as presented in the summer institute. Garvey set both personal and professional goals for what she had learned in the summer. She wished to change the way she taught by incorporating more writing into her courses and made this formally important by setting these as her professional development goals for the year.

Patricia Garvey taught five classes each day, four periods of U.S. history and one of world history. She set a goal of offering eight writing assignments to each class in the 1983–84 school year. By mid-year, she had incorporated process-centered writing assignments into the curriculum of all five classes, providing time for precomposing discussions of assignments, for writing in class, and for peer editing. She had also infused questions into all of her unit tests. Garvey felt pleased at meeting her goals, yet she was distressed by the mounds of paperwork generated by her efforts. As the weeks passed, she also realized that her efforts went unrecognized, both by her peers who had attended the institute and by her principal. Furthermore, she often felt uncertain about the way she was proceeding with an assignment and was dismayed at the lack of feedback from peers, administrators, and WWP project staff. Garvey was further frustrated by the school schedule, with its frequent interruptions for public address system announcements and assemblies which often drew away some, but not all, class members. She was also distressed by the enduring, inflexible nature of the forty-minute class period. All these factors undermined her efforts to provide sustained opportunities for students to compose thoughtfully and to respond to one another's work.

CONCLUSION

The stories of these four teachers illustrate three significant points concerning staff development and school change:

1. School change is not easy to effect because teachers' personal biographies, subject matter teaching assignments, and prior experiences predispose them to particular beliefs not readily altered by isolated experiences, even when these are populated by other capable, thoughtful, and informed people. Such changes in practice require what

has been called "the resocialization of key actors in the implementation process" (Fullan and Pomfret 371). This resocialization calls for not only inservice experiences but also resource support (time and materials), feedback mechanisms, and a vehicle for participation in decisionmaking. Research focusing on the implementation of innovation strongly supports frequent meetings of the personnel involved. Time to meet, talk, think, and work together is needed if teachers are to implement the curriculum changes required of an innovation.

2. Those who seek school change need to rely on a developing body of literature that focuses attention on the need for collegial, collaborative efforts of administrators and teachers who plan and work together to achieve long-term goals. Findings clearly demonstrate the importance of collaborative planning strategies made jointly by teachers and district and building administrators. Such collaboration is necessary for both short- and long-term success of an innovation. According to Judith Little, collaboration makes important contributions to a program of innovation:

- opportunity to build known and shared aims;
- opportunity to build trust by demonstrating reciprocity, deference;
- opportunity to develop a shared language for describing, analyzing, and refining practice;
- opportunity for observing and assisting actual practice; and
- building of faculty morale and a sense of individual and group efficacy over time. (97–98)

Teachers working within a single school building or within a school district require this collaboration, with each other, with administrators, and with the staff development project personnel.

3. Schools with rigid scheduling patterns and physical design constraints isolate teachers from one another and prevent the sort of encouragement, support, and inquiry necessary if collegiality, collaboration, and peer feedback are to occur. The batch processing of students who move at regular intervals through the public spaces occupied by individual teachers fails to provide the time, space, and other ergonomic considerations necessary for teachers' sustained reflection on curriculum and students. The secondary school culture constrains teachers attempting to implement an innovation. Frequent interruptions to the daily routine of school decrease the amount of time available for academic pursuits. Furthermore, the practice of scheduling all but one or two class periods per day for class instruction inhibits interactions among teachers. The absence of offices and the sharing of small, cramped spaces by several teachers create environments that prevent successful collaborative endeavors.

RECOMMENDATIONS

First, the multiweek summer institutes with stipends for participating teachers clearly provide a haven for the kinds of thinking required if school change is to occur.

By bringing teachers together for sustained interaction, opportunities to sort through problems and apply a range of potential solutions are made possible. However, the groups brought together in these institutes need to represent teachers and administrators from school districts who have come to learn and plan together for change. The NWP-affiliate sites need to encourage local school districts to formulate commitments and plans for initiation, adoption, and implementation of the process model prior to attending the summer institute. For example, a district committee might identify the need to develop a district skills continuum to be met in new ways by writing instead of workbook practice. Time for meetings to occur over the summer and the following academic year must be scheduled; key personnel identified; staff trained in the process model; and released time provided for faculty to develop and disseminate the curriculum. Those districts with preplanned agendas for their work can come to the summer institute with particular problems and use the resources of the NWP staff to help them acquire a range of possible solutions.

Second, time is required during the school day for teachers to meet regarding their concerns, problems, and successes as they pay greater attention to writing in their district. Without such time, individual teachers will continue to benefit from their new expertise and from the benefits of community afforded by the National Writing Project, but they will largely work in isolation. This situation can change only if teachers within school buildings and school districts have the opportunity to interact during the school day, not merely on a few designated days scattered throughout the school year. This time needs to be set aside for both the informal sharing of teachers' concerns and for peer observation and feedback.

In addition to this support, the NWP must also provide the time *during the summer institute* to focus on local district needs. Not only must NWP sites support team planning for increased attention to writing in a district, but also the summer institute staffs must relinquish time from their agendas to teachers and administrators. The norms of the summer institute (e.g., lectures and writing activities led by the institute staffs, past participants' retelling of their successes in writing) need to be altered to support a fresh focus on local district team planning and problem-solving. Less time needs to be focused on reviewing the good practice of others and more time devoted to the identification of local district needs and goals.

These suggested changes in the NWP would also require rethinking the manner in which teachers are invited to the summer institutes. Rather than encouraging the attendance of those teachers already known for their excellent teaching, priority might go to those districts that have identified and organized teams of teachers and administrators ready to work on problems concerning writing. The staffs of the summer institutes then must respond with information concerning both the teaching of composing and good practices of staff development. Such a refocusing of the summer institute coupled with new enrollment procedures will expand the community of teachers who participate in decisionmaking, increase the number of teachers who work on curriculum, and offer opportunities to thousands of capable teachers. The NWP has already made a significant impact on many teachers throughout the country, yet it can do more: the NWP network can seize the moment and lead the way in helping all teachers to respond thoughtfully to problems of curriculum and classroom practice.

Note

1. All public school teachers' names are pseudonyms. The name of the school and community have also been changed.

Works Cited

Bay Area Writing Project Staff. *National Writing Project: An Overview.* Berkeley CA: University of California, School of Education, 1979, ERIC Document Reproduction Service No. ED 184 123.

________. *National Writing Project Evaluation Portfolio.* Berkeley CA: University of California, School of Education, 1983.

Berman, P., and M. W. McLaughlin. *Federal Programs Supporting Educational Change, Volume III: Implementing and Sustaining Innovations.* Santa Monica, Calif.: Rand Corporation, 1978.

Braddock, Richard, Richard Lloyd-Jones, and Lowell Schoer. *Research in Written Composition.* Champaign, Ill.: National Council of Teachers of English, 1963.

Caplan, Rebekah. Personal interview. December 1986.

Carnegie Task Force on Teaching. *A Nation Prepared: Teachers for the 21st Century.* New York: Carnegie Forum on Education, 1986.

Daniels, Harvey, and Steven Zemelman. *A Writing Project: Training Teachers of Composition From Kindergarten to College.* Portsmouth, N. H.: Heinemann Educational Books, 1985.

Edelman, M. "Language, Myths, and Rhetoric." *Society* 12 (5):14–21.

Effrat, Marcia P. "Approaches to Community: Conflicts and Complementarities." *The Community-Approaches and Applications.* New York: Free Press, 1974. 1–32.

Emig, Janet. "Writing, Composition, and Rhetoric." *Encyclopedia of Educational Research,* H. E. Mitzel, ed. London: The Free Press, 1982. 2021–36.

Fulwiler, Toby. *Teaching with Writing.* Upper Montclair, N. J.: Boynton/Cook Publishers, 1987.

Fullan, M., and A. Pomfret. "Research on Curriculum and Instruction Implementation." *Review of Educational Research* 47 (1977): 355–97.

Gere, Ann Ruggles. "Teaching Writing: The Major Theories." *The Teaching of Writing.* Chicago, Ill.: The National Society for the Study of Education, 1986. 30–48.

Gomez, Mary Louise. "The Wisconsin Writing Project: An Exemplar of Planned School Change Through Staff Development." Madison, Wis.: University of Wisconsin–Madison Ph.D. dissertation, 1985.

Gray, James. Telephone interview. February 1985.

Griffin, Gary A. "Thinking About Teaching." *Improving Teaching,* K. K. Zumwalt, ed. Alexandria, Va.: Association for Supervision and Development, 1986.

Hillcocks, Jr. George. *Research on Written Composition—New Directions for Teaching.* Urbana, Ill.: ERIC Clearinghouse on Reading and Communication Skills and National Conference on Research in English, 1986.

Jalongo, Mary R. "Decisions That Affect Teachers Professional Development." *Childhood Education* 62 (1986): 351–56.

Lieberman, Ann, and L. Miller Lynn. *Teachers, Their World, and Their Work—Implications for School Improvement.* Alexandria, Va.: Association for School and Curriculum Development, 1984.

Little, Judith W. "Seductive Images and Organizational Realities in Professional Development." *Teacher's College Record* 86 (1984): 84–102.

McLaren, Peter. *Schooling as a Ritual Performance.* London: Routledge and Kegan Paul, 1986.

McLaughlin, Milbrey W., and David Marsh. "Staff Development and School Change." *Teachers' College Record* 80 (1978): 69–84.

Myers, Miles, and James Gray, eds. *Theory and Practice in the Teaching of Composition: Processing, Distancing, and Modeling.* Urbana, Ill.: National Council of Teachers of English, 1983.

North, Stephen M. *The Making of Knowledge in Composition—Portrait of an Emerging Field.* Upper Montclair, N. J.: Boynton/Cook Publishers, 1987.

Perl, Sondra, and Nancy Wilson. *Through Teachers' Eyes—Portraits of Writing Teachers at Work.* Portsmouth, N. H.: Heinemann Educational Books, 1986.

Popkewitz, Thomas, B. Robert Tabachnick, and G. Wehlage. *The Myth of Educational Reform.* Madison: University of Wisconsin Press, 1982.

Smith, Mary Ann. Telephone interview. December 1987.

Tomorrow's Teachers: A Report of the Holmes Group. East Lansing, Mich.: The Holmes Group, 1986.

Willis, Paul. *Learning to Labor.* London: Saxon House, 1977.

Maia Pank Mertz

6. Testing Teachers: Current Issues and Their Implications for Evaluating English Teachers

The 1980s have been characterized by calls for educational reform at a diversity of levels. While the reports and mandates on educational reform in the early 1980s focused on efforts to raise standards for student achievement, the latter half of the decade has witnessed an emphasis on the improvement of the teaching force. As noted in *The Evolution of Teacher Policy,* "During the 1980s, virtually every state enacted legislation to reform teacher education, licensing, and compensation. In all, more than 1,000 pieces of legislation regarding teachers have been developed over the course of the decade, and a substantial fraction have been implemented" (Darling-Hammond and Berry v).

Increasing emphasis on teacher competency tests as a means to define professional competence and to eliminate those not qualified to teach has begun to have a direct impact on the teaching force available for America's schools. Almost every state uses tests to evaluate teachers at some level: "By 1986, forty-six states had mandated teacher competency tests in basic skills, subject matter, or professional knowledge as a requirement for admission to teacher education or for certification or both" (Darling-Hammond and Berry ix). Perhaps the most significant development concerning teacher testing was the formation of the National Board for Professional Teaching Standards which resulted from the recommendation of the Carnegie Report called *A Nation Prepared: Teachers for the 21st Century*. This report states that "A National Board for Professional Teaching Standards should be created to establish standards for high levels of competence in the teaching profession, to assess the qualifications of those seeking board certification, and to grant certificates to those who meet the standards"

(Executive Summary). While the precise directions this board will take is yet to be determined, most educators agree that it will have a significant impact on the way future teachers will be evaluated and certified. Furthermore, depending on the significance that educators and state policymakers give to these examinations, the content of these tests probably will begin to influence teacher education programs. As the history of testing has demonstrated, "teaching to the test" is not an uncommon phenomenon in education.

The purpose of this chapter, therefore, is twofold: to identify and discuss some of the major issues that teacher testing presents to the profession as a whole; and to discuss the implications of these issues for testing teachers of English. Some of the questions to be considered include (1) What is the nature of the current tests and how are they used? (2) What is the impact of these tests on minority teachers? (3) What is the role of tests in current efforts to "professionalize" teaching? and (4) Who will determine how English teachers will be tested? This discussion will include some recommendations for ways to assess the competence of English teachers. The chapter concludes with a summary of the major issues discussed.

NATURE AND USE OF TEACHER COMPETENCY TESTS

As noted, the use of competency tests is growing rapidly. Not only are state agencies involved in developing policies that require teachers to be tested, various educational organizations have also called for assessments of prospective as well as experienced teachers. Leaders of the nation's largest teacher organizations, the American Federation of Teachers (AFT) and the National Education Association (NEA) have supported the idea of a national test controlled by teachers and other professionals in education. Members of both the AFT and NEA are included in the National Board for Professional Teaching Standards, as are members of various subject matter organizations, including the National Council of Teachers of English (NCTE). The testing movement has been given additional impetus by the new standards of the National Council for Accreditation of Teacher Education (NCATE), which now require both entry and exit criteria for teacher education students as a precondition for an institution's eligibility for accreditation (8). In many colleges, "entry and exit criteria" are interpreted to mean entry and exit "tests." Consequently, NCATE member institutions will be moving rapidly to find tests that meet this criterion for accreditation.

The Holmes Group, a consortium of leading research institutions that advocates the professionalizing of teaching through various means, including the elimination of teacher certification at the undergraduate level, also recommends teacher testing as one means to improve the profession. In April 1986, *Tomorrow's Teachers: A Report of The Holmes Group* was issued. This document states that the Holmes Group "commits itself to develop and administer a series of Professional Teacher Examinations that provide a responsible basis for decisions on entry to the profession" (65).

While the professional teacher examinations have not yet been devised—and recent developments suggest that the Holmes Group will be working closely with the National Board for Professional Teaching Standards to do so—the emphasis on testing is in concert with other national and state-level efforts. Although it recommends teacher testing, *Tomorrow's Teachers* warns against reliance on only one kind of testing: "Because of the limitations of standardized testing in predicting the future performance of teachers, the Holmes Group commits itself to require students to demonstrate mastery of important knowledge and skill through multiple evaluations across multiple domains of competence" (65). This caution is important in light of the rapid growth of testing nationwide. Clearly, the test must not consist of a single, paper-and-pencil measure. Furthermore, as "multiple evaluations" are devised, test makers must take into consideration the special nature of the subject matter the teacher teaches and the classroom context in which the "test" is given.

Although the Holmes Group and the National Board present broad interpretations of how testing can be accomplished, most current efforts represent the use of "examinations or standardized tests, authorized by some authority external to particular institutions of higher education and school districts" (Haney, Madaus, and Kreitzer 171). Often the "external" agencies are the state departments of education who use these tests for one of the following purposes:

1. to control entry of students into teacher-education programs;
2. to certify successful completion of teacher-training programs;
3. to control the initial certification or licensure of teachers; or
4. to inform decisions regarding recertification or promotion of experienced teachers. (Haney, Madaus, and Kreitzer 171)

Given the multiplicity of ways these tests are used, it is important to consider what information about teachers' abilities is obtained from such examinations. Do they provide information about the teacher's knowledge of the subject matter to be taught? Do they indicate a teacher's knowledge about pedagogy? Or are they used primarily for political purposes—as indications that teaching really is a "profession" such as medicine or law? Are they more similar to "charms and talismans for diverse hopes and interests than reasonable instruments of public policy?" (Haney, Madaus, and Kreitzer 171). While attempting to extricate teacher testing from public policy and legislative issues is futile, it is important to ask whether the current testing practices serve an educational purpose or whether they are instruments by which policymakers attempt to ensure the public that they are contributing to the improvement of the teaching force. An examination of the ways teacher tests are used provides some insights into these questions.

Currently, the National Teacher Examination (NTE) is the most common test required for testing prior to certification. The NTE program began in 1940 as the National Teacher Examination of the American Council on Education (ACE). It developed as a result of a "request for help in selecting teachers by a group of large-city superintendents. When ACE and others formed the Educational Testing Service (ETS) with a grant from the Carnegie Foundation, the examination became its responsibility" (Krathwohl 75).

The current NTE consists of a Core Battery and twenty-eight speciality tests. The Core Battery comprises three two-hour tests: the test of communication skills, the test of general knowledge, and the test of professional knowledge.

> The Test of Communication Skills measures listening, reading and writing. As part of the test, examinees are required to write a thirty-minute essay. The listening section uses audiotaped materials, including some classroom dialogue to evaluate the teacher's ability to process both cognitive and affective messages.
>
> The Test of General Knowledge includes questions on literature and fine arts, mathematics, science, and social studies. The goal is to identify the well-educated problem solver who possesses a body of factual knowledge and can apply it to a wide range of important issues within and outside the classroom. . . .
>
> The Test of Professional Knowledge includes questions related to the context and process of teaching. The former deals with the social and cultural forces that influence curriculum and teaching, the latter with general principles of learning and instruction. (Krathwohl 75–76)

The preprofessional skills tests in reading, writing, and mathematics were added recently. They function primarily as tests of basic skills and are often used with college sophomores. Although it has been nearly fifty years since the first NTE, these tests continue to be controversial for a diversity of reasons. Criticisms concerning the 1976 NTE continue to be made against the tests:

> The items on the Professional Education Test should be carefully scrutinized by potential users. Some of the items seem to smack of professional shibboleths, others have a shaky research foundation, others seem to reflect the values of the writer more than the substance of the field, others are simplistic, others are debatable, others seem like classic examples of social desirability items, and still others are combinations of these. Some items, of course, are wholly acceptable. But if the items are taken as a whole, it is in fact difficult to believe that these items adequately sample from the professional preparation provided by most teacher training programs. (Mitchell, qtd. in Haney 211)

Other major challenges have also been advanced against the tests. Issues concerning content validity, predictive and concurrent validity, cut-off scores, as well as concerns about the way the tests are used continue to be among the major issues confronting these examinations.

Instead of the NTE, some states use tests developed for their particular needs by groups within the state. Some states request agencies such as the ETS or National Evaluation System (NES) to develop tests for them although the costs of such efforts are generally too prohibitive. As pointed out in *The Evolution of Teacher Policy*

(1988), "Of the most prevalent types of competency tests—basic skills, subject matter knowledge, and professional knowledge—states have most readily enacted and implemented basic skills tests.... In recent years, a few states have added on-the-job performance assessments of first-year teachers as a requirement for continuing certification" (Darling-Hammond and Berry 25–26). Yet by far, paper-and-pencil tests continue to dominate the ways teachers are tested. As the use of these tests proliferates, so do the criticisms, ranging from legal concerns to charges that the tests have a cultural bias and discriminate against minorities.

Not only are serious concerns voiced about the value of the test content, but also ample evidence suggests that test cut-off scores are often manipulated by states to enable them to meet the need for teachers:

> In some states, particularly in the Sunbelt region, growing shortages of teachers have intersected with competency testing to produce the various certification loopholes.... One state—Louisiana—was forced to lower the test cut-off score. In 1985, the state lowered its NTE cut-off scores in order to remedy teacher shortages in math and science. The lowering of the cut-off scores was opposed by the state's business lobby, but without question, the policy change has positively affected the state's teacher supply. In 1978, only 60 percent of Louisiana's teachers passed the NTE, whereas in 1986, 87 percent passed. (Darling-Hammond and Berry 23)

Such manipulations make even more suspect the value of these tests in helping to improve the quality of teachers entering the profession.

Perhaps the best summary of the many criticisms concerning current measures can be found in Patricia M. Lines's essays on "Testing the Teacher: Are There Legal Pitfalls?": "[t]ests may measure the wrong things, introduce their own biases, or be otherwise poorly designed. They are also one-dimensional—measuring only knowledge and not other characteristics that make for an effective teacher, such as compassion, love of children, energy, wisdom, dedication, and similar qualities" (618). Lines also points out that teacher testing raises legal questions under the Fourteenth Amendment to the U. S. Constitution, Titles VI and VII of the Civil Rights Act of 1964, and Title IX of the Education Amendments of 1972. Because of these laws, "teacher testing programs must be equitable and fair. Primarily such programs must measure what teachers should know in order to be effective teachers, and the tests must not be used to discriminate by race or sex" (Lines 622). (Similar concerns about the legal issues concerning testing are found in Richard R. Hammes, "Testing the Teacher: A Legal Prospective." *Action in Teacher Education* [Fall 1988]: 13–19.)

A key legal decision concerning teacher testing occurred in the case of the *United States v. South Carolina* in 1977. It concerned the use of the NTE in determining certification and compensation. Haney, Madaus, and Kreitzer summarize the case and its immediate implications:

> In question was South Carolina's use of cut-scores on the NTE to determine certification and classification of teachers. The state raised the cut-scores on the NTE several times, resulting in increasingly disproportionate disqualification of candidates from historically black colleges. . . . The state of South Carolina had commissioned the ETS to conduct a validation study of the NTE for use in teacher certification in the state. The study, which documented a relationship between the content of the NTE and the content of teacher training programs in South Carolina, was accepted by the federal district court as demonstrating the job-relatedness of the NTE for use in initial teacher certification. . . . In effect, *United States v. South Carolina* established content validity of teacher tests as the prime basis for determining the legal permissibility of teacher tests, whatever their disparate impact on blacks and other groups protected under Title VII of the Civil Rights Act. (189–90)

While the *South Carolina* case seems to have established that the test be job-relevant, other legal challenges to teacher-testing programs have had mixed results; see, for example, *Allen v. Alabama State Board of Education,* 1985, and *Newman v. Crews,* 1981. The *South Carolina* case highlights one of the most serious charges against teacher testing—accusations of test bias and the resultant discrimination against minorities.

THE IMPACT OF TEACHER TESTS ON MINORITIES

One of the most serious issues regarding teacher testing concerns the overwhelming evidence that current paper-and-pencil tests discriminate against minority teachers and are "leading to a severe reduction in black teachers from the nation's classrooms" (Mercer 70). In "The Gathering Storm: Teacher Testing and Black Teachers," Mercer reports the following:

> In Georgia, for example, slightly more than 85 percent of the whites taking the [teacher certification] exam pass the first time, compared with less than 40 percent for blacks. . . . In Louisiana in the last few years, 70 to 73 percent of the students from predominately white public colleges passed the certification test, while 10 percent of the graduates of predominately black institutions succeeded the first time. . . . During six administrations of the Florida Teacher Certification Examination, the passing rate for whites has ranged from 80 to 90 percent, compared to a range of from 32 to 37 percent for blacks. (70–71)

Various explanations exist as to why so many minority teachers do poorly on these tests. Some propose that inferior performance is the result of the poor education minorities have historically received in this nation. Others blame test bias. Yet, whatever the reasons, the results present a bleak future for black public school teachers for our schools. Many are concerned that we will soon have a shortage of minority teachers to serve the increasingly large minority populations of school children.

Minorities currently "constitute 26 percent of the U. S. population, but less than 12.5 percent of K–12 teachers. By the 1990s, even without considering the possible effects of a national teacher certification test, the minority proportions are predicted to be 30 percent of the population, but only 5 percent of the teaching force" (Menacker, Hurwitz, and Weldon 124).

Some black institutions are trying to combat this problem. Grambling State University, a black institution in Louisiana, had fewer that 5 percent of its graduates attain the qualifying score on the NTE in 1980. Yet, "major reforms in the institution's teacher education program resulted in the proportion passing rising to 85 percent in 1985" (Haney, Madaus, and Kreitzer 194). Similar gains were obtained when the University of Arkansas, Pine Bluffs, began education reforms and the pass rates on the NTE rose "from 42 percent in 1983 to 73 percent in 1984" (Hackley 19). As encouraging as these gains appear to be, questions remain concerning the cause of these improvements. As Haney, Madaus, and Kreitzer point out, "While these accounts are highly suggestive, they fail to examine seriously the issue of whether increased pass rates on the NTE are indicative of general improvements in the quality of teacher preparation. An alternative explanation is simply that coaching for the test, rather than better educated teachers, led to the dramatic increases in pass rates" (194).

In addition to institutional efforts to improve the pass rates of students, some states such as Texas have begun programs to help minority candidates pass teacher competency tests. (See, for example, the discussion in Nava, 33–34; Heger and Salinger, 58–60.) Yet the most recent figures still indicate that minority teachers are being eliminated from the teaching force at alarming rates. In May 1986, 18.4 percent of black teachers and administrators as compared to only 1.1 percent of white educators failed the Texas Examination of Current Administrators and Teachers (TECAT) (Rodman 13).

Recent reports from the American Association of Colleges for Teacher Education (AACTE) indicate that since 1978 the number of "new teachers produced by forty-five predominately black AACTE member institutions in the South declined by 47 percent (Smith, 1972). George (1985) reports that in Louisiana, from 1972 to 1982, 85 percent of black student teachers failed the NTE (1985). As a result, an average of only forty blacks a year have become teachers in Louisiana, a state in which 37 percent of the school-aged children are black" (Haney, Madaus, and Kreitzer 192). These results, as well as state-testing policies, are discouraging minority students from entering the profession. All the consequences—political as well as educational—of the decreasing number of minority teachers remain to be seen.

THE ROLE OF TESTING IN PROFESSIONALIZING TEACHING

Many of the proponents of teacher testing argue that some form of evaluation is necessary if teaching is to be accepted as a true "profession." The recent reform proposals have emphasized the necessity to professionalize teaching through vigorous preparation, certification, and selection to ensure that quality teachers will be trained. Darling-Hammond and Berry point out that the "first American reforms to professionalize teaching occurred over a century ago when Horace Mann established the first state normal school for the training of teachers in 1839" (vi). Later, the progressives worked toward professional schools that would be "analogous to those in law, medicine, and the applied sciences, to support universal education" (vi). Efforts to professionalize teaching have continued throughout the century. As can be seen in this account from the 1856 *Massachusetts Teacher,* issues raised more than a century ago continue to be discussed today:

> "Ought not teaching," the speaker asked, "to be raising [*sic*] to the rank of a liberal profession, distinctly recognized as such?" To accomplish this end persons entering teaching from "caprice" or temporarily from financial motives should be barred in the future. Professionalization would be assured "by a high standard of preliminary requisition," "emoluments corresponding to its true dignity and value," and protections "from the intrusions of the incompetent and unskillful." The time had arrived for the employment and evaluation of teachers to be freed from "the verdict of men engaged in other occupations"; the teaching force had to secure its own professional faculty or appropriate body, of whatever name, competent and empowered to grant professional certificates, licenses or diplomas. (Katz, qtd. in Haney, Madaus, and Kreitzer 203)

The observation that the employment and evaluation of teachers be freed from "the verdict of men engaged in other occupations" reflects the tensions between public and professional control of teaching that has permeated the evolution of teacher policy. One can argue that whoever controls the tests that result in entry to the profession will, in fact, control the profession. Whether the medical and legal professions provide the appropriate models for teacher testing remains to be seen. Unlike physicians and attorneys, however, teachers have diverse groups who want to establish control over their profession. Currently, teacher organizations, schools and colleges of education, state departments of education, subject matter organizations, as well as state legislators establish policies that affect the teaching profession. Therefore, issues concerning public or professional control of teaching will continue to be at the forefront of teacher testing until some kind of resolution or compromise is established among the various groups that establish policy concerning teacher training and teacher testing.

While most educators support efforts to professionalize teaching, others have noted some of the negative aspects to professionalization. Sykes, for example, points out that the social status of law and medicine have been established through explicit discrimination and that access to these professions, until recently, has been limited to all but white, middle-class males. The use of teacher tests that eliminate minorities from the profession is one manifestation of the problem that concerns Sykes. He also notes that the medical model of professional standards has become a model for education. Graduation from an accredited professional school, completion of a rigorous examination, and the completion of a residency or internship represent the current directions of educational reform. Irrespective of the possible drawbacks of professionalization pointed out by Sykes, the current reform documents express strong support for testing as one major aspect of professionalizing teaching. Haney's observation represents the view of many educators: "What better way to provide tangible evidence that entrants to the profession have mastered the specialized body of knoowledge—which forms the essential basis for professional claims—than to have a specialized, objectively graded professional certification exam?" (204).

The two major teacher education documents of the 1980s—the Carnegie Report on *A Nation Prepared: Teachers for the 21st Century* and the Holmes Group report on *Tomorrow's Teachers*—emphasize the need for teacher testing as a part of professionalization. According to the Carnegie report, the key to success in achieving far more demanding educational standards is through "creating a profession equal to the task—a profession of well-educated teachers prepared to assume new powers and responsibilities to redesign schools for the future. Without a profession possessed of high skills, capabilities, and aspirations, any reforms will be short lived." The National Board for Professional Teaching Standards has the responsibility to establish high standards and to certify teachers who meet that standard.

Tomorrow's Teachers echoes the recommendations of the Carnegie Report. One of the five major goals of the Holmes Group is "to create standards of entry to the profession—examinations and educational requirements—that are professionally relevant and intellectually defensible" (4). The report is critical of the level of testing that is currently in effect in some states: "America cannot afford any more teachers who fail a twelfth-grade competency test. Neither can we afford to let people into teaching just because they have passed such simple, and often simpleminded, exams" (4). Instead of these "simple" or "simpleminded" examinations, the Holmes Group, as noted, proposes the Professional Teachers' Examinations. For the Holmes Group, testing is definitely seen as a means by which teaching can be made a true profession, for "the hallmark of a profession is its responsibility for the quality and competence of its members" (65).

Looking at the history of other professions, as well as analyzing the rhetoric of recent teacher education reform documents, one realizes that teacher testing is a phenomenon that will not disappear in the near future. If teaching continues its struggles to become a profession analogous to law and medicine, testing of some kind will be one of the rites by which individuals will be inducted into the profession. Because the tests' importance for professionalization has also been argued, what remains to be determined is the nature and extent of the tests that teachers will be required to take. The issue is no longer, "Should teachers be tested?" Instead, the question of concern ought to be "What kinds of tests should be given to teachers?" From the perspective of English educators, a corollary question is "Which groups or organizations should develop the tests and also establish the criteria for successful performance on these tests?" Issues related to these two questions will be the focus of the next section.

WHO SHOULD DEFINE "COMPETENCY" FOR ENGLISH TEACHERS?

As the previous discussion has revealed, several organizations and educational reform groups see teacher testing as part of their agenda. Aside from the tests currently being used, the National Board—given the organizations represented in its membership—clearly will provide leadership in defining professional standards for teachers. The Holmes Group, with member institutions representing many of the leading research institutions in the nation, also has the potential for providing leadership in teacher testing. While it is too early to tell, it would not be unexpected if the National Board and the Holmes Group work in concert because many leading educators are members of both groups. An important question that both groups must deal with is "What role will subject matter organizations have in determining the nature of testing in their discipline?"

NCTE's concern about the current testing movement resulted in the formation of its Task Force on Teacher Competency Issues in the summer of 1986. Comprised of English educators from both the public school and university level, the committee prepared a summary report on the recent trends in teacher testing and presented some guidelines for testing English teachers. This document, the "Report of the NCTE Task Force on Teacher Competency Issues," released in November 1986, voiced concern about many aspects of the current testing movement. It also asserted that "we [the task force] oppose any teacher assessment/testing/evaluation program that does not conform to NCTE guidelines for general test use, teacher certification, and program accreditation" (*NCTE Report* 182). The report goes on to delineate five general guidelines that must be considered in teacher assessment:

> The assessment program must not focus on minimums; it must address comprehensively the skills and knowledge central to success in teaching reading, writing, literature, and other English-language related subjects.
>
> The program must be more than a "test," though a good examination might well be part of it. Candidate data should include observational materials, written work, interviews and other indicators necessary for making reasonable and fair judgments.
>
> One dimension of the program must address instructional and individual improvement. Feedback from evaluation must be useful for those evaluated.
>
> The program must be developed by responsible faculty in each institution, working with teachers who are active in the classroom.
>
> The program should not be standardized across institutions. Complicated as this requisite may make decisions, it is a necessary safeguard to protect diversity in higher education (NCTE *Report,* 187–88).

The recommendations of this task force clearly support forms of teacher testing that are more comprehensive than the tests currently used.

The task force report also expressed concerns about who defines competency for teachers, about the legal implications of teacher tests, and about the impact of testing on minority teachers. While the report was highly critical of several aspects of current testing, it was fully in support of efforts to upgrade the profession: "As a group, we welcome efforts to recruit outstanding students into teacher education programs and encourage experimentation in teacher education programs. Therefore, we encourage NCTE to affirm the importance of high admission standards for teacher education programs and for strong inservice programs to support teachers' professional growth" (*NCTE Report* 187–88). The report also asserts that NCTE is the "organization which is best qualified to define competency for English language arts teachers" (188). The NCTE report highlights the issue concerning the relationship between the National Board—or any other testing organization or agency—and the various subject matter organizations. Questions concerning who determines appropriate testing procedures must be addressed and solutions found if teacher testing is to have credibility among subject matter specialists.

Currently, the predominant way that NCTE influences the competency of English teachers is through the guidelines for teacher education programs such as the 1986 *Guidelines for the Preparation of Teachers of English Language Arts.* As noted in the introduction to the 1986 *Guidelines,* "During every decade in its seventy-five-year history, the [NCTE] has advanced recommendations for the preparation of teachers of English language arts. Working from a rich tradition of ideas about teacher education, the Council has developed various recommendations in response to changing educational conditions, new perceptions of the nature of English Education, and emerging views on the essential components and arrangements of teacher education programs" (*Guidelines* 1). Throughout the history of these documents, colleges and universities have used the guidelines to set standards for their teacher education programs for English teachers. The influence of the 1986 *Guidelines* probably will be broader than that of earlier versions of this document because NCATE recently adopted these guidelines for accrediting English teacher certification programs in its member institutions. These guidelines, therefore, present the standards which English teacher education programs must meet in order to be in compliance with NCATE.

The 1986 *Guidelines* present characteristics and competencies of English teachers that cannot be assessed through current modes of testing. Of the three sections in Part I of the *Guidelines*—knowledge, pedagogy, and attitudes—only *knowledge* could be tested by paper-and-pencil tests. The section on *pedagogy* stipulates things that teachers must be able to *do;* and the *attitudes* sections describes desireable attitudes that teachers of English need to possess. Clearly if English teachers are to be tested in ways that are compatible with the goals of teacher education programs, new methods of testing must be developed.

The guidelines for teacher assessment described in the "Report of the NCTE Task Force on Teacher Competency Issues" present a number of alternatives to the current standardized tests. As the report notes, a good paper-and-pencil test might be part of the assessment, but teacher candidate data must include a variety of measures. For example, given the diversity of English as a subject matter, the teacher should be observed a number of times teaching different aspects of the curriculum. Interviews with teachers would be particularly helpful in obtaining the information concerning attitudes necessary for English teachers. Samples of written work, rather than tests which merely purport to measure knowledge of writing and literature, could provide information about the teacher's ability to apply the skills that he or she is expected to teach. Teachers could be asked to prepare portfolios that include samples of their written work, evaluations by their college instructors, descriptions and evaluations of their work experiences with children or adolescents, as well as any other pertinent information. These portfolios would be evaluated and used in conjunction with the results of subject matter tests and evaluations of their classroom performance. By using multiple and diverse measures, the chances of obtaining an accurate assessment of the teacher candidate is increased. Undoubtedly, some of these measures would require a great deal of time and would be quite costly. But they would result in much more accurate and meaningful evaluations of an English teacher's competence. These measures would be a great improvement over current modes of testing teachers.

CONCLUSION

The educational reform movements of the 1980s have resulted in pressures from state legislatures, state departments of education, and various educational groups for greater accountability in all aspects of public education. Consequently, standardized tests have increased their emphasis on teacher accountability. Although teacher testing is not new, its current magnitude is. The growing demand for assessing teacher competence by means of tests is having a detrimental effect on some aspects of the profession. The use of tests such as the NTE is affecting the number of minority teachers entering the teaching force. The negative impact of the test has also resulted in a decrease in the number of minorities entering teacher education programs.

Several other problems exist concerning the use of these standardized tests. Legal challenges to these tests continue. Some educators question the content validity of the tests; others pose serious questions concerning predictive and concurrent validity. Particularly problematic is the manipulation of cut-off scores to control the number of teachers that enter the profession. When there is a shortage of teachers, the cut-off scores are lowered; when there is a surplus, the scores are raised.

Prospective teachers, classroom teachers, and teacher educators need to be informed about the National Board for Professional Teaching Standards, which is in the process of preparing standards for certification. Furthermore, subject matter specialists need to work with all certifying agencies to oversee the special needs of their discipline. English teachers, with the aid of organizations such as NCTE, must work to ensure that state-level, as well as future national-level, tests appropriately measure those characteristics and abilities that result in good English teachers.

Perhaps the best summary of the elements necessary for reasonable and appropriate teacher testing are found in Lee Shulman's essay on "Knowledge and Teaching: Foundations of the New Reform":

> If teachers are to be certified on the basis of well-grounded judgments and standards, then those standards on which a national board relies must be legitimized by three factors: they must be closely tied to the findings of scholarship in the academic disciplines that form the curriculum (such as English, physics, and history) as well as those that serve as foundations for the process of education (such as psychology, sociology, or philosophy); they must possess intuitive credibility (or "face validity") in the opinions of the professional community in whose interests they have been designed; and they must relate to the appropriate normative conceptions of teaching and teacher education. (5)

Teacher testing will have something to contribute to the advancement of the profession only when all of these elements are in place. Using tests whose content is questionable, manipulating test scores to control the market supply of teachers, and eliminating many minority teachers from the teaching force due to test bias will ultimately harm teaching as a profession. As Shulman says, "We have an obligation to raise standards in the interest of improvement and reform, but we must avoid the creation of rigid orthodoxies. We must achieve standards without standardization" (20). As a starting point, paper-and-pencil tests must be supplemented or replaced by evaluation procedures that take into account the complexity of teaching. Reform in teacher testing must accompany reform in teacher education.

Works Cited

"A Nation Prepared: Teachers for the 21st Century" (Executive Summary). The Report of the Task Force on Teaching as a Profession of the Carnegie Forum on Education and the Economy, May, 1986.

Allen v. Alabama State Board of Education, 612 F. Supp. 1046 (M.D. Alabama 1985).

Darling-Hammond, Linda, and Barnett Berry. *The Evolution of Teacher Policy.* New York: The Rand Corporation, JRE-01 (March 1988).

George, Pamela. "Teacher Testing and the Historically Black College." *Journal of Teacher Education* (November–December 1985): 54–57.

Guidelines for The Preparation of Teachers of English Language Arts. Urbana, Ill.: National Council of Teachers of English, 1986.

Hackley, L. V. "The Decline in the Number of Black Teachers Can Be Reversed." *Educational Measurement: Issues and Practice* 4 (1986): 17–19.

Hammes, Richard R. "Testing the Teacher: A Legal Prospective." *Action in Teacher Education* (Fall 1988): 13–19.

Haney, Walter, George Madaus, and Amelia Kreitzer. "Charms Talismanic: Testing Teachers for the Improvement of American Education." *Review of Research in Education,* Ernst Z. Rothkopf, ed. Washington, D.C.: American Educational Research Association, 1987. 169–238.

Heger, Herbert, and Terry Salinger. "Responding to Teacher Candidate Testing through Program Development." *Journal of Teacher Education* (November–December 1985): 58–60.

Katz, M. *The Irony of Early School Reform: Educational Innovation in Mid-nineteenth Century Massachusetts.* Cambridge, Mass.: Harvard University Press, 1968.

Krathwohl, David R. "The NTE and Professional Standards." *Educational Leadership* (October 1983): 75–77.

Lines, Patricia M. "Testing the Teacher: Are There Legal Pitfalls?" *Phi Delta Kappan* (May 1985): 618–22.

Menacker, Julius, Emanuel Hurwitz, and Ward Weldon. "Teacher Upgrading: Policy Alternatives." *The Educational Forum* (Winter 1986): 123–35.

Mercer, Walter. "The Gathering Storm: Teacher Testing and Black Teachers." *Educational Leadership* (October 1983): 70–71.

Mitchell, J. V. *The Eighth Mental Measurement Yearbook* 1978. Reported in Walter Haney, George Madaus, and Amelia Kreitzer. "Charms Talismanic: Testing Teachers for the Improvement of American Education." *Review of Research in Education,* Ernst Z. Rothkopf, ed. Washington, D.C.: American Educational Research Association, 1987.

National Council for Accreditation of Teacher Education. *Standards, Procedures, Policies for the Accreditation of Professional Education Units.* Washington, D.C.: National Council for Accreditation of Teacher Education, 1987.

Nava, Robert. "Caveat: Teacher Competency Tests May be Hazardous to the Employment of Minority Teachers and the Education of Language Minority Students." *Thrust* (October 1985): 33–34.

Newman v. Crews. 651 F 2d (4th Cir. 1981).

"Report of the NCTE Task Force on Teacher Competeny Issues." *English Education* (October 1987): 181–92.

Rodman, B. "At Grambling: Fighting Scores Instead of the Tests," *Education Week* 20 (November 1985): 13.

Salganik, Laura Hersh. "Why Testing Reforms Are so Popular and How They are Changing Education." *Phi Delta Kappan* (May 1985): 607–10.

Shulman, Lee S. "Knowledge and Teaching: Foundations of the New Reform." *Havard Educational Review* (February 1987): 1–22.

Sykes, Gary. "Evolution of the Professions." *The Holmes Group Forum I.* (1987): 10–12.

Tomorrow's Teachers: A Report of the Holmes Group. East Lansing, Mich.: The Holmes Group, 1986.

II

Textual Relationships and Pedagogy: Literature and Writing

Robert E. Probst

7. *Literature and Literacy*

Literature's place in the curriculum has always been questioned. Plato thought the poet dangerous, his poetry immoral, and kicked him out of the ideal society; Bacon persuaded us that truth could be found only through objective, scientific investigation, and allowed him back in because he was too insignificant to worry about. The poet—and literature—have remained on uncertain ground until this day.

In a scientific, mathematical, computerized era, that is perhaps to be expected. We have achieved our greatest, or at least our most visible successes, through the rigorous, objective, quantifying procedures of the scientists and engineers. They have built bridges, eliminated polio, travelled to the moon, sent probes to the edge of the galaxy. Poets do not build rocketships.

Nor do they help us with our checkbooks, insurance policies, or real estate ventures. Poets—and their comrades, novelists, dramatists, and so forth—are an impractical lot, contributing apparently little to the gross national product. Lacking useful skills, they are seldom asked to govern us, to run our corporations, or to participate in the major debates of the culture, although their distant associates, actors, seem occasionally able to make second careers for themselves as politicans.

The schools, as uncertain as the rest of the society, have had a problem figuring out exactly why it is that they spend so much time on literature. Mathematics, physics, and driver training have fairly clear reasons for being, but the purposes for teaching literature have evaded us. We teach it... because it is there.

CONCEPTIONS OF LITERACY AND LITERATURE INSTRUCTION

Extracting Information

Our failure to articulate our purposes satisfactorily has allowed literature instruction to be bastardized in several ways. In some cases, particularly in the elementary schools, literature has been reduced to the vehicle by which reading skills may be taught. Sadly, the phrase *reading skills* usually implies a very narrow conception of the act of reading, a conception in which comprehension—the extracting of information from texts—is the goal.

When our purpose in reading instruction is to teach students to extract information, our focus tends to fall most heavily upon the text. The text itself provides us with our measures of performance. It becomes the benchmark by which we may judge the reading—one that is "true" to the text is food, and one that omits from or adds to the text is faulty. We can teach students those skills that will help them get data from texts efficiently, and then test the quality and accuracy of the information they have managed to plunder to tell how well they are performing. Because literature is a source of experience, not information, such reading is inadequate for it, as Louise Rosenblatt has effectively argued for years.

Information about Literature

In other cases, we have most highly valued information about literature. This case exists more often in the secondary schools, where English teachers—literature majors —influenced by their professors, have tried to teach literary history and criticism. After all, a great deal of information is available about the lives of writers, the periods of literary history, the nature of the genres, and the critical assessments of writers and works. Organizing our teaching around that already well-organized information is tempting.

What, for example, could be more orderly and logical than a course organized historically? It moves smoothly from year to year, everything falling into place as neatly as the days on a calendar, everything assigned its place by the simple principle of sequence. In the high schools, the junior and senior years have often been so arranged, usually with American literature in the eleventh grade and British in the twelfth—Beowulf to Virginia Woolf.

There is, of course, nothing wrong with learning about the history of the literature —it is a fascinating study, if one happens to take an interest in that sort of thing, as many of us do. There is a danger, however, that arranging the course historically may draw our attention to literary history and away from literary experience—that unique transaction between the reader and the text. If we find ourselves emphasizing dates, sequences, influences, characteristics of periods, and so forth, then we may suspect that we are working, and asking our students to work, as historians rather than as readers.

Names, Places, and Dates

A third view, fairly similar to the second, has recently been proposed by E. D. Hirsch under the rubric *cultural literacy*. Although his more moderate statements seem palatable enough, in his list of items everyone needs to know he may have reduced the concept of culture—and of literacy—to the absurdly trivial. He speaks of cultural literacy in terms of little, discrete, particles of information. Do we know

Achilles, the Treaty of Versailles, Appomatox, . . . ? Hirsch reduces literacy to a list of names. If students' eyes do not glaze over in bewilderment when someone mentions Milton or Miller or Blake, Hirsch would take that as evidence that they are satisfactorily trained —literate people.

Does this nodding acquaintance, however, really indicate that students have reflected on those matters that occupied Milton and Miller and Blake, or does it simply give the impression, as with successful cocktail-talk, that they know something they really do not know? After all, one can dress someone in an elegant three-piece suit, add a leather briefcase and a car-telephone, and yet not have a successful corporate executive officer or CEO. No matter how much one looks like one, without the understanding, skill, and attitudes of the professional, one is simply an impressive (visual) imitation.

Culturally literate students, as conceived by Hirsch, similarly might be mere imitations of educated people. Acquainting students with the names, without engaging them in the dialogue and reflection that those names represent, will make students only the shadow-shapes of educated men and women, and reduce education to little more than a tedious television game show. One danger of Hirsch's vision of cultural literacy is that it is too simple. It assumes that literacy is a matter of possessing unassimilated information, when it is much more complex than that.

Of course another and greater danger is that such a vision might actually achieve some of its desired effect. It might actually serve to defne *literacy* and *the literate,* and if it does it will have clamped shackles on both the curriculum and the minds of the students. Lists such as those Hirsch offers are static and restrictive, defining one perspective, on vision, as literate, and others as something less. No such list can be responsive to a culture as fluid as ours, and no such list is likely to respect the unique and rapidly changing cultures of the students in the schools. (For an interesting analysis of the dangers inherent in Hirsch's notion of literacy see Chris M. Anson, "Book Lists, Cultural Literacy, and the Stagnation of Discourse," *English Journal* 77 [2] February 1988: 14–18.)

Even when he most cautiously defends his vision of cultural literacy, however, Hirsch acknowledges its adequacy as a guiding concept for education. Cultural literacy, he asserts, consists of that extensive but shallow background knowledge literate people should be expected to have. That "background information," he admits, "is usually sketchy and vague. Our students should know this, and not be disheartened by the sheer number of things literate people know. Our students need know only a smattering about some things, and this gives them and their teachers time to go into more detail about other things" ("Core Curriculum" 48).

Conceived of as a list of titles, names, events, allusions, and so forth, cultural literacy is not, then, the core of education—teachers and students should have time for other things. Hirsch says quite clearly that cultural literacy, as he represents it, should not be at the center of the curriculum: "There is a fundamental difference in function between intensive information, which is the staple of the curriculum, and extensive information, which is the staple of cultural literacy. Intensive teaching is where real learning occurs" ("Core Curriculum" 49). Its role, in other words, is small. His list of items reflects the periphery of the curriculum—the miscellany floating around the edges and not the central elements. We might need some common background, and Hirsch's list might contain many of the items that should be in that background, but to conceive of literacy in such simple terms is to reduce literature and literacy to the inconsequential.

In the absence of a competing vision of purpose, however, such a simplistic notion as cultural literacy might come to be seen as the ultimate goal of our teaching. Just as the "basics" crept through the educational enterprise like an insidious vine, choking out more substantial enterprises, such a reductive concept of literacy as Hirsch is proposing, apparently so compelling to many, perhaps because it seems easy to teach and to assess, is likely to insinuate itself into the educational landscape, establishing as destructive a stranglehold as the back-to-basics movement once held (and might still hold).

LITERACY

Then what is literacy? It must be more than the ability to dig shards of information out of texts—that conception banishes our entire literary heritage to the periphery. We do not, after all, go to literary texts to practice our decoding skills, or to gather practical information. And it must be more than the ability to remember data about writers or books—that conception, although it seems to respect the literature, ignores the experience of reading it in favor of reading around it. And it must be more than superficial acquaintance with lists of names—that conception reduces education to mere social deceit. Yet we clearly need a shared language, a common way of speaking and writing that enables someone from New York to communicate with someone in San Diego, and we might also need some shared pool of knowledge or intellectual experience—some shared culture—that enables us to understand ourselves and one another. If that culture is to join us together in any significant way, however, it must be more than mere information.

Arthur Applebee has cautioned us about too simplistic a notion of literacy, arguing that cultural heritage has to be viewed as more than a pile of books:

> Any definition of a literary heritage in terms of specific books or authors distorts the cultural significance of a literary tradition by failing to recognize that what the Great Books offer is a continuing dialogue on the moral and philosophical questions central to the culture itself. The usefulness of the heritage lies in the confrontation with these issues which it provides; any acquaintanceship which avoids the confrontation is both trivial and irrelevant, an observation often subsumed in the comment that each generation takes from the past what it needs, reconstructing the literary hierarchy on contemporary terms. (284)

The vision of literacy implicit in Applebee's remark is more active and involved. He suggests that the literate person is not one who can name the approved names, but rather one who is engaged in the "ongoing dialogue" of the culture, one who has dealt with the ideas and issues of the culture. Although the approved names in some way represent those ideas and issues, mere acquaintance with the names is no sign that a student has engaged in the dialogue. Might it not be more sensible for the schools to plan their instruction in literacy and literature with attention to that dialogue, rather than to such lists as Hirsch has offered?

For example, Shakespeare and *Macbeth* are on the list, and without doubt, justifiably so—people need to be aware of relationships that have to do with power, of the overwhelming desire for power that afflicts some, and Shakespeare's *Macbeth* reflects on those matters. But does that necessarily mean that all students have to read *Macbeth?* Could some of them read *All the King's Men* or *The Chocolate War* and address some of the same questions? Are there not other works, perhaps Hispanic or Oriental, that might encourage reflection on the same issues and to which students from those cultures might be even more receptive? The point after all is not to be able to drop Shakespeare's name into polite conversation but to be able to think intelligently about life.

Everyone needs to deal with issues of personal responsibility and personal choice, but does that mean all have to read *Portrait of the Artist as a Young Man?* Could they read instead *Bless the Beasts and Children* or *True Grit* and engage in the same kind of dialogue about the same general issues. Both *Beckett* and *The Crucible* (and, for that matter, historical treatments of the witchcraft trials or the McCarthy era) are ways of getting at broader issues—religious freedom, rules of evidence, due process, respect for individual rights and freedoms—more important than either title alone. Again, the crucial matter is not that students be able to name McCarthy, to cite *The Crucible,* or to tell us about the witchcraft trials, although that probably is material we would expect an educated person to know something about. Rather, engaging in the dialogue about due process, religious and political freedom, and the other issues is more important.

As long as students are invited to reflect on the broader questions that permeate the great works, the questions that are central to their culture, we may be satisfied that they are developing literacy. This argument, of course, is not against the great works—rather, it is an argument for conceiving of the literature curriculum as a series of intellectual encounters or experiences, rather than as a list of titles.

James Squire has suggested that to sustain the culture we do need a common body of reading, a shared cultural base:

> We talk much about our common heritage and our responsibility for teaching it, but the common heritage is significantly uncommon if children and young people do not share some literary experiences in common. Whether Dr. Seuss or E. B. White in the primary school, Mark Twain or John Steinbeck in the secondary, key works serve as benchmarks for our culture. (19)

But he is moderate in his call for a set of common readings, suggesting that perhaps between 10 percent and 25 percent of selections should be shared, and reminding us further that "the selections taught to all children should not only meet criteria of excellence, but should also be those works likely to speak most directly to all of our children" (20–21). He is concerned, in other words, that our curriculum not be designed with attention only to the content or quality of the works, but that the students—their attitudes, interests, and needs—also be respected. More important, he calls not for the memorizing of literary names and titles so much as for a sharing of literary experiences.

MAKING SENSE OF EXPERIENCE

The vision of literacy as the piling up of bits and pieces of information is deficient, then, in part, because it ignores the crucial task of helping students learn to make sense of their own experience. Literacy is not simply a matter of knowing that others have done so, and being able to name some of them—rather, it demands participating in the act of making meaning. A vision of literacy as mere acquaintance with what others have done is hopelessly inadequate.

We need to conceive of literacy not as fragments of information, as Hirsch has depicted it, or as reading skills, as the elementary schools have seen it, or as knowledge of particular literary works or authors, as the high schools have presented it. Instead, we need to conceive of it as involvement in the ongoing dialogue of the culture about the issues or questions or problems that have occupied its people. Literacy should imply not only that we know something of what others have thought and done but also that we think and do ourselves. If we are to have literate people, rather than people who appear literate, we must get students to do more than receive the literature of the culture. We must get them to participate in the culture, to join the conversation.

FIVE KINDS OF LITERARY KNOWING

To reconceive the literature curriculum in such a way that students and teachers would see that their goal is to join in the dialogue of the culture might be helpful. Such a reconception would pay attention to the literary heritage—the great works and the great authors, and the themes that they dealt with—and to the interests and abilities of the students, and to the nature of the transaction between the student and the texts. We might think of the goals of that curriculum in these terms:

Knowledge of Self. One outcome of literary study should be, it seems, knowledge of one's self. We read imaginative literature, after all, not just to satisfy someone else—a teacher or an employer—but for personal reasons. We might read for escape, or pleasure, or for a chance to reflect on another's visions. The only people who read imaginative literature for rewards extrinsic to the experience itself are students, forced to read for grades, and literary professionals, critics, teachers, or scholars, who may read as part of their work. Free citizens, however, read for themselves.

Such reading has the potential of yielding insight into the self. As readers encounter ideas or visions or experiences, they have the opportunity to balance them against their own, and they might, as a result, see their own more clearly. They might even come to modify their own notions, perhaps slightly, perhaps drastically.

The literature curriculum should explicitly acknowledge the personal significance of literary experience, rather than ignore or deny it, as it has often done in the interest of teaching skills or information. It should make provisions for students to focus on that personal element, by inviting them to respond to literature with personal associations, memories, judgments, stories of their own. If it does so, the literature classroom will then enable students to forge some understanding of their own place in the culture, inviting them to join as equal partners, rather than as mere listeners, in the dialogue of the culture.

Knowledge of Others. Literacy serves also to create a society. That, perhaps, is the ultimate goal implied in Hirsch's notion of cultural literacy—a group, sharing certain values and intellectual experiences, able to communicate efficiently and clearly within itself. Literature has an important role to play in socializing members of a society. Its role, however, is not merely to give them a common set of names to refer to, but rather to provide them experiences in which they come to see and understand one another more fully.

If knowing more about one's self is the first goal of the literature curriculum, then knowing more about others might well be the second. As students read—*The Chocolate War,* let's say—they might reflect upon their own confrontations with others who want to control them, and the reflections might enable them to understand how they react or how they might react. They might also, however, come to see more clearly how their classmates think about the same issues. Students indifferent to pressures to conform and strong enough to resist the group, might, in talking about *The Chocolate War,* come to understand students who fear the group's strength, or who are too confused to make decisions and judgments for themselves, and who thus capitulate. Students who fear the group and its more powerful leaders might come to see that even the most aggressive and powerful share some of their fears.

We need not predict what knowledge of others students will forge as they read and talk—it is beyond our authority to decide that—but we should acknowledge that reflection upon the thoughts, values, and feelings of the others in the classroom, as well as upon our own, is part of the literary experience. Clearer understanding of others, sharpened knowledge of the groups to which we belong, should be one of the explicit goals of the literature program.

Knowledge of Texts. Traditionally, this is probably where the emphasis in most literature instruction has fallen. Students have always been required to learn something about the texts. Occasionally, what they have been asked to learn seems of little significance. When students are asked to remember the imaginary facts about imaginary characters or imaginary events, we have reason to suspect that teachers either have inadequate criteria for judging the importance of information or simply want to assure themselves that the students have, in some minimal way, read the text.

More significant ways of knowing about texts exist, however. It is crucially important, for instance, for students to learn to draw inferences about the values and assumptions inherent in literary works. If they do not, if instead they accept the works at face value, unquestioningly, then they are vulnerable to manipulation. Robert Scholes has warned us about the danger:

> In an age of manipulation, when our students are in dire need of critical strength to resist the continuing assaults of all the media, the worst thing we can do is to foster in them an attitude of reverence before texts. . . . It is the attitude of the exegete before the sacred text; whereas, what is needed is a judicious attitude: scrupulous to understand, alert to probe for blind spots and hidden agendas, and finally, critical, questioning, skeptical. (16)

And it is not a new warning—J. Mitchell Morse devoted an entire book to cautioning us about the fraudulent and inadequate assumptions of even the world's greatest writers, urging us to teach students to examine their assumptions and biases, so that we are not trapped by them:"Let us not be overawed, even by Shakespeare, so far that we can't recognize vulgarity for what it is when it solicits our participation . . ." (193).

Students need to learn how texts work, which is not to suggest that they need to memorize the three (or is it four?) techniques by which an author creates character. Rather, they need to learn how texts suggest values and beliefs, how they push us, subtly or obviously, to accept the writer's assumptions and ideas. If we fail to teach them that, we leave them vulnerable to the manipulations of the culture.

Knowledge of Contexts. All discourse takes place in, and to some extent is dependent upon, a context. A book is read at a certain time in the student's life and takes on meaning that is determined not only by the text itself or by the student but, at least in part, also by the surrounding events.

We might imagine how vastly different the readings of Cormier's *The Chocolate War* might be under different circumstances. In a school dominated by a gang, for example, the reactions would be predictably different from those elicited by the same text in a school where harmony and order prevailed. Perhaps we would see differences even between schools in which there was a great deal of pressure to conform to certain group norms and those in which students were allowed to express their individuality more openly.

Similarly, a text that deals with the relationship between parent and child—Simpson's "My Father in the Night Commanding No" is a good example—might be read in dramatically different ways by a student whose mother just bought her a car, by one whose father just threw him out of the house, by one who has recently lost a parent, by one who is an orphan. . . . And those who are themselves parents might read it in still other ways. The possibilities are infinite.

The context—the circumstances in which the text is read—helps to shape the reading. Students need to learn how that happens, and they can do so if the discussions of and the writing about literature move beyond the text itself and into the responses and associations of the students. If they are asked to observe not just how the text is put together but also how they make something of it, then they may begin to see all the variables at work.

Knowledge of Processes. Finally, students should come to know something of the processes they employ in making sense of literature. In part, this means learning about the nature of statements and the differing obligations different statements impose upon us. For example, the two statements, "This text made me happy" and "The writer wanted me to feel happy," similar as they may be, commit the speaker to different courses. The first, a description of an internal state, a comment about one's own feelings, requires no defense. We may assume that individuals are the authority on their own states of mind. Of course, the possibility exists that other evidence will indicate that they are deceiving us, or themselves, and we might want to suggest that, but for the most part such assertions about the self do not require justification or proof.

The second statement, however, is an inference about the writer's intention. Rather than offering information about the speaker, this statement purports to tell us something about the world outside the speaker, and so it demands evidence or explanation. The reader who makes this statement is committed to give evidence for it. Rather than describing an attribute of thought or feeling, such a statement makes claims about matters outside the mind. Because such matters are accessible only through observation and reasoning, we may ask to see the observation and reasoning.

The two statements represent, in a crude way, two different processes for making meaning of literary texts. The first, expressive and introspective, looks into the emotions, associations, and thoughts awakened by the reading, and might lead the reader down paths that stray far from the text that opened them. One path, for instance, might lead to the writing of journals or personal narratives exploring memories evoked. Although, clearly, those memories are in no way in the text, and the writer may not have planned to evoke them, they may nonetheless be part of the transaction with the text, and the student may profit from examining them. If Hamlet leads us to productive reflection on our own impulses to vengeance, we may have profited as much from the reading as if it had led to a critical essay on Hamlet's vengeance.

Another path might be into the writing of imaginative literature of one's own. Surely reading one story might inspire an idea for another, or reading one poem might awaken a feeling or sharpen a perception that could become another poem. Students should not be so deceived by the curriculum, with its habitual insistence upon critical and expository writing about literature, that the explication of texts is the only appropriate culmination of reading.

On the other hand, inference and explication are legitimate options, and students should come to see that critical analysis is a powerful and productive way to deal with texts. Although it has often been reduced to a frustrating and fraudulent attempt to replicate the thinking of teacher or critic, when it is instead a vigorous effort to arrive at some understanding of the workings of the writer's mind, of the values implicit in the portrayal of human events, or of the uniqueness of the perception of the world, then it can be a stimulating activity.

This bipolar division into expressive and inferential processes for dealing with literary texts is too simple and crude, probably omitting many other possibilities, but it is suggestive. We might, for example, look at much smaller differences. Asking students to read a short story, dictating their responses into a tape recorder for later transcription and analysis, and then asking them to read another, making a record of their thoughts and feelings in the margin (a very wide margin in a specially prepared text), revealed several differences within a small group of students. Some liked the process of talking aloud, if only to a tape recorder, about the reading; others could barely tolerate the noisy interruptions they were required to make to their own reading. Some easily wrote lengthy reactions in the story's margins as they were reading; others refused to do so, and finished the reading first, then returned to make their notes. Some responded almost entirely in questions; others responded almost entirely with personal associations and memories. Some focused on ethical questions raised by the text; others concentrated on the emotional turmoil of the characters rather than on their ethical dilemmas; others reflected on the implications of decisions and choices made by the author.

All these variations represent subtle differences in the ways in which readers approach texts, the processes by which they create meaning from them. Students are likely to be better readers if they are aware, first of all, that the process is not magical—although it might appear to be in those classes where the teacher reveals the single acceptable interpretation—and second, that there are many ways of dealing with literary texts, that all have virtues and limitations, that some readers are more comfortable with one approach than with another, and that broadening our repertoire, and enjoying the game, might be what we should work for in the literature class.

CONCLUSION

If students learn to judge the success of their reading only by the degree of their submission to the text, by what they remember of it or extract from it, then they are likely to ignore the uniqueness in themselves and in their circumstances that strongly shapes the act of reading—especially, perhaps, the reading of imaginative literature. Both the emphasis on reading skills and the emphasis on literary information encourage readers to neglect personal response. They encourage them to submit to the text, but not to make it their own. But when we enjoy literature, when it strikes us so forcefully that it becomes more than an opportunity to exercise our skill at "defining through context" and more than an artifact to be fitted into a historical pattern, we do make it our own, and we are conscious of our presence in the act.

Rosenblatt has suggested that we distinguish between efferent and aesthetic reading, and respect both in the curriculum. Efferent reading—whose purpose is to carry something away from the text, to extract some information, idea, principle, or whatever, that we will employ after the reading—is, of course, vitally important. It enables us to deal with political speeches, insurance policies, contracts, and computer manuals. Aesthetic reading, on the other hand—that reading in which our focus is on the present moment, the ongoing experience with the text—is equally important. It is the process by which we define ourselves and our relationship with the world. If literary studies are to be humanizing, are to yield truly literate men and women, then we must invite a full engagement, mind and spirit, with literary texts.

Works Cited

Applebee, Arthur N. *Tradition and Reform in the Teaching of English: A History.* Urbana, Ill.: National Council of Teachers of English, 1974.

Hirsch, Jr., E. D. "'Cultural Literacy' Doesn't Mean 'Core Curriculum'," *English Journal* 74 (1985): 47-49.

________. *Cultural Literacy: What Every American Needs to Know.* Boston: Houghton-Mifflin, 1987.

Morse, J. Mitchell. *Prejudice and Literature.* Philadelphia: Temple University Press, 1976.

Rosenblatt, Louise M. *The Reader, the Text, the Poem: The Transactional Theory of the Literary Work.* Carbondale, Ill.: Southern Illinois University Press, 1978.

________. *Literature as Exploration,* fourth edition. New York: Modern Language Association, 1984 (1938).

Scholes, Robert. *Textual Power: Literary Theory and the Teaching of English.* New Haven, Conn.: Yale University Press, 1985.

Squire, James R. "The Current Crisis in Literary Education," *English Journal* 74 (1985): 18–21.

George E. Newell

8. *Exploring the Relationships between Writing and Literary Understanding: A Language and Learning Perspective**

Whenever English teachers have assigned writing about literature, they have been compelled to do so to teach students writing skills, such as particular forms of organizing and presenting arguments, and to teach students how to conduct close, objective textual analysis. These relationships between the two central activities of the English classroom have continued because they support the assumption that formal or new critical interpretation of literature prepares students for academic success and for their lifelong experiences with literature and with writing. Consequently, discussions of writing about literature have usually focused on specific skills of practical criticism assumed to be elements of adult performance: "Literary analysis is no different from any other kind of analysis: it attempts to find truth. The process of analysis begins by dividing a problem into parts. Once the parts are separated and considered singly, it is easier to study their natures, functions, and interrelationships" (Roberts 6).

Coupled with a concern for close textual analysis is yet another enduring tradition in English teaching: our conceptualization of literary education as cultural heritage. Arthur Applebee explains the roots of this heritage approach:

> The teaching of literature began as an attempt to introduce students to the best authors and writing of the English tradition, with instruction at times concentrating wholly on biographical and historical data. Such studies were thought to have several justifications: they would provide a common set of reference points for the culture at large; they would teach the student to respect the culture by giving him a sense of his "heritage"; and they would improve his personal system of values. (*Tradition and Reform* 247)

* I would like to thank Chris Pappas, Ken Daub, Linda Levstik, and the editors for comments on earlier drafts of this chapter.

Because cultural wisdom and knowledge contained in the literary canon are thought to lie beyond the grasp of students' intellectual powers, teachers assume the role of purveyors of information about literature and students are held accountable for that information. The interrelationships among the study of literature, the maintenance of the culture, and personal value systems are thought to be simple and direct—teaching becomes a matter of ensuring that students are "exposed" to the right kinds of literature. Writing, in turn, serves as a means for testing students' ability to recite what they have been taught: "In a well-organized essay of 200-250 words, answer the question that follows: Homer considered that Odysseus was a hero, a representative of Greek ideals. How is Odysseus a model for youths of all times" (Applebee, *Writing in the Secondary School* 75)?

The continuing dominance of these two traditions (Applebee, *Tradition and Reform;* Purves, *Reading and Literature*) indicates that while literature has been and continues to be the main constituent of the English classroom, we have had very few changes in instruction. Teaching methods seem a rather incoherent mix of traditional approaches (new critical and heritage) with some scattered attempts at reader response. In one sense it seems ironic that English educators (teachers and researchers alike), who were very likely drawn to the field through literary studies, should have allowed the teaching of literature to stagnate. But now, after nearly two decades of heavy emphasis on writing research and instruction, the English teaching profession has again returned to unanswered questions regarding literary education: What knowledge about literature should be taught directly? What literary works do we select for use in the classroom and on what basis? How can we evaluate literary understanding?

At the same time, as we begin to struggle with questions of how we might enable students to understand and build upon the knowledge and wisdom of our cultural heritage, a clear danger exists that we might forget what we have learned from our absorption in writing instruction: the central role of student ownership in the acquisition of new skills and knowledge.

Research into the development of oral and written expression has produced compelling evidence that, rather than merely "echoing" adult language, children learn to use language through continual interaction with adults in contexts in which both child and adult negotiate control over the communicative event. This process begins with an "expressive" or personal language that children learn in the context of home and extends to more formal literacy events in school settings. Thus, the assumption is that reading and writing are extensions and reformulations of earlier language learning processes. Rather than viewing children's oral and written language as lacking adult sophistication, development is now seen as accumulative, ongoing, and collaborative, beginning with the context-bound communication of personal intent and evolving to more highly conventionalized uses of language found in academic disciplines.

While we have begun to embrace the significant parallels between oral and written language development, we have been less willing to view the experience of reading literature in such a way. As a profession with many differing traditions and perspectives, we have always struggled to understand how the parts of the English curriculum fit together. This is especially evident in the ways we have conceptualized our teaching agendas for writing and literature curriculum. We have developed a new process-oriented writing pedagogy which rides uneasily with a heritage approach to the reading of literature—an approach that is often coupled with the concern for a single, correct literary interpretation. Rather than calling for the rejection of one approach to literature instruction in favor of the other, the purposes of this discussion are to take stock of the way new conceptualizations of literary interpretation can be used to explore theoretical and empirical bases for the notion that when students' responses to literature are constructed out of their own reasoned interpretations, their arguments become richer and more sophisticated.

These purposes raise four questions:

1. What do we mean by literary interpretation?
2. What advantages do we gain for both writing development and literary education if we view writing as a way to foster literary understanding?
3. What is the nature of the research base that might support such a perspective?
4. When adopted into classroom life, how successful is the implementation of writing and learning approaches to literary study?

And, as a corollary, what are the forces that engender teacher "resistance" to such an approach? Following an exploration of these issues, I offer an instructional framework for using writing to explore ideas and experiences students encounter in literature.

ASKING NEW QUESTIONS ABOUT LITERARY INTERPRETATION

In recent years, a growing tension has also emerged between the traditional assumptions concerning what constitutes appropriate ways of interpreting and analyzing literary texts and discussions of what constitutes meaningful acts of reading and writing.

In literacy research, both writing and reading are currently construed as constructive activities that occur as writers/readers build meaning by integrating their prior knowledge and new ideas. In literary criticism, discussion has centered on the tensions between text- or reader-based interpretations and on the need for a more pluralistic view of interpretation (Booth), a view that holds that as readers interact with texts they construct differing text-worlds (Iser). These perspectives fit uncomfortably, at best, with the assumption that the study of literary texts should lead toward the acceptance of a received body of knowledge, whether formulated by the teacher or by literary criticism.

Traditionaly, writing about literature has been construed as a test in which students' written responses are evaluated according to how well they report interpretations transmitted by the teacher. In such a context, students' interpretations are considered appropriate only as they correspond to some ideal model, rather than as constructions shaped by students' own attempts to make sense of their reading. Consequently, as English teachers we need to develop a new conceptualization of writing about literature based on the constructive nature of understanding literary discourse as distinct from other forms of discourse and the role of writing in fostering that understanding. While writing might well be the most valuable way of evaluating learning, it can also be used to help students think about and reformulate their interpretations.

WHAT ADVANTAGES ARE GAINED BY TAKING A WRITING AND LEARNING PERSPECTIVE?

The assumption underlying the relationship of writing and learning is that writing is a constructive act that fosters topic understanding as writers build verbal representations of relationships between previous and new ideas. On the other hand, theoretical models have described the reading process as constructive in that an interaction is established between the text and the reader's purpose and knowledge. Thus, the "blueprint" of written language must be enriched and embellished by the reader if meaning is to be constructed.

These parallels between writing and reading suggest that writing about reading may provide a means for enriching and embellishing the meanings students tentatively construct from text. Accordingly, not only do students develop a fuller meaning of the text but also, in their attempts to argue for that meaning, might broaden their procedural knowledge for discourse strategies and structures. This thinking has become the basis for process approaches to writing, with their emphases on variety in form and audience and on the importance of students' personal knowledge.

Major changes in writing pedagogy occurred in the 1970s and 1980s when research began to examine how writers compose. Janet Emig's study of the writing processes of twelfth graders led to a watershed of studies focused primarily on the complex and recursive processes that writers rely on while composing various tasks. More recent work by John Hayes and Linda Flower has focused on the development of more formalized models of composing, allowing researchers to generate and to test specific hypotheses about the nature of the writing process. In general, studies of composing have led to three important findings:

1. Writing involves subprocesses (generating, drafting, revising, and editing) that operate recursively throughout the process.
2. Writing processes vary according to the demands of the task, including the writer's topical knowledge.
3. Writing processes differ across various kinds of writers (e.g., experts versus novices).

A process orientation, with its focus on meaning construction where ideas literally take shape at the point of utterance, seems to relate to the notion of writing as a way of reasoning and learning. Both assume an active writer who must integrate and reformulate ideas as the process unfolds. In this sense, learning is tentative and constructive rather than hurried and reproductive. Perhaps most important, a process-oriented view of writing seems most powerful as a way to integrate scholarly positions on how learning occurs, including literary understanding (Rosenblatt), with the realities of the classroom.

WHAT IS THE NATURE OF THE RESEARCH BASE?

As English teachers, we may take for granted that writing can and should play an important role in learning. Our own experiences as writers and teachers of writing often suggest that writing can be a powerful tool for rethinking, revising, and reformulating what one knows.

The strongest evidence about the effects of writing on learning should come from studies that have examined connections between writing and learning directly. Yet only a few studies have been conducted to explore when, what, or how people learn from writing. Earlier studies on reading comprehension and study skills, with simpler forms of writing such as answering adjunct study questions (e.g., Anderson and Biddle) and notetaking (e.g., Fisher and Harris), indicate that the nature of the study technique is related to the nature of improvement in recall of text material, with some tasks enabling the retention of a full but superficial spectrum of text information and others a more in-depth understanding. However, studies of prose learning have not examined the effects of composing more complex forms of writing such as extended essays on learning. Others fall short as studies of direct effects of writing on learning as a consequence of their primary focus on composing processes.

In recent years, writing research has begun to develop a compelling theoretical base and a slender but promising empirical base for the relationship between writing and learning (Applebee, "Writing and Reasoning"). What began as an effort to examine writing-to-learn from informational text has expanded to include studies of writing and literary understanding. One of my own studies (Newell) examined the effects of various school writing tasks on the process of composing a response to informational text and the understanding of passage-specific knowledge that results. Using a measure that examines students' understanding of specific concepts in prose passages, (Langer, "Examining Background Knowledge"), I found that analytic essay writing enabled students to orgainze their understanding of the passages significantly better than taking notes or completing short-answer exercises.

In another study, Judith Langer ("Learning through Writing") found that when students wrote essays about expository text, their meaning-construction processes enabled them to reconceptualize passage content in ways that focused on larger issues and topics as compared to the results obtained from notetaking and answering study questions. Langer reported that essay writing allowed students to engage in conceptually more complex thoughts than the other two tasks as reflected in her measure of topic-related knowledge. This finding was augmented by a series of studies by Langer and Applebee (*How Writing Shapes Thinking*) that examined the relationships of writing and learning in a larger sample.

James Marshall's study of how the instructional context influences what students take from discussing and writing about literature and the effects of writing on literary understanding represents the first attempt to examine the factors that shape both the type and quality of literary response. The instruction Marshall observed was marked by an academic approach to literature, leading students to close textual anaylsis that required them to ignore their personal reactions. When Marshall had the students who had studied literature within that context respond to stories using study questions, personal analytic essays (drawing on personal experiences and values to interpret the text), formal analytic essays (drawing on text only to interpret), and a read-only condition, he found that essay writing in either mode led to a better understanding of the texts than either the read-only or study question conditions.

To pursue some of the issues raised by Marshall, my colleagues and I (Newell, Suszynski, and Weingart) examined the effects of Marshall's conceptualization of formal analytic writing and personal analytic writing on tenth graders' understanding of short stories. With the understanding that the teacher had encouraged personal explorations of literature, we speculated that the students would respond to the two types of tasks quite differently. When the essays written in the two conditions were scored for quality of response using a holistic measure, results favored the personal tasks. An examination of the written products revealed that the personal analytic writing contained a fuller range of responses, resulting in richer, more compelling, top-down interpretations than the formal writing. We suggested that formal writing requiring a public presentation of an objective interpretation might demand too much too early in the process of understanding the text. Personal writing, on the other hand, may function as a "thought piece" to clarify students' tentative interpretations, delaying the need for immediate certainty and permitting students to develop more sophisticated responses.

The underlying assumption of this discussion is that writing tasks that allow students to apply personal frames of reference in interpreting texts provide opportunities to elaborate upon meanings they have tentatively created in their reading. Consequently, contexts in which students write as a reasoned and tentative exploration of their own analyses contribute to a deeper understanding of text.

That such compelling research findings should play a role in educational change might seem obvious. But as we look to a research base to support the notion that writing fosters literary understanding we immediately face two problems: (1) the research has just begun, requiring us to pose only the most tentative implications for instruction; and (2) we must move cautiously to understand the contexts of classroom life. Consequently, any change based on research must include practitioners' judgment about the appropriateness of our extrapolations from research findings. Across the studies reviewed here runs the understanding that the advantage of essay writing lies in the process the tasks engender: constructing an interpretation, locating and integrating evidence to support it, and selecting language to represent it—each step suggesting the need for a process-oriented pedagogy. Yet to be explored, however, are the features necessary for successful implementation of the process approach to writing and reasoning about literary text.

HOW EFFECTIVELY IS A PROCESS APPROACH TO WRITING ABOUT LITERATURE IMPLEMENTED?

Thus far we have reviewed studies focused primarily on learning, but the current discussion is also concerned about instruction that might support how students read and write in school settings. While a long tradition of research on classroom practice and literacy education exists (Fillion and Brause; Smith-Burke), I want to examine a new and promising line of work in the development of language pedagogy. After reviewing some of the basic features of instructional scaffolding, I use this conceptualization of instruction as a backdrop for discussion of a recent study on how English teachers implement writing and learning strategies in literature instruction.

Applebee and Langer have, over several years of research on writing in U.S. schools, formulated a set of features they believe are necessary for effective instruction. Based on the studies of children's language development and Vygotsky's (*Thought and Language; Mind in Society)* social learning theory, they have posed the notion of instructional scaffolding (Applebee and Langer; Langer and Applebee "Language, Learning, and Interaction"; Langer and Applebee, *How Writing Shapes Thinking*). The power of this metaphor resides in its use in analyzing "essential aspects of instruction that are often missing in traditional approaches" (Applebee, "Problems in Process Approaches" 108) and its heuristic powers for developing new instructional approaches.

Furthermore, new skills and knowledge are learned collaboratively in tasks that are too difficult for the learner to manage alone but that can be successfully managed with the interactive assistance of a teacher, or can be provided in other forms such as group-oriented instruction, teachers' written responses, and class discussion. While cautioning that instructional scaffolding is merely suggestive of what a more fully conceptualized model might include, Applebee and Langer offer five aspects of effective instruction. (For a full explanation, consult the works by Applebee and Langer cited above.)

1. *Student ownership of the learning event.* Rather than simply following teacher demands or repeating ideas drawn from the text or the teacher,

students must be given tasks and activities that offer opportunities for their own ideas and opinions.

2. *Appropriateness of the tasks.* While the tasks must derive from students' knowledge and skills, the teacher must also present new tasks requiring teacher support for successful completion.
3. *Structured learning environment.* Students must encounter tasks that require the help of a more knowledgeable adult (the teacher) capable of organizing activities around a natural sequence of thought and language to guide student learning.
4. *Shaped responsibility.* In the role of collaborator, the teacher's role must shift from testing of previous knowledge to assisting with new learning.
5. *Internalizations of routines and strategies.* As students internalize structures and strategies for reading and writing, instruction must be altered to ensure that students continue to develop their own purposes in the completion of newer and more complex tasks.

How might instructional scaffolding be applicable to the issues we have raised concerning literary education? If we assume what Jerome Bruner has termed a "negotiatory, or 'hermeneutical' or transactional view" (122) of meaning, literary interpretation can be understood as the sharing of views between teacher and students. Bruner explains that contemporary views of culture hold that, rather than simply a matter of transmitting knowledge and values from experts to novices or from teachers to students, culture is constantly in flux requiring its members to direct and shape it through interpretation and renegotiation. Thus, in a very real sense, talk around text can become "culture making." Rather than focusing on either the students' experiences or the culture as represented in the text, a reciprocal relation exists between being a maker of meaning and culture and being a receiver of cultural wisdom. "He [the student] becomes at once an agent of knowledge making as well as a recipient of knowledge transmission" (Bruner 127).

INSTRUCTIONAL SCAFFOLDING IN THREE CLASSROOMS

Guided by assumptions underlying the concept of instructional scaffolding and questions concerning the nature of support teachers extend during instruction, my associates and I recently completed a study of the way three high school English teachers at three grade levels (9, 10, and 11) use writing in literature instruction (Newell and MacAdam). Our goals were to examine how teachers conceptualize the relationship between writing tasks and the reading of literature and to explore problems associated with using writing as a supportive strategy in the study of literary texts. We also saw our work as an opportunity to examine the constraints we might face as we presented the teachers with new ways of thinking about writing tasks and about what counts as literary understanding.

After about three months of classroom observations and interviews with the three teachers and case study students from their classes, we spent two months conducting planning meetings with the teachers. We worked collaboratively with them, drawing on their teaching experience and our theoretical and practical sense of writing-to-learn strategies. Our discussions focused on their instructional goals and the way a variety of writing tasks might be used to further those goals.

Our observations are necessarily condensed here. We would, however, like to share our main discoveries and understandings: First the teachers' implementation strategies were to a large extent shaped by their prior understanding of their roles in the instructional process, their perceptions of the functions of literature in the school curriculum, and the skills and knowledge of their students.

Second, the three teachers revealed very strong beliefs about the value of literature, but their beliefs took three different forms: (a) that literature was to be studied as body of knowledge about "the most important ideas and knowledge of our civilization"; (b) that students deserve a chance to read and enjoy literature and to use literature to understand their own lives; and (c) that the teacher's role is to "do what I can to make aesthetic reading possible for the students, even if it seems impossible at times." Given these three attitudes and beliefs about literary education, the teachers employed our suggestions for writing about literature in different ways.

We also explored the teachers' perceptions of the role of the writing process approach in fostering their students' thinking and reasoning about literary texts. Again, we found considerable diversity in these perceptions. One downplayed the role of process strategies in her pedagogy, arguing that it takes time away from "covering literature content." Beth Cummings[1] saw her primary role as instructing students on strategies for "getting it all down and in correct form and content immediately rather than waiting for inspiration."

On the other hand, Mary Bennett and Don Swenson were more open to the use of writing process strategies as part of literary study. Initially, both teachers were skeptical of close, textual analysis, regardless of the types of students they taught. Swenson remarked that "literature is not a subject matter. It's people writing about experiences they want to share with other people." Bennett's resistance to what she described as a "professor's view of literature rather than kids'" was clearly articulated when she admitted that, "Even if I did assign lit. crit. papers, and even if the kids did them okay, what would that mean to them . . . and to me?"

Beyond simply describing the teachers' definitions of literature and writing and examining the bases of their beliefs, we also observed them using writing as part of literature instruction. While we noted vast differences in the beliefs of Cummings and the other two teachers, we also recognized that as in other studies, the most process-oriented teachers suffered to some degree the constraints of tradition and the conditions of their instruction.

Swenson, who experimented willingly with writing to encourage students' reflections upon their interpretations, turned to more formulaic assignments when he taught "formal writing that analyzes." Furthermore, he believed that objective tests were necessary to evaluate if the students "really got it or were still just thinking about it." Both Bennett and Swenson distinguished between personal writing tasks to interest and encourage students in the study of literature and more formal tasks that had to be teacher controlled "if the students are going to survive academically."

Thus, as their students attempted more difficult language and thinking tasks, Bennett's and Swenson's usually supportive strategies were suddenly dropped. Their reasons for such a shift in their roles were clearly justified in their minds. They felt that the writing their students generated as a result of our exploratory strategies was inadequate as a true indicator of literary understanding as institutionalized by their schools.

In summary, even when the teachers took the time to reflect and to collect their thoughts about teaching, they struggled to find ways to act on the results of their reflection. Quite often in our discussions, Swenson and Bennett expressed concern that a language and learning orientation requires a great deal of time—"time we often don't have when there's so much at stake." Our work with the three teachers raises the question of whether substantive change in teaching is possible given the kinds of constraints we observed.

How might we, as teacher educators, explain some of these seemingly contradictory teacher beliefs and these somewhat mixed forms of instruction? Recent discussions of improving preservice and in-service teacher education (Zeichner and Liston) suggest that assuming we can simply provide teachers with pedagogical skills and techniques derived from a preexisting body of knowledge might be misleading. While the instructional context might seem easily known and manipulatable, a complex dynamic usually operates just below the surface. The results from our study remind us that we find many conceptions of what is worth knowing and what counts as knowledge, and that when the call for reform is sounded we must try to understand the complexities of classroom life. Given those complexities, effective teaching requires practitioners to base their instructional decisions on deliberate thought rather than impulse. Accordingly whether we work with prospective teachers or experienced practitioners, we must view teaching as a reflective and dynamic activity rather than routine and static.

The results of our interviews and observations also suggest the need for a more careful examination of the contexts that shape the way teachers learn to manage process approaches to writing about literature. While they need a compelling conceptualization of the role of writing in enhancing literary understanding, they also need to think about evaluation in some rather new ways.

How might we as teachers and teacher educators develop assessment techniques more in line with present notions of the constructive nature of learning and literary understanding? On the one hand, formal testing with its emphasis on easily scored, multiple-choice tests tends to emphasize breadth of coverage rather than depth of understanding (Langer and Applebee, *How Writing Shapes Thinking*) On the other hand, a writing and learning perspective argued for in this chapter focuses on more complex analysis and understanding of literary text. What might such evaluation techniques that have such a focus entail? English teachers have become more willing to rely on holistic evaluation of writing—methods that rely on the quality of the overall structure of the argument or presentation rather than simply the citing of fragmented bits of information. Modifying such approaches to include a balance between the quality of students' reasoned interpretation of texts and the appropriateness of the supporting evidence they draw from the text and from their own intellectual and experiential knowledge seems possible. Such a modification in our testing methods in school districts and classrooms should ensure that process-oriented writing and literature pedagogy finds support rather than resistance in our work as teachers and teacher educators.

As a first step in modifying the way we teach and evaluate literary understanding, the next section suggests a framework for using the heuristic powers of writing in literature teaching so that teaching and evaluating are complementary. Rather than a set formula, our framework requires continued assessment of the meaning-making students engage in throughout the process of coming to terms with the text. The quality of their responses is based not only on citing specific information but also on the effectiveness and structure of the interpretation as a whole.

TOWARD AN INSTRUCTIONAL FRAMEWORK FOR USES OF WRITING IN TEACHING LITERATURE

Our review of a theory of writing and learning, of the research base for that theory, and of a study of how teachers implement writing-to-learn strategies in literature classrooms leads to the inevitable question—how might we reconceptualize the relationship of writing and literature? In this section, I step from the more comfortable footing of theory to the precarious ground of informing practice. As I do so, I depend upon what I have argued for thus far about the heuristic powers of the writing process, upon recent discussions of literary understanding, especially Rosenblatt's transactional theory of reading, and upon recent attempts to reconceptualize reading and writing instruction (Langer and Applebee, *How Writing Shapes Thinking*). To an even greater extent, however, the framework derives from what we have learned in our work with the three teachers: Cummings, Bennett, and Swenson. Many of the uses of writing described here came from two sources: what the teachers were already using before the project began and the new activities that came from our collaborations.

Since the components of a more adequate conceptualization have been discussed in earlier sections of this chapter, let me summarize them here:

1. Literary understanding is a constructive process that begins when the reader engages in personal-aesthetic reading of a text that requires the reader to call upon knowledge and experience to be integrated with the content of the text.
2. Writing and learning routines requiring students to marshall an argument or

point-of-view and to garner reasons for that perspective based on the text and on the writer's experential knowledge are more likely to support literary understanding than writing requiring unelaborated responses focused on text elements only.

3. Effective instruction occurs when the teacher assumes the role of informed collaborator, who allows students to acquire understanding of the text by employing strategies that support the students' effort at meaning. Evaluation is formative and ongoing and employed as a measure of students' reasoning, including an even mix of both the quality of the conceptualization and the use of supporting details.

Based loosely on Langer's (*Children Reading and Writing*) model of construction of meaning and Applebee and Langer's notions of instructional scaffolding, Table 8.1 represents a framework for employing a process approach to writing about literature. Analogous to components of process-oriented writing pedagogy, the features of this framework are ordered around the learner's gradual and tentative attempts at coming to know a text and the learner's eventual evolution to a more public, shared meaning, as well as the instructional activities that might support that process. Our first readings, as our first drafts, often begin with only the most skeletal understanding; only through multiple readings and attempts to write about that evolving understanding do we flesh out a fuller grasp of the text containing a consistent pattern of meaning. As a respondent to what the learner has tentatively construed from the reading and writing about the text, the teacher facilitates the development of the learner's intentions using supportive advice and questions. Thus, the form and structure of the learner's written interpretation are understood, not as arbitrary and given formulations of academic prose, but as "signposts that the reader will understand to cue meanings that the writer intended" (Langer, *Children Reading and Writing* 4).

Instructional support requires the teacher to take the role of collaborator who establishes the context for reading and interpreting the text; to call for personal reflection on what meaning the students have begun to develop; to help students toward new learning by modeling, questioning, praising, correcting, and so forth; and finally to evaluate the students' more public meanings of the text. Throughout the instructional process, writing-to-learn strategies contribute to these efforts. Four types are outlined in Table 8.1: preparing, formulating, reformulating, and evaluating. Accordingly, as the roles of the teacher and student change, the pedagogical uses of the writing change as the students build their interpretations. In this framework, the teacher retains the more traditional role of planner and initiator of reading and writing tasks. In contrast to traditional strategies, however, the activities operate as means for providing student ownership over the evolving meaning rather than for evaluating and grading according to preset objectives.

How might we make the notion of ownership a more practical concern in our teaching? To illustrate the nature of the teacher's role in the collaborative process, I

Table 8.1

An Instructional Framework for Writing and Learning about Literature: A Process-Oriented Approach

The Students' Role: Understanding the Text	The Teacher's Role: Providing Instructional Support	Writing-to-Learn Strategies
1. Anticipating and planning to read.	1. Providing a context for an initiating reading.	1. *Preparing Tasks:* Reconstructing experiences and knowledge that parallel those represented in the text (e.g., writing about experience).
2. Engaging and refining initial responses to the text and finding the language to represent them.	2. Supporting attempts to read the text aesthetically by providing routines and strategies leading to an integration of students' knowledge and experience and the text.	2. *Formulating Tasks:* Composing initial attempts at understanding the text (e.g., writing a narrative account of a reading of a text to resolve difficulties).
3. Monitoring the evolving meaning and reformulating meaning when understanding breaks down.	3. Teaching students to monitor their evolving meaning. Delaying evaluation to allow for work-in-progress.	3. *Reformulating Tasks:* Reorganizing and reflecting on new learning by finding causes and effects, explaining motivations, and speculating about other possibilities (e.g., writing an essay).
4. Presenting a fuller interpretation of the text.	4. Requesting and evaluating public presentation of literary interpretation.	4. *Evaluating Tasks:* Revising an interpretation after self-analysis, peer review, or teacher response, culminating in a formal essay.

want to review a brief example of the way Swenson, one of the three English teachers in the study discussed earlier (Newell and MacAdam), supported a student's effort to analyze Holden Caulfield by assigning a journal entry comparing Holden's values to his own. Swenson allowed the student Michael to sort through his experiences as a way to explore Holden's values (a preparing task in the table).

INITIAL DRAFT

> A similarity between Holden and me is that we both like reading. But Holden likes Shakespeare and I like mystery stories over Shakespeare. But I'll read it if necessary.

In his journal, Michael merely lists similarities and differences between his and Holden's reading. Swenson realized that Michael was still formulating his analysis of Holden and responded: "Now that you have a particular thing to say about Holden, consider what you really want to say about what Holden's attitude toward reading suggests about him as a character." Michael's first attempt to draft a more formal analysis of Holden suggests a fuller understanding, not only of Holden's different attitude toward reading but also of his reflective nature.

FINAL DRAFT

> To understand Holden's love of reading, especially reading Shakespeare, I considered what I like about mysteries. Holden seems more intelligent to me now that I thought about how different it is to read Shakespeare versus mysteries. Ackley was bugging him and he tried to ignore him so he could read. This says that Holden was dedicated to reading. Maybe I'm not. Holden had a lot of depth to him it seems.

Apparently, Michael's more well-argued analysis of Holden grew out of Swenson's facilitative remarks asking Michael to elaborate on his initial response. While responding to work-in-progress is only one strategy for instructional scaffolding, Swenson's response demonstrates the way well-shaped remarks can help students think through problems encountered in a specific task while also providing the student with strategies that can be used in similar situations. Swenson's support allows Michael to complete the task on his own terms and as part of the process of coming to know his own interpretation. He is also learning to develop an argument of his own. We can only speculate on how Swenson's strategic use of a remark might contrast with a more typical request that Michael's second draft be more organized and more detailed, requiring that he guess what the teacher expects to see in a final product.

This approach to writing about literature, as represented in the framework, does not necessarily imply a radical shift in pedagogy. Rather it represents a synthesis of a long-standing tradition of calling for students to offer an interpretation of the text and to marshall support for their point-of-view with more recent developments in writing and reading instruction. Again, as in more traditional approaches, the teacher's role is central, but in a rather different way. Although the teacher retains control over the syllabus and the activities that form the contexts for the reading and writing that occur, the students take an active role in determining what will be written and discussed. The developing knowledge is negotiated between teacher and student. Within this process orientation, the teacher's role is collaborative rather than evaluative, the students' role is active rather than passive, and the outcomes are more appropriately conceived as understanding a literary text rather than as learning information about literature. Traditionally we have thought of literature as content for students to write about or as a way to test students' ability to analyze texts, but as we work our way toward a clearer conception of the relationship between writing and literary understanding we may attain a more compelling pedagogy and a clearer notion of what literary education might include.

Note

1. Pseudonyms are used throughout this chapter.

Works Cited

Anderson, Richard C., and W. Barry Biddle. "On Asking People Questions About What They Are Reading." *Psychology of Learning and Motivation.* Gordon Bower, ed. Vol. 9. New York: Academic Press, 1975.

Applebee, Arthur N. *Tradition and Reform in the Teaching of English: A History.* Urbana, Ill.: National Council of Teachers of English, 1974.

———. *Writing in the Secondary School.* Urbana, Ill.: National Council of Teachers of English, 1981.

———. "Writing and Reasoning." *Review of Educational Research* 53 (1984): 577–96.

———. "Problems in Process Approaches: Toward a Reconceptualization of Process Instruction." *The Teaching of Writing.* Anthony Petrosky and David Bartholomae, eds. Chicago: The University of Chicago Press, 1986.

Applebee, Arthur N., and Judith A. Langer. "Instructional Scaffolding: Reading and Writing as Natural Language Activities." *Language Arts* 60 (1983): 168–75.

Booth, Wayne. *Critical Understanding: The Power and Limits of Pluralism.* Chicago: University of Chicago Press, 1979.

Bruner, Jerome. *Actual Minds, Possible Worlds.* Cambridge, Mass.: Harvard University Press, 1986.

Emig, Janet. *The Composing Process of Twelfth Graders.* NCTE Research Monograph #13. Urbana, Ill.: National Council of Teachers of English, 1971.

Fillion, Bryant, and Rita Brause. "Research into Classroom Practices: What Have We Learned and Where are We going?" *The Dynamics of Language Learning: Research in Reading and English.* James Squire, ed. Urbana, Ill.: ERIC Clearinghouse on Reading and Communication Skills and National Conference on Research in English, 1987.

Fisher, John L., and John R. Harris. "Effects of Notetaking on Recall." *Journal ıl of of Educational Psychology* 65 (1973): 321–25.

Hayes, John R., and Linda Flower. "Identifying the Organization of Writing Processes." *Cognitive Processes in Writing.* Lee W. Gregg and Erwin R. Steinberg, eds. Hillsdale, N. J.: Lawrence Erlbaum Associates, 1980.

Iser, Wolfgang. *The Act of Reading: A Theory of Aesthetic Response.* Baltimore, Md.: The Johns Hopkins University Press, 1978.

Langer, Judith A. "Examining Background Knowledge and Text Comprehension." *Reading Research Quarterly* 14 (1984): 468–81.

________. *Children Reading and Writing: Structures and Strategies.* Norwood, N. J.: Ablex, 1986.

________. "Learning through Writing: Study skills in the Content Areas." *Journal of Reading* 27 (1986): 400–06.

Langer, Judith A., and Arthur N. Applebee. "Language, Learning and Interaction: A Framework for Improving the Teaching of Writing." *Contexts for Learning to Write: Studies of Secondary School Instruction.* Arthur N. Applebee, ed. Norwood, N. J.: Ablex, 1984.

________. *How Writing Shapes Thinking: A Study of Teaching and Learning.* NCTE Research monograph #22. Urbana, Ill.: National Council of Teachers of English, 1987.

Marshall, James D. "The Effects of Writing on Students' Understanding of Literary Texts." *Research in the Teaching of English* 21 (1987): 30–63.

Newell, George E. "Learning from Writing in Two Content Areas: A Case Study/ Protocol Analysis." *Research in the Teaching of English* 18 (1984): 265–87.

Newell, George E., and Phyllis MacAdam. "Teachers' Perceptions of the Role of Process in Writing about Literature." *The Quarterly* 10 (1988): 4–8.

Newell, George E., Karen Suszynski, and Ruth Weingart. "The Effects of Writing in a Reader-Based and Text-Based Mode on Students' Understanding of Two Short Stories." *Journal of Reading Behavior* 21 (1989): 37–57.

Purves, Alan. *Reading and Literature.* Urbana, Ill.: National Council of Teachers of English, 1981.

Roberts, Edgar. *Writing Themes about Literature (fifth edition).* Englewood Cliffs, N. J.: Prentice-Hall, 1976.

Rosenblatt, Louise. *Literature as Exploration.* New York: Barnes and Noble, 1976.

________. *The Reader, the Text, the Poem: The Transactional Theory of the Literary Work.* Carbondale, Ill.: Southern Illinois University Press, 1978.

Smith-Burke, M. Trika. "Classroom Practices and Classroom Interaction during Reading Instruction: What's Going On?" *The Dynamics of Language Learning: Research in Reading and English.* James Squire, ed. Urbana, Ill.: ERIC Clearinghouse on Reading and Communication Skills and National Conference on Research in English, 1987.

Vygotsky, Lev S. *Thought and Language.* Cambridge, Mass.: Harvard University Press, 1978.

________. *Mind in Society.* Cambridge, Mass.: Harvard University Press, 1978.

Zeichner, Kenneth M., and Daniel P. Liston. "Teaching Student Teachers to Reflect." *Harvard Educational Review* 57 (1987): 23–48.

Ron Fortune

9. *Literature as Writing: Integrating Literature and Writing Instruction through Manuscript Studies*

Teachers and scholars have attempted to integrate the different strands of English studies—literature, composition, and language—for a long time, but despite the persistence of their efforts they generally have not been very successful. A variety of explanations can be offered both for the persistence of their efforts and for their lack of success. One likely explanation for the former is the recognition that, as long as the three strands remain separate, English curricula will be fragmented. Many high school and college English courses attempt to teach literature and writing together, for example, but either the two are assigned to different units within the course or one is made subservient ot the other and is not taught effectively. Even when the different strands are assigned to different courses, teachers often must cover two or all three of the strands in their teaching assignments and students take three different kinds of English courses that do not seem to have very much to do with one another. Thus teachers and their students often experience the same sense of fragmentation in moving from one course to the next.

Arguably, this fragmentation is not necessarily problematic, especially when the different strands are covered in different courses. However, the essential problem with fragmentation—from both the teacher's and the students' perspectives—is that it denies the opportunity to have different lessons reinforce and enrich one another. So, even if literature and composition, for example, are covered in different courses and the internal integrity of the different courses seems maintained, neither the teacher nor the student can allow the knowledge developed in the literature course to reinforce and even extend that nurtured in the composition course and vice versa. The absence of this reinforcement and reciprocal enhancement, in turn, diminishes the quality of learning that can occur for the teacher and the students through their studies.

In his *Tradition and Reform in the Teaching of English,* Arthur Applebee suggests one primary reason for the failure to integrate literature, composition, and language. The failure has resulted, he argues, from attempts to treat the different strands as subject matters and from defining the subject matter of each strand in terms sooner or later incompatible with the subject matters of the other strands. Again with regard to literature and composition, their separation has be founded on the perception of literature instruction as that which acquaints students with selected literary works and their backgrounds while composition instruction has been seen as that which involves students in the exercise of specific skills embedded in rules to be learned. In traditional classrooms, neither literature nor composition instruction has been defined in terms of giving students experience with the complex range of activities involved in processing text both from the reader's and the writer's perspective. Significantly, Applebee does not argue that the strands are necessarily different but rather that the ways they have been traditionally defined as subjects makes their integration in the classroom problematic.

One response to the situation described above and the response pursued herein is to identify ways in which the different strands overlap and share essential features and then to suggest how curricula designed to cover the different strands can be based on their commonalities. As long as the integrated curricula remain sensitive to and can accommodate the individuality of each strand, they will not sacrifice that individuality to the overriding desire to bring the different strands together within a single conceptual frame.

Developing a comprehensive program for integrating literature, composition, and language is beyond the scope of this discussion. Rather, given the available space, the discussion concentrates on integrating literature and composition and investigates the possibilities of a particular approach for doing so. This neither means that language, as the third strand, must be omitted because the proposed approach cannot accommodate it nor that the approach described below is the only way to integrate the strands of English. Concentrating on literature and composition simply reflects a current exigency in the discipline. To the approach outlined here others can and should be added because the more approaches at a teacher's disposal, the richer the integration he or she will be able to manage in the classroom.

The particular exigency connected to the integration of literature and composition comes from the widespread perception that current circumstances encourage their separation. Indeed, Winifred Horner's introduction to a recent collection of essays concerned with "bridging the gap" between composition and literature expresses "a deep concern about the widening gulf between research and teaching in literature and research and teaching in composition," a gulf that finally threatens the continuing vitality of the discipline as a whole (1). Katharine Ronald has also observed at the college level a trend toward "departments in which literature and composition people studiously avoid encroaching on each other's territories" (231). The reasons for the separation are varied, and some would argue that they have more to do with the politics of the discipline than with the characters of the different strands comprising it. However, even if this were true, the absence of well-articulated programs for bringing literature and composition together feeds the agenda of those who would keep them apart for political reasons. A first step, then, must be the articulation of integrated disciplinary models.

The approach to integrating literature and writing offered here looks at both literature and composition from the viewpoint of the writing activities an author, whether professional or student, goes through in producing a text. Much can be gained, both for the teaching of literature and the teaching of writing, by looking at the creation of great literary texts and student texts together. Some might argue that students' texts and great literary texts are too different to be connected in any meaningful way. The argument that follows, however, suggests that their difference is more one of degree than of kind and that, for this reason, they can help illuminate each other in the classroom. The program described here was originally developed through a three-year series of summer institutes for high school English teachers funded by the National Endowment for the Humanities (NEH). The rationale and classroom applications provided below reflect the work of high school teachers who participated in the NEH Institute and had the opportunity to experiment with this program's approach in their classrooms.

RATIONALE

The direction taken in this discussion toward connecting instruction in literature and writing has been suggested, ironically, in an analysis of reasons why composition and literature must remain separate. In his overview of the emergence of composition as a field, Stephen North argues that unifying literature and composition will require a new "pattern of inquiry" involving "concerns about how [literary] texts, or any texts, were produced" (369). While North is not optimistic about the chances for such a new pattern of inquiry to emerge, the components for such a pattern already exist within the discipline, and one of these—manuscript studies—has a long tradition in English studies. The other—composition studies—has developed dramatically in the last fifteen years or so and in that time has assumed an increasingly important role in the discipline. Thus, for the approach to integrating literature and writing to be developed in this discussion, the problem is less a matter of an entirely new way to perceive the discipline and more a matter of synthesizing existing patterns of inquiry and bringing the synthesis to bear on the problems students experience in learning to read literature and learning to write.

Manuscript studies and composition studies have as a common denominator their focus on the nature of text and the activities through which a text comes into being. Manuscript study manifests this interest in its concentration on the materials—notebooks, early versions of a work, its various drafts, and its various editions—that great writers generated in producing texts studied in high school and college English courses. Fredson Bowers's introduction to *Whitman's Manuscripts: Leaves of Grass (1860)* typifies this orientation when he defines his purpose as reconstructing "in these manuscripts the revisory process from first inscription to the final achieved version" (vii). In an introduction to Dostoevsky's notebooks for *Crime and Punishment,* Edward Wasiolek describes what can be found in these notebooks in terms that echo discussions of the composing experiences of student writers found in professional journals of composition theory and practice:

> What do the wrong turns, mistakes, blind alleys, and unmined possibilities tell us? How do we go from the possibilities to the fact itself? They remind us . . . that the marvelous coherence of *Crime and Punishment,* the creative logic that takes us with what seems to be inevitable movement from beginning to end, was once uncertain, halting, and far from clear. . . . The notebooks tell us . . . what was left out, what was different, what was undeveloped, and what was at some point more fully developed (6).

Getting a chance to see the composing activities in which great writers engaged while composing their well-established texts can transform teachers' and students' understanding of what texts are and how they came to take their published form. Suddenly, instead of just seeing the text in its published form as if it had sprung from nowhere, they can see the writer experimenting with different strategies to solve particular content and formal problems that emerge at various points in the creation of the given text. Transforming the teachers' and students' perceptions of the text, in turn, can enrich students' literary responses as well as their understanding of what they are about when they compose their own texts.

Strictly speaking, manuscript studies should be restricted to the actual drafting of texts as reflected in an author's manuscripts. For the purpose of this discussion, however, the phrase will be extended to include the study of other materials—letters, diaries, journals, other published writings—indicating a writer's activities in the genesis as well as the composition of a text. Without such an extension, developing a literary text might seem limited to actual drafting activities only. Clearly, drafting activities exist in a rich milieu, and appreciating them depends in part on seeing their connections to the composing activities that surround them.

Connecting writing and literature through manuscripts also requires a clarification of what *writing* means in the context of a writing class. Many of the changes that have occurred in what has been called the *revolution* in the teaching of writing are collectively known as the "process approach" to writing instruction (Hairston). This terminology, however, is problematic because it "implies a linearity, a finiteness, a rule-governed structure that many researchers have suggested simply does not exist" (Purves 52). Even if "process" itself did not suggest linearity, the concept of "the writing process" has become so formulized in textbooks and discussions of strategies for teaching writing that the phrase now signifies a collection of abstracted activities supposedly capable of developing students' understanding of writing and their ability to do it well. The formulization of "writing process," however, works against the qualities of fluidity, spontaneity, and recursiveness that all writers associate with composing and that must be a part of the experience of writing cultivated in writing classes. Referring to "writing activities" instead of "the writing process" has the advantage of allowing discussions of what writers do when they compose without harnessing writing into a set of procedures that do not realistically convey the complexity of composing (Purves 52).

Manuscripts and the Problems in Teaching Literature and Writing

Manuscripts in literature and writing instruction only provide resources capable of solving certain teaching and learning problems more effectively than other resources but that work best when used in conjunction with those other resources. Understanding how and when to use manuscripts in conjunction with other resources involves perceiving the general types of teaching and learning problems in literature and writing that they seem most suited to helping solve.

Manuscript Studies and Instruction in Literature

The value of manuscripts in helping to develop students' literary responses is reflected in a student's evaluation of a lesson on Blake's "The Tiger" and "The Poison Tree" in which manuscripts were used extensively. The student wrote, "I enjoyed the lesson yesterday because I became interested in the poems. It was a new twist, instead of the boring study questions that fail to involve students. It's a tricky way to get a student to enjoy poetry." This student's reaction represented the reactions of most of the other students in the same class, and it suggests that the teacher used the manuscripts successfully to overcome one major obstacle in developing students' literary responses —involving them actively with the literature in a way that does not at the same time make the literature merely an occasion for discussions in which the literature itself gets lost.

Alan Purves and Victoria Rippere's breakdown of the constituents of literary response helps to articulate the problems that manuscripts can assist in addressing. In *Elements of Writing About a Literary Work: A Study of Response to Literature,* Purves and Rippere classify literary response into four basic types: engagement, perception, interpretation, and evaluation. The use of manuscripts pertains most directly to difficulties students have with the second of these. The authors' characterization of this aspect of literary response is worth quoting at length:

> [Perception] encompasses the ways in which the person looks at the work as an object distinct from himself and, except that it is the product of an author about whom the

> writer might have knowledge, separate from the writer's consideration of the world around the writer. This perception . . . is analytic and deals with the work either in isolation or as an historical fact needing to be related to a context. If the perception is of the work in isolation, it may be of the work either as a self-enclosed entity or as the product of a craftsman. (6)

Typically, students learn to perceive the text more precisely than they generally do because manuscripts give them the opportunity to compare the published version to an earlier version that is at once close to but critically different from it. This helps to concentrate their attention on the details of the text as text and thus to get beyond the purely subjective reaction to the text.

To some teachers, focusing on developing the students' perception of text might seem counterproductive because it appears to undercut the current emphasis on the students' personal and subjective engagement with the literature they read. The actual effect, however, is to extend their engagement with the text by balancing their subjective contributions to the transaction with the text with an attention to the text's contributions to that transaction. Those who cite Louise Rosenblatt's stress on the reader's subjective response to a literary text often forget that she is reacting to critics, literary theorists, and literature teachers "who have lavished attention on authors and texts" (ix) to the exclusion of the reader's contributions to the literary transaction. In fact, the aesthetic reading she promotes highlights a balance between the reader's and the text's contributions to the reading of a literary work.

Significantly, Purves and Rippere do not put their four constituents of literary response in a particular sequence but instead suggest that "any category may precede any other" (8). As an example they add that "one's engagement in a work may precede or follow from one's analytic perception or one's interpretation" (8). Thus, making students more aware of a text's contributions to their literary responses can be a means of increasing rather than diminishing their involvement with it. The movement from perception to engagement is implicit in the student evaluation cited earlier. This student and others in the class suggested that, rather than diminishing their engagement with Blake's poetry, their perceptions of these texts, enhanced by their comparisons of different drafts of the manuscript, actually intensified their involvement with the poems.

Manuscript Studies and Instruction in Writing

Even as manuscript studies can prove effective in developing students' literary responses, they can also prove useful in dealing with certain problems that interfere with students' efforts to become better writers. Often, the greatest problem students face is that they do not have a realistic sense of how texts evolve. They become weighted down with textbook exercises and formulations that simplify the task of writing to the point of making it a poor imitation of the real thing. As a result, they often produce artificial texts that answer to a form but do not articulate a thoroughly examined and well-reasoned discussion that they can make meaningful for themselves and their readers. Or, in some cases, they recognize the gap between the simple formulations and the real demands of writing but lack the experience that lets them see how to work through or get around the problems they face. The result is writer's block, as they finally give up on the possibility of producing anything they consider good (Rose).

Manuscript studies exemplify writers working through all aspects of composing and, therefore, can be useful in addressing most of the writing problems learning writers experience. Classroom applications of the approach suggest two areas in which manuscript studies can prove particularly helpful. One of the first areas in which students experience difficulty as writers and are susceptible to simple formulations is in their efforts to find something to write about. Many teachers, with the best of intentions, try to suggest possible topics to students and help them develop their responses to these topics. Unfortunately, such an approach only aggravates the problem by bypassing the task of figuring out what is meaningful for the writer and how it can be made meaningful for a reader. Manuscript studies exemplify the arduous efforts great writers undertook in initiating literary works and in the process not only suggest the activities involved in exploring subjects for composition but also suggest the valuable resources students have within them and at their disposal.

A second area in which manuscripts can be especially useful is suggested by another comment made by a student in the same class as the one quoted earlier: "Studying poetry using manuscripts makes it easier to accept yourself as a writer and your work, knowing that not everyone can just sit down and write a 'perfect' poem. Almost everyone has to write a rough draft." Improving students' abilities to revise begins with making them aware of both the necessity and the function of revision. Seeing the authors revise literary works that students have often seen only in their published form can dramatically influence their sense of the importance of revision and even the activities they engage in when revising their own texts. In *Errors and Expectations,* Mina Shaughnessy specifically promotes the use of literary manuscripts in basic writing instruction, arguing that it has two major advantages. First, it teaches students the often-hidden notion that the "process that creates precision is itself messy." Second, seeing facsimile copies of Keats's *Eve of St. Agnes,* for example, shows students how writers carry on the debates that lead to the finished work, which in turn, she suggests, encourages students to engage in similar debates in composing their own texts (222). Again, the debates evident in these manuscript materials range over the entire spectrum of rhetorical and textual decisions writers make, something that typically cannot be said of the formulized representations of writing embodied in many process approaches to writing instruction. So, seeing great writers revise through exposure to their facsimiles more than primes students to revise in their own writing; it also exemplifies the kinds of activities entailed in revision.

The students quoted earlier, one commenting on the value of manuscript study for the study of literature and the other on its value for learning to write, were in the same class and were responding to the same lesson. This again suggests that a genuine integration of literature and writing instruction was occurring. The teacher was able to use the manuscripts to develop students' insights either into literature or into writing or into both at the same time. The specific direction was determined by the emphasis the teacher gave the particular lesson.

APPLICATIONS

A discussion of some of the issues that teachers should consider in planning lessons in writing and literature using manuscripts is in order before getting on to the applications themselves.

The first and, in some respects, the most problematic issue for many teachers is the availability of manuscript materials. In fact, these materials are more available for literary works commonly taught in high school and college English courses than many teachers believe. Garland Press, for example, has completed or is completing many volumes in a series of facsimilies for the complete novels of modern British and American novelists, including Faulkner, Fitzgerald, and Hardy. Furthermore, the complete and definitive scholarly editions of an author's work often contain extensive facsimile sections from an author's manuscripts as well as source materials the writer used for a given work. Examples of these editions include the Northwestern/Newberry edition of the works of Melville, the Cambridge University Press edition of the works of D.H. Lawrence, and the Cornell edition of Wordsworth's poetry. Other presses have produced facsimilies of individual works in a writer's canon, including Gale Press's facsimile edition of *Adventures of Huckleberry Finn,* the Bruccoli-Clark facsimile editions of *The Red Badge of Courage* and *The Great Gatsby,* The M&S Press's facsimile edition of *Nineteen-Eighty-Four,* and the Harcourt Brace facsimile edition of *The Waste Land,* including the editorial annotations of Ezra Pound. In addition, critical studies of the composition of many literary works offer both a critical analysis of the author's composing practices and generous selections from the materials drawn from and generated in the creation of a text. Examples include Michael Reynolds's *Hemingway's First War: The Making of A Farewell to Arms,* Judith Barlow's *Final Acts: The Creation of Three Late O'Neill Plays,* Sholom Kahn's *Mark Twain's Mysterious Stranger: A Study of the Manuscript Texts,* and J. Lyndon Shanley's *The Making of Walden with the Text of the First Version.* The widespread production of these materials indicates that they can be attained readily in most university libraries and even in many public libraries.

The use of manuscripts to teach literature and writing loses some of its value if a teacher attempts to make manuscripts the core of every lesson. A steady diet of manuscripts can cause students to lose their natural curiosity in seeing Dickens or Hemingway or Frost at work, struggling just as the students must struggle with their own texts. Manuscripts work best when used regularly (as opposed to constantly) but selectively. Regular use allows the special advantages derived from manuscript study to accumulate from lesson to lesson and therefore to have a long-term effect on how students read and write. Selectivity is necessary because these materials—especially the manuscripts themselves—can be inherently confusing. That is, their very messiness, highly useful from one perspective, can also make them difficult to follow. The best lessons match focused "debates" implicit in segments from a writer's notebooks or manuscript, for example, to the kinds of knowledge and experience students need to become better writers and readers of literature.

A third issue suggests how a teacher's own critical biases can interfere with the effective use of manuscripts in the teaching of literature. Specifically, for some literature teachers, a New Critical bias against going outside the work itself lingers and promotes the belief that interest in anything outside the published text, including manuscripts, is misplaced and even harmful. Often a corollary to this formal critical bias is the feeling that examining an author's letters, diaries, notebooks, and manuscripts violates the writer's privacy. The thinking underlying these concerns suffers from two limitations. The first and perhaps more basic is the notion that teaching literature should make students good literary critics who follow a particular set of critical principles. This approach misrepresents one central aspect of the task facing literature teachers and their students in high school and college. The task should primarily involve helping students learn to perceive the literary text. Without perception, the students' interpretation and evaluation, concerns that might be more closely related to reader's critical philosophy, are problematic. If students already knew how to perceive the text, then perhaps teachers could concentrate on inculcating a particular critical stance. Most students in high school and college, however, must learn to perceive the text, and anything that helps them do this, including materials outside of the text itself, has a legitimate and even crucial role in the literature classroom.

The second limitation, connected with the concern for a writer's privacy, again suggests a misperception of the writing teacher's task. The same teachers who might object to the invasion of a professional writer's privacy often have no qualms about requiring students to submit their drafting materials with the final versions of the writings they complete for a course. They would defend this practice by saying that their ability to help students develop as writers depends on their access to all the materials that students produce in their composing activities. This argument implies, however, that a particular student's writing ability can exist and develop in a vacuum. As recent studies of writing as a social and collaborative activity (Bazerman; Bruffee) and of intertextuality (Porter) suggest, a writing course cannot restrict itself to the individual writing activities and texts of individual students because these activities and texts must be informed by the activities and texts of other writers. Without a sense of the world of texts and text-making activities, students cannot finally develop as writers capable of fully participating in that world. The justification for using writers' manuscripts must be the same as that used to explain why a teacher might require students to submit all drafts with their final texts—it is needed to help students learn to write.

A final issue is the writing teacher's fear that a great writer's manuscript materials might establish a caliber of performance that so vastly exceeds what students can do that it demoralizes students and undercuts their efforts to learn to write. This concern misses one of the key virtues of literary manuscripts in a writing class. The objection is a remnant of pedagogies in which students were shown models of finished professional pieces and then expected, at least implicitly, to imitate these models and use them to judge their own writing. With such an approach, teachers had reason to fear that their students would be intimidated by the standards set by the professional text. Manuscripts, however, have just the opposite effect, humanizing literary authors and texts and allowing students to develop a sense of kinship with the writer when they see the struggles involved in producing that professional text. The result, as the statement from the student cited earlier suggests, is that students learn to accept themselves and develop more realistic expectations of themselves as writers.

Sample Lesson Using *The Waste Land*

This first sequence of activities was created for an English class of eleventh and twelfth graders, focusing on both literature and writing. The teacher had a threefold purpose: (1) to teach students about using their own earlier writing and the writing of others as resources to draw on in writing their own texts, (2) to teach students what truly useful peer editing entails, and (3) to use the first two lessons to enrich their reading of poetry in general and *The Waste Land* in particular.

The approach to teaching writing that stresses prewriting, writing, and revising in that order undermines students' abilities to write by suggesting that each essay begins anew without regard to texts students have previously written and read. This negates the notion that writing is an ongoing intellectual undertaking in which writers regularly take ideas from their own earlier writings and from texts they have read. Denying students the opportunity to take advantage of their earlier reading and writing experiences deprives them of rich intellectual resources necessary to good writing and misrepresents the nature of writing.

In this particular lesson, then, the teacher begins, after having students read *The Waste Land* once, by having students read lines from Eliot's "The Death of Narcissus" (1915) and "Dans le Restaurant" (1916), two of his earlier poems from which Eliot incorporated lines into *The Waste Land.* She also has them read selections from the Bible, sections from Jessie Weston's *From Ritual to Romance,* and Shakespeare's *The Tempest.* While examining the common themes Eliot might have found engaging in these works, class discussion and assignments stress Eliot's activities as writer, the ways in which he might have absorbed and worked over these materials as he approached the composition of *The Waste Land.* As these discussions are occurring, the teacher also asks students to go back to their own earlier essays, to their journals, and to readings that have stayed with them for some reason and then to see how these materials suggest themes and strategies for a new piece of writing of their own.

From here, students simply begin to write their new texts. Although discussions to this point have accentuated the students' own earlier writing and reading as a repository of ideas and themes always available to them as writers, the teacher does not require them to draw from these materials as they write. The point of the lesson is to make them aware of the materials as one resource rather than to force them to follow a particular practice. As they write, they must feel free to draw on all the resources available to them according to their needs. Interestingly, the most significant outcome of this lesson is that students begin to use materials from their own earlier writing and even from works they have read as effective generative resources. Mostly, they learn how writers work for their ideas in particular ways rather than passively waiting for inspiration to hit them.

After students have completed drafts ready to undergo the scrutiny of an editor, the teacher has them exchange papers for peer editing. Before doing this, however, she uses Vivien Eliot's (Eliot's first wife) and Pound's annotations on Eliot's draft of *The Waste Land* both to help students understand the function of an editor and to improve their editorial abilities. Often students do not benefit from peer editing because they do not understand the relationship between editor and writer, a problem reflected in the tendency of many student editors to be uncritical in their comments for fear of hurting the writer's feelings. Then, even after they come to understand that constuctive critical comments can help a writer more than unsubstantial positive comments, they must learn what constitutes a constructive comment.

To solve both problems at the same time, the teacher has students compare Vivien Eliot's comments with Pound's. As they do so, they learn that editors are most helpful when they view the writer's text from the writer's point of view and try to help the writer bridge the gap between the writer's apparent intention and the written text. Sometimes, the editor can even help the writer define more precisely ill-defined intentions. Vivien Eliot's comments stay outside the writer's task while Pound's indicate that, as he edits, he is involved in composing the poem with Eliot. To the opening section of the draft version of "A Game of Chess," Vivien Eliot states, "Don't see what you had in mind here." Pound's comments suggest that Eliot delete phrases and transpose lines and, at one point, even tell Eliot that a particular line is a "dogmatic deduction but wobbly as well." Vivien Eliot's comments leave the writer at a loss; they do not specify the source of the problem or suggest strategies Eliot might use in dealing with the problem. Pound's comments, on the other hand, both identify why the problems are problems and suggest alternatives Eliot might pursue. A brief list of some of the major changes Pound's comments brought about suggest his effectiveness as an editor: (1) the deletion of the first fifty-four lines of draft one, (2) the deletion of seventy-two lines of rhymed couplets at the beginning of "The Fire Sermon" section, and (3) the deletion of eighty-two lines in the section, "Death by Water" that Eliot based on Dante's description of the Voyage of Ulysses. The difference between Vivien and Pound, then, is that between a passive and an active editor, a distinction important to students because, unless they are active peer editors, they not only minimize the help they can give each other but also diminish the value of peer editing as a means of enabling them to become better editors of their own texts.

Peer editing is followed by the students' completion of their own texts and their returning to the poem to study it as a literary work. Students' work with the poem as an exemplar of writing activities has by this time given them a good overview of the poem, so the teacher uses the manuscript to focus their attention on particular aspects of the poem to sharpen their perception of it. Using passages whose revisions from draft to published version are particularly significant, the teacher divides the class into several groups and assigns each group a particular section, asking them to identify the changes, to determine whether or not the changes should have been made, and to explain their reasoning. The purpose here is not that students learn to give the "right" answers but rather that they become engaged with the literary text through their focused perception of it. This approach seems particularly successful because students are not asked to look at the poem in a vacuum but instead have something concrete, indeed an earlier version of the same poem, with which to compare it, and this gives them a foothold that makes discussing the poem in a meaningful way possible.

Sample Lesson Using Updike's "A Sense of Shelter"

This second sample lesson is considerably more focused than the first. It concerns the students' awareness of the role of detail in their reading and writing and uses drafting materials from John Updike's "A Sense of Shelter." The course textbook, *On Writing, By Writers,* includes five drafts of various sections of Updike's story and his comments about why he made many of the draft-to-draft changes.

The lesson begins with a simple observation assignment in which students are given a week to draft a character sketch, a description of a setting, or a description of a character in a setting. The purpose of the assignment is to help them learn to select details from notes they have taken as they work toward a focused, coherent representtion of a character or scene. They are reminded, as they draft this paper, of the importance of making the paper's details work toward a single overall effect.

On the same day these drafts are due, class discussion focuses on the themes of Updike's story, especially as they relate to the students' own lives. This phase of the lesson establishes students' prior knowledge and primes them for reading the story. For the next class meeting, students are asked to read the first five paragraphs of "A Sense of Shelter," in which the main character's character is established. Class discussion focuses on predicting what will happen in the story and specifically on what Mip's, the main character's, fate will be, based on the details in this opening section. The teacher follows this discussion by directing students' attention to the five earlier versions of this opening section and having the class list on the board the distinctive details of each version and the changes made from one version to the next. Then, students finish reading the story and discuss which version of the opening is most appropriate given what happens in the rest of the story. Often, the students settle on the final version as the best, but the critical point here is that students look at the text itself and allow the details of the text to participate in their literary responses.

After they have finished discussing the story, they return to their own papers. Having seen the way Updike debates over the details most appropriate to the character he wants to create, especially as that character becomes increasingly clear to him as he moves from draft to draft, the students undertake their own debates regarding the details most suited to the central impressions they intend to create in their character sketches or scene descriptions. As they do this, the teacher is particularly careful to allow the details they have recorded lead them to new insights that may become the central impressions they pursue in their revisions.

The sample lessons based on *The Waste Land* and on "A Sense of Shelter" together illustrate the flexibility of approaching literature and writing instruction through manuscripts. The lessons on the former cover a wide range of reading and writing activities as the teacher brings manuscripts to bear on different problems encountered at different points during the students' reading and writing experiences. The latter focuses on a particular problem in reading and a related problem in writing, using manuscripts to help students recognize the problem and then learn to deal with them in their reading and writing.

CONCLUSION

Many English teachers at both the secondary and postsecondary levels have long regarded manuscript studies as a rather arcane specialty in the discipline having little or no applications in classes concerned with developing students' abilities to write and to respond to literature. Indeed, most teachers who have participated in the NEH Institutes report never having seen or worked with authors' manuscripts in their professional education, a fact made more significant by their having at least master's degrees in English. But using materials generally considered at a distance from the mainstream of literature and writing instruction to teach literature and writing suggests more than anything the essential unity of the discipline. However, before that unity is reflected in teachers' approaches to literature, writing, and language instruction, an effort must be made to see the strands of the discipline in new ways in light of the problems teachers and students must solve in English classes.

Works Cited

Applebee, Arthur N. *Tradition and Reform in the Teaching of English: A History.* Urbana, Ill.: National Council of Teachers of English, 1974.

Bazerman, Charles. "A Relation Between Reading and Writing: The Conversational Model." *College English* 41 (1980): 656–61.

Bowers, Fredson. "Foreword." *Whitman's Manuscripts: Leaves of Grass (1860).* Chicago: University of Chicago Press, 1955.

Bruffee, Kenneth. "Writing and Reading as Collaborative or Social Acts." *The Writer's Mind: Writing as a Mode of Thinking.* Janice Hays, Phyllis Roth, Jon Ramsey, and Robert Foulke, eds. Urbana, Ill.: National Council of Teachers of English, 1983. 159–71.

Eliot, T. S. *The Waste Land: A Facsimile and Transcript of the Original Drafts Including the Annotations of Ezra Pound.* Valerie Eliot, ed. New York: Harcourt Brace, 1971.

Hairston, Maxine. "The Winds of Change: Thomas Kuhn and the Revolution in the Teaching of Writing." *College Composition and Communication* 33 (1982): 78–86.

Horner, Winifred Bryan. "Historical Introduction." *Composition and Literature: Bridging the Gap.* Winifred Bryan Horner, ed. Chicago: University of Chicago Press, 1983. 1–13.

North, Stephen. *The Making of Knowledge in Composition: Portrait of an Emerging Field.* Upper Montclair, N. J.: Boynton-Cook, 1987.

Purves, Alan. "Commentary." *The Dynamics of Language Learning: Research in Reading and English.* James Squire, ed. Urbana, Ill.: National Council of Teachers of English, 1987. 52–54.

Purves, Alan, and Victoria Rippere. *Elements of Writing About a Literary Work: A Study of Response to Literature.* Urbana, Ill.: National Council of Teachers of English, 1968.

Ronald, Katharine. "The Self and the Other in the Process of Composing: Implications for Integrating the Acts of Reading and Writing." *Convergences: Transactions in Reading and Writing.* Bruce Petersen, ed. Urbana, Ill.: National Council of Teachers of English, 1986.

Rose, Mike. *Writer's Block: The Cognitive Dimension.* Carbondale: Southern Illinois University Press, 1984.

Rosenblatt, Louise. *The Reader, the Text, the Poem: The Transactional Theory of the Literary Work.* Carbondale: Southern Illinois University Press, 1978.

Shaughnessy, Mina. *Errors and Expectations: A Guide for the Teacher of Basic Writing.* New York: Oxford University Press, 1977.

Wasiolek, Edward. "Introduction." *The Notebooks for Crime and Punishment.* Chicago: University of Chicago Press, 1967.

West, William. *On Writing, By Writers.* Boston: Ginn, 1966.

III

Rhetoric and Composition: Designs for Integration

Martin Nystrand

10. On Teaching Writing as a Verb Rather than as a Noun: Research on Writing for High School English Teachers*

The traditional focus of writing instruction has been on good written texts. More recently, emphasis has been given to the composing process. New researchers are studying writing as a communicative process. In doing this, they are refocusing on written texts and the essential role they play in mediating between the needs of the writer for expression, on the one hand, and the reader for comprehension, on the other. This chapter reviews these trends and explains the importance of teaching writing as a continuous process of drafting, rewriting, and discussing drafts with readers. Particular attention is given to the context of these activities.

THE WRITING PROCESS

Janet Emig was the first researcher to stress the fundamental nature of writing as a process. In research reported in her seminal little book, *The Composing Process of*

* This paper was prepared at the National Center on Effective Secondary Schools, Wisconsin Center for Education Research, School of Education, University of Wisconsin-Madison, which is supported in part by a grant from the Office of Educational Research and Improvement (Grant No. G–008690007). Any options, findings, and conclusions or recommendations expressed in this publication are those of the authors and do not necessarily reflect the views of this agency or the U. S. Department of Education.

Twelfth Graders, she asked eight twelfth graders to "compose aloud," uttering in her presence each thought and word that came to mind in the process of writing. In this research, she attempted to capture the dynamics of the composing process of these students by recording and transcribing the resulting monologues. By studying writing in this way, she hoped to gain some insight into the nature of the composing process. As it turned out, the composing processes of her subjects were not very elaborate, a result that seemed to suggest as much about the nature of school writing as the composing process itself. Nonetheless, in a 1981 retrospective, she emphasized the following points:

1. Writing is predominantly learned rather than taught.
2. There is no monolithic process of writing: there are processes of writing that differ because of aim, intent, mode, and audience.
3. The processes of writing do not proceed in a linear sequence: rather, they are recursive.... ("Non-magical Thinking" 26)

By *recursive,* she meant that such phases of writing as planning, rereading, writing, and so forth continuously recur as writers work.

To understand the general import of Emig's research on composing, it is useful to note an equally seminal work in reading research that was published in the same year as Emig's study: in 1971, Frank Smith published his influential *Understanding Reading.* In this important synthesis of research from psycholinguistics and cognitive psychology applied to reading, Smith argued that comprehension is essential information processing. Rather than extracting meaning from the text, the process is just the reverse: readers bring meaning to the text in the form of expectations and test these expectations through reading.

To a large extent, the significance of both Emig's and Smith's works lies in their concern with education reform. Both Emig and Smith argued that the key to this reform involved not new curricula or instructional techniques but rather a reorientation of the instructor's traditional concerns from what is taught to what is learned, from classroom practices to cognitive processes, from concrete outcomes (such as analysis and imitation of certain kinds of texts in writing and correct pronunciation of words in reading) to the generative and interpretive processes of engaged writing and reading.

Indeed, at the heart of each study was nothing less than the terms by which writing and reading might be defined. Emig argued that historically high school writing instructors had taught writing not as a process at all but as so many texts; teachers had overemphasized completed texts—especially exemplary texts—to the near exclusion of the composing process. In reaction to this, Emig stressed the central role of the writer in the composing process: any text, she argued, is far more than just an example of description, narration, exposition, or persuasion. Emig was uneasy about formulaic, prescriptive approaches to writing, especially the one embodied by the five-paragraph theme: "One could say that the major kind of essay too many students have been taught to write in the American schools is algorithmic, or so mechanical that a computer could readily be programmed to produce it" (*Composing Processes* 52). In order to understand the composing process, as well as to play a positive role in its development, Emig argued, we need to consider the text properly within the context of the composing act itself. The text is an important consequence of this fundamental process, she argued, and it is mistreated (and misconceived) when it is red-marked into a *cause célèbre* of neglected amenities.

Smith's arguments about reading are similar. Like Emig, Smith made a sharp distinction between instruction and learning. He argued that too often schools teach reading as a matter of correctly pronouncing words rather than as a process of finding meaning. He was particularly opposed to phonics instruction because "reading is not accomplished by decoding to sound—meaning must usually be grasped before the appropriate sounds can be produced" (*Comprehension* 195). By emphasizing "word-perfect reading," he argued, teachers inhibit comprehension, which often involves risk-taking and requires processing words in terms of overall meaning rather than word-by-word decoding and pronouncing. Most fundamentally, he noted, reading is a cognitive process, an active process whereby readers interpret what they find in terms of what they already know.

It is not completely by accident that these two seminal studies should bear important similarities, that they should both be influential for similar reasons, and that they should both be published in 1971. Both Emig and Smith were graduate students at Harvard University in the 1960s, and largely their works reflect "the heady psycholinguistic atmosphere of Cambridge, Massachusetts" at the time, as Smith notes in his preface to *Understanding Reading* (x). (*Psycholinguistics* is the combined study of language and psychology.) Both the Emig and Smith studies start from several essential tenets about the nature of language espoused at that time by linguist Noam Chomsky and psychologists George Miller and Jerome Bruner.

Among the most important of these tenets is the idea that fundamentally language use is a cognitive, generative process in which the meaning of any text depends seminally on the purposes of the user. That is, the meaning of any text depends not only on the intentions of the writer but also, in the final analysis and in any given case, on the purposes and expectations of the reader. According to cognitive/psycholinguistic theory, the language user brings order to experience by formulating representations, or *schemata,* of the world. These formulations, much as the files in a filing cabinet or on a floppy disk, help individuals (1) organize their perceptions, understandings, and memories of the past and (2) focus their expectations for the future because generally what individuals find in experience is partly a result of what they expect to find. Hence, for Emig, as for other composing process researchers, writing is an act of meaning-making whereby the writer transforms ("Transcribes") his or her thoughts into text, whereas for Smith, as for many other reading researchers, reading is the interpretive act whereby readers test their expectations for the author's meaning in terms of actualities of text.

As often happens in the history of important ideas, Emig was not the only writing researcher to articulate a model of writing as a meaning-making activity at about this time. In 1970, British scholar James Britton published a major work, titled *Language and Learning,* in which he argued that language is fundamentally *expressive.* By this, he meant that speaking and writing are typically motivated by closely held concerns and interests. As we act on these interests, the more conventional forms of language arise: he termed these forms *transactional language* (for language used to get things done, as in the cases of *informative* and *conative* language) and *poetic language.* Like Emig, Britton located the origins of written discourse within the writer and argued that writing teachers could best help their students learn to write when they promoted expressive writing, essentially the same as Emig's *reflexive writing* (which she defined as self-sponsored writing tasks), Too often, Britton et al. said, school writing tasks are *dummy runs* wholly unrelated to writer concerns, whose main purpose is to display the status of the writer's knowledge and writing skill.

Research on the composing process has many implications for instruction, especially given the fact that experienced writers spend most of their time involved in it. The writing process is "where most of the action is," and compared to it, the text seems almost an afterthought. Experienced writers especially spend considerable amounts of time planning, rehearsing, and revising their thoughts and texts. Moreover, the writing processes of experienced writers are often recursive as Flower and Hayes ("Problem-solving") note: writers plan some, write some, plan some more, revise as a result of rereading what they have written, and so forth. Novice writers spend far less time, and their composing processes are far more simple: (1) their planning takes little if any time ("Cognitive Process Theory"); (2) their revision is typically cursory and superficial, less concerned with actual rewriting than editing, limited to correcting misspellings and punctuation errors (Sommers); (3) little recursiveness or interplay is found among the components of their writing processes; and (4) their conception of writing is recipe-like and linear: when asked to describe how they typically write a paper, they claim first to think, then to write, and finally to check over their texts before submitting them ("Learning to Write"). Clearly, learning to write well requires mastering and managing an intricate, recursive composing process, and because the process is thoroughly disguised by the finished product, teaching writing well requires raising students' consciousness not just about their texts but more fundamentally about this process that undergrids their texts.

The second important reason for giving pedagogical attention to the writing process is that too often students' notions of writing have almost entirely to do with finished texts: consequently many students have either no idea or very stylized conceptions of how to go about composing a paper. In research at the University of Wisconsin, for example, Nystrand ("Learning to Write") found that many college freshmen have very superficial conceptions of how they write papers. These writers typically said, first they thought, then they wrote, then they sometimes looked over their texts for spelling and typographical errors, and finally they turned them in. Only rarely did they report any variation in this scheme, that is, any sophistication or sense of intricacy concerning the way they wrote. When students have so little insight into composing, they become easily discouraged and are unable to write easily, their writing skills often overwhelmed by papers requiring any complexity at all, for example, most college term papers. Helping students to insights about the complexities of composing—understanding that writing frequently is a messy business, even for the most practiced writers—is important because such insights help them cope with and manage what can be an unwieldy experience. Flower and Hayes make this important point in their article, "The Dynamics of Composing: Making Plans and Juggling Constraints."

Many students, furthermore, have misconceptions about writing. For example, they believe that writing can be good only when the writer is inspired (i.e., when the muse alights); that good writing conforms rigidly to formulas; that all essays must have three main points formulated in five paragraphs; that all paragraphs must have a certain minimum number of sentences; that good writers do not use dictionaries or handbooks (because they already know all the words and rules); that good writers are continuously fluent and never have problems knowing what to say (i.e., they never have "writer's block"). Many students assume that skillful writing is akin to a genetic trait ("You either have it or you don't")—not a learned skill and a cultivated art. Needless to say, only experience and insights into actual writing can significantly remedy such fallacious assumptions.

WHAT TEACHERS CAN DO TO PROMOTE THE WRITING PROCESS

What kind of attention should teachers give to their students' writing process? Should teachers teach the writing process the way they do parts of speech? That is to say, is "the" writing process yet another thing students must learn about? These questions are important, but the pedagogical implications of knowledge about the composing process have not to do with *what* to teach students about writing so much as *how* to engage students in the process itself. The following are some of these implications.

1. Raise Students' Consciousness about the Composing Process. Teachers can promote students' understanding of their composing processes in many ways. One way is to raise students' consciousness about the importance of their writing process by talking and asking their students to talk candidly about the surprisingly interesting details of how they write. Teachers can read interviews of famous writers (Plimpton) talking about how they write and/or talk about their own composing process to get things started, and they can ask students to write about how they usually compose a paper or a letter. Teachers can also ask students to make notes about how they write their next paper. The class can then compare these accounts, which students read aloud to each other or otherwise share.

2. Model the Composing Process. Another way teachers can promote their students' awareness of their composing process is to model the process for students. The teacher can offer to do some writing on the board in response to a topic that students provide and then, while composing, talk aloud every thought and word and every decision for accepting, rejecting, and revising the piece as it unfolds before students. Teachers will exhibit the full scope of their writing activity particularly if they do not prepare a writing topic in advance but rather work (courageously!) with an impromptu topic the class provides on request.

3. Promote Prewriting. Because a direct relationship exists between planning and writing well (Flower and Hayes, "Cognitive Process Theory"), teachers are well-advised to foster prewriting in their students' writing. Prewriting has to do with whatever writers do to collect and focus their thoughts before they write; examples include brainstorming, trying out ideas by talking about them, and such forms of writing as making notes. In the linear model of writing proposed by Rohman and Wlecke, prewriting referred to that part of the writing process that comes immediately before writing (according to Rohman and Wlecke, first one *pre*writes, then one writes, and finally one *re*writes). Although researchers such as Emig, and Flower and Hayes, recognized that writing is a recursive, not a linear, process, the writing research community has retained the concept of prewriting to refer to any phase of composing that helps writers collect and focus their thoughts—even if this phase occurs in the midst of composing. Indeed, the concept of prewriting as we now understand it recognizes that the very act of writing can often cause one to think of things and to reconsider one's original intention and meaning—what Britton et al. call "shaping at the point of utterance." When this happens, prewriting occurs *in the midst* of writing. Also, any draft that a writer chooses to revise is by this definition prewriting. In so far as prewriting has to do with collecting and focusing thoughts (i.e., a rehearsal of discourse; premeditation), it can occur at any time during composing, even after drafting is well underway.

Of course, not all writing involves or requires prewriting. Routine kinds of writing tasks, such as particular short-answer tasks, homework assignments, and many class tests—that is, writing tasks that probably entail (indeed, are designed to elicit) the straightforward recitation of previously mastered material—should not require prewriting. But teachers should promote and allow time for prewriting whenever they want their students genuinely to wrestle with a writing topic or to find a useful thesis, or whenever a writing task is of special importance to the writer—in short, whenever students encounter writing tasks that require lots of thinking. In Robert Stevenson's two studies of high school language activities that students reported as both engaging and challenging, writing ranked highest of all, and essay tasks in which the writers were required to take a position on an issue and defend it were ranked highest of all writing activities. To the extent that teachers especially want to challenge their students with writing tasks that they find intrinsically rewarding, they should anticipate recursiveness and the need for prewriting—and consequently allow time for it—in their most important assignments. Prewriting is important for teachers to promote because the discoveries writers make during prewriting are among the few true rewards available to writers.

4. Brainstorm with Students. One form of prewriting that teachers can engage in with students is brainstorming. Teachers can brainstorm with their students for writing topics in class, perhaps playing devil's advocate, periodically pausing to evaluate the ideas and their potential for development into papers.

5. Promote Both Prewriting and Revision with a Multiple-Draft Policy. Perhaps the most effective way a teacher can promote prewriting and rewriting is by establishing a multiple-draft policy at the start of the school year. When a student has obviously struggled with a topic with poor results, it often is useful to return the piece to the student with a note explaining the problem(s) and asking the author to revise what is "obviously only a draft." One virtue of this policy is that, rather than penalizing writers for poor work, it teaches them to recognize key distinctions between drafts and final copies.

6. Diagnose Writing Problems in Terms of Process Difficulties. Teachers help students become aware of their writing processes when, in writing conferences, they ask them how they wrote a particular problem paper and also how they generally write their paper(s). Not infrequently, when asked to discuss their writing process in this way, students can shed light on problems that might otherwise be misdiagnosed. The teacher may learn that awkward syntax and misspelled words are the result, not of missing or sagging skills, but rather of a student's failure to manage his or her composing processes wisely, for example, trying to write and watch television at the same time; or perhaps some insecurity about being in high school and having to write formal papers. When students have problems writing, the causes are frequently in the process of writing, not the text. But discussing these, teachers can help students learn to manage the problem itself, not just the symptom, and consequently help students gain insight into their composing and avoid such problems in the future.

7. Other Miscellaneous Techniques. Other miscellaneous techniques that promote the composing process are free writing, journal keeping, and outlining. Outlining especially helps students learn to manage their writing process efficiently if it is practiced mainly whenever students get stuck. Hence, outlining *before writing* can help writers organize their thoughts; outlining when stuck *in the middle* can help writers sort out what to say next; and outlining *upon completion of a draft* can help writers see if they have left any important points out and plan revisions accordingly.

WRITING AS A COMMUNICATION PROCESS

As important as the writing process is, it is not the whole story, for writing is not only a cognitive and expressive process in which writers put their thoughts into writing; it is also a communication process involving readers as well as writers. This important insight explains much about the activity of writing and has many important implications for instruction.

From the point of view of research on the composing process, texts are the final result of composing, and they are noteworthy as manifestations or embodiments of the writers' thinking and planning. But, of course, texts are much more than this. In addition to representing writers' intentions, texts must effectively balance the thinking and planning of the writers with the comprehension needs and expectations of the readers. Hence, the points that writers make, the very examples they use, the patterns of organization they deploy, all reflect not only what they have to say but also what they assume their readers expect and need in order to understand them. (In this chapter, for example, I have worked to balance research findings on writing with what I assume high school English teachers need to understand these ideas.) In other words, effective writing presumes reciprocity between writers and readers, an idea spelled out in some detail in Nystrand's *Structure of Written Communication.*

Teachers frequently exhort their students to develop their ideas explicitly, explaining that writing must "speak for itself" because the writer cannot expect to help readers out if they are puzzled by the text. Some researchers, echoing this sentiment, have proposed that writing is essentially different from speech in just this way: whereas speech is "fragmentary" and "context-bound," written texts must be explicit and "autonomous" (cf. Olson). But this distinction is valid only, of course, if one compares formal essays and idle gossip; it is not a valid distinction for written and oral language generally for which many counterexamples are readily available, for example, abbreviated written notes, explicit oral lectures.

Nonetheless, it is not easy for beginning writers to learn to write explicit texts. And this fact reveals a very important aspect of written communication: a text is explicit not because it says everything all by itself but rather because it strikes a careful balance between what needs to be said and what may be assumed. To know what may be assumed requires writers to anticipate correctly what their readers already know, on the one hand, and what will be new to them, on the other. In other words, explicitness is not really an aspect of texts but rather *a judgment that readers make when they find all their questions addressed by the text.* Not only young, novice writers find learning to be explicit difficult but also experienced writers, who must learn to address new audiences, for example, many graduate and professional students in law and medicine (Williams, in press). The writer's problem is not just being explicit but also knowing what to be explicit about (Nystrand, "The Role," *Structure of Written Communication*). Because writers must balance their own needs for expression with their readers' needs for comprehension, writing is fundamentally a social act.

WHAT TEACHERS CAN DO TO PROMOTE WRITING AS A COMMUNICATION PROCESS

If students are to master writing as a communicative process, they must not only write regularly but also systematically try their drafts out on others and get feedback from readers. Ideally this feedback should come from a wide variety of readers; they should certainly write for more than just their teachers (Freedman and Sperling). Most high school students do not write enough, nor do they write for enough teachers to receive nearly the amount and diversity of feedback that is desirable for learning to write well. Also, while English teachers may be experts in rhetoric, grammar, and mechanics, and can consequently offer their students sound advice on these aspects of their writing problems, they are typically perceived by their students (and rightly so) as *judges* of their writing and their knowledge of subject matter. Rarely must student writers ever explain to their teachers something about which the teacher really does not understand or know. While such writing may help students master and recall essential course information, it unfortunately gives them little if any real experience writing informative prose because teachers who read their papers in this way do not read their student papers to be informed. Arthur Applebee comments:

> For learning to write well, the most effective writing situation will be one in which the effectiveness of the writing matters—where the student can savor the success of having presented a convincing argument or struggle with the problems of having failed to do so. In such situations the teacher can sometimes intervene directly, helping students develop their writing skills by demonstrating the effects of different methods of organization and presentation. If all that really matters, however, is that the right items of information can be cited, then the development of such new writing skills will be essentially irrelevant, and they will be ignored by student and teacher alike. (101)

Teachers can give their students experience with writing as a communicative process in several ways. The key to them all is establishing audiences for their students that transcend teachers. For example, teachers can ask students to try out their texts with each other and provide classtime for such draft swapping. Some high school English teachers establish class newspapers and magazines in which they "publish" their students' writing. Other teachers arrange for their students to be pen pals with students in other schools. Some teachers, in schools with networked computers, provide for peer writing using microcomputers (Huston and Thompson).

1. Use Peer-Conferencing Groups. Perhaps the most easily available audience for student writers is that comprised of in-class peers. Considerable research has been conducted on the effectiveness of peer-conferencing where groups of four or five students regularly meet in class to present their papers for discussion with each other. In writing about elementary and high school English teaching, James Moffett originally justified peer conferencing on the grounds that it was "the only way, short of tutorial, to provide individual students enough experience and feedback" (12). The regular use of writing groups is a seminal idea for reducing the paper load of high school English teachers who regularly must deal with 150 students or more and still want their students to write regularly. But aside from this practical consideration, other important benefits are associated with peer conferencing.

In one study, Nystrand (*Structure of Written Communication*) found that college freshmen wrote significantly better exposition after a semester of intensive peer conferencing than did students who had written only for their instructors. One of the differences between the two groups was that students writing just for their instructors increasingly came to see revision as a matter of editing (finding typographical errors and correcting misspelling and punctuation errors) whereas students writing regularly for their peers increasingly treated revision as a matter of "reconceptualization," rethinking the purpose and development of their papers. This difference between the two groups related to the fact that students writing for their teachers increasingly saw their teacher/reader as a "judge" of their work whereas students writing mainly for each other came to see their peer readers as collaborators and helpers. Consequently, students in peer groups developed more positive attitudes toward writing.

Other research on peer conferencing, including studies of high school students, have demonstrated its effectiveness in contributing to gains in (a) critical thinking, (b) organization, and (c) appropriateness (Lagana); (d) revision skills (Benson; Nystrand and Brandt); (e) attention to prewriting; (f) awareness of writers' own writing process (Nystrand "The Role of Context"); (g) ability to evaluate the probable success of writers' own texts (Nystrand and Brandt); and (h) increased writer confidence (Fox).

2. Use Journals and Learning Logs. Another easily available audience for writers is themselves, and teachers can help their students tap the potential of this audience by having them keep personal journals and/or learning logs in which students regularly summarize and react to whatever they are reading and learning. Students keep these journals and logs mainly for their own purposes, but when teachers read and respond to them, they do so not as judges of content but rather as trusted, interested adults, and their marginal comments, together with the student entries, read like an extended conversation. In an eleventh grade learning log in English, for example, a student may write tentatively, "I'm not sure what caused Macbeth's downfall. It was his ambition. But it was also Lady Macbeth's ambition. But what did the witches have to do with it???" The writer may also digress: "Maybe if I went back and looked at the soliloquies, this might make more sense. Let's see. . . . " Such a learning log, of course, could never be submitted as an exam answer: the "tentativeness" would be judged as a sign of "uncertainty" and the digressions viewed as an indication of "incoherence." Neither, despite its importance to the learner's engagement with the subject, would be allowed, let alone encouraged, in an exam-driven curriculum.

This sort of language, as I noted, is what James Britton termed *expressive.* In his analysis of student talk about a Hemingway short story, he writes:

> The language remains "expressive" throughout, in the sense that it is relaxed, self-presenting, self-revealing, addressed to a few intimate companions; in the sense that it moves easily from general comment to narration of particular experiences and back again; and in the special sense that in making comments the speakers do not aim at accurate, explicit reference (as one might in an argument or sociological report) and in relating experience they do not aim at a polished performance (as a raconteur or a novelist would). ("Talking to Learn" 96)

This sort of discourse is pedagogically important, Britton notes, because in the process of talking the students work through just those concepts that need to be internalized, and they have the opportunity to do so precisely in terms of what they already know. This discussion, like the discourse of learning logs, is noteworthy not as a report of what has been learned or assigned but rather for *its potential as a mode of learning itself.*

For psycholinguists, given and new information are defined in terms of what information the speaker/writer and listener/reader share (e.g., Haviland and Clark). *Given information* is what both know, and *new information* is what one knows but the other does not. Difficult technical writing, for example, is usually difficult because it has too much new and not enough given information vis-à-vis what the readers already know.

In a learning log that the writer keeps, the writer and reader are one and the same; the writer is also the reader. This fact affects what given and new information the writer is required to balance. In written exams or homework questions, the writer must discuss new concepts in terms of whatever *the teacher* assumes to be given, presumably previous course content. In a learning log, by contrast, students have an opportunity more fully to appropriate new concepts because they may deal with them not only in terms of previous course content but also in terms of anything else that seems relevant to *them.*

Learning logs occupy a middle ground between journals that students keep for themselves, on the one hand, and exams where students must recite particular information that the teacher checks for mastery, on the other hand. The teacher reads the logs as an interested party who is genuinely open to what the writer has to say and responds much as a conversant would, that is, by adding to what the writer has said. This latter kind of discourse is *authentic* (cf., Nystrand and Gamoran, "Instruction as Discourse," "Instructional Discourse") because it allows students as well as teachers to have input into instruction. (An authentic teacher question, for example, is a question for which the teacher has not prespecified an answer; it is an open-ended question to which the teacher really does not know the answer. Authentic questions are opposite of *test questions*). When teachers are clearly open to student ideas and opinions, they create a positive atmosphere for learning because they treat what students say as important, thereby promoting greater authority among them.

An excellent introduction for teachers on the use of journals and learning logs is Toby Fulwiler's *The Journal Book.* An excellent companion volume examining research on dialogue journal keeping is Staton, Shuy, Peyton, and Reed's text.

CONCLUSION

Perhaps the most important insight from recent research on composition is that effective writing instruction is less a matter of teaching knowledge about composition, rhetoric, or grammar to students and more a matter of promoting and refining the process of writing. English teachers need to think of writing as a verb, not as a noun. In any case, information about writing (e.g., parts of speech, principles of rhetoric, types of paragraphs, etc.) makes sense to students only in the context of the activity itself. This is why writing teachers' primary responsibility concerns initiating and sustaining appropriate writing activities and arranging for effective feedback.

Although the traditional focus of high school writing instruction has been on good written texts, recent developments have emphasized the composing process. The major pedagogical implications of research on composing processes have to do with ways of fostering the writing process, including prewriting, writing, and rewriting. Writing researchers are currently broadening this perspective by examining the relationship of the process to its product, the text. Specifically, they are examining the role that written texts play in mediating between the needs of the writer for expression, on the one hand, and the reader for comprehension, on the other. From this point of view, texts "bridge" the respective purposes and concerns of writers and readers. The major pedagogical implications of this work have to do with broadening the audiences that students address, mainly through the use of peer conferencing and journal keeping. Both cognitive and social views of writing stress the importance of the instructional setting teachers create in their classrooms, requiring students to write frequently for each other and to respond to each others' writing.

Works Cited

Applebee, Arthur. *Writing in the Secondary School: English and the Content Areas.* Urbana, Ill.: National Council of Teachers of English, 1981.

Benson, N. The Effects of Peer Feedback during the Writing Process on Writing Performance, Revision Behavior, and Attitude Toward Writing. Unpublished Ph.D. dissertation, Boulder, Colo.: The University of Colorado, 1979.

Britton, James. "Talking to Learn." *Language, the Learner, and the School,* Douglas Barnes, James Britton, and Harold Rosen, eds. Harmondsworth: Penguin, 1969.

———. *Language and Learning.* London: Penguin Press, 1970.

Britton, James et al. *The Development of Writing Abilities (11–18).* London: Macmillan, 1975.

Emig, Janet. *The Composing Processes of Twelfth Graders.* Urbana, Ill.: The National Council of Teachers of Englihs, 1971.

________. "Non-Magical Thinking: Presenting Writing Developmentally in Schools." *Writing: Process, Development, and Communication.* C. H. Fredericksen, and J. F. Dominic, eds. Hillsdale, N. J.: Lawrence Erlbaum, 1981.

Flower, Linda, and John R. Hayes. "Problem-Solving Strategies and the Writing Process," *College English,* 39 (1977): 449–61.

________. "Dynamics of Composing: Making Plans and Juggling Constraints." *Cognitive Processes in Writing.* L. Gregg and E. Steinberg, eds. Lawrence Erlbaum, 1980.

________. "A Cognitive Process Theory of Writing," *College Composition and Communication.* 32 (1981): 356–87.

Fox, R. "Treatment of Writing Apprehension and Its Effects on Composition," *Research in the Teaching of English.* 14 (1980): 39–49.

Freedman, Sarah, and Melanie Sperling. "Teacher-Student Interaction in the Writing Conference: Response and Teaching," *The Acquisition of Written Language: Revision and Response.* S. Freedman, ed. Norwood, N. J.: Ablex, 1985.

Fulwiler, Toby. *The Journal Book.* Portsmouth, N. H.: Boynton-Cook, 1987.

Haviland, S., and Clark Herbert. "What's New? Acquiring New Information as a Process of Comprehension." *Journal of Verbal Learning and Verbal Behavior.* 13 (1974): 512–21.

Huston, Barbara, and Diane Thompson. "Moving Language around on the Word Processor: Cognitive Operations upon Language," *The Quarterly Newsletter of the Laboratory of Comparative Human Cognition.* 7/2 (1985): 57–64.

Lagana, J. "The Development Implementation, and Evaluation of a Model for Teaching Composition which Utilizes Individualized Learning and Peer Grouping. Unpublished doctoral dissertation. Pittsburgh, Pa.: University of Pittsburgh.

Moffett, James. *Teaching the Universe of Discourse.* Boston: Houghton-Mifflin, 1968.

Nystrand, Martin. "The Role of Context in Written Communication." *The Nottingham Linguistic Circular.* 12/1 (1983): 55–65.

________. "Learning to Write by Talking about Writing: A Summary of Research on Intensive Peer Review in Expository Writing Instruction at the University of Wisconsin-Madison." Unpublished final report to the National Institute of

Education. *Resources in Education,* 20/6 (1985). (Eric Reproduction Service No. ED 225 914.)

________. *The Structure of Written Communication: Studies in Reciprocity between Writers and Readers.* Orlando and London: Academic Press, 1986.

Nystrand, Martin, and A. Gamoran. "A Study of Instruction as Discourse." Paper presented at the 1988 Convention of the American Educational Research Association. Madison: The National Center on Effective Secondary Schools, 1988.

________. Instructional Discourse and Student Engagement." Paper presented at the 1989 Convention of the American Educational Research Association. Madison: The National Center on Effective Secondary Schools, 1989.

Nystrand, Martin, and Deborah Brandt. "Response to Writing as a Context for Learning to Write." *Responding to Student Writing: Models, Methods, and Curricular Change.* C. Anson, ed. Urbana, Ill.: National Council of Teachers of English, 1989.

Olson, David R. "From Utterance to Text: The Bias of Language in Speech and Writing," *The Harvard Educational Review,* 47 (1977): 257–81.

Plimpton, George, ed. *Writers at Work: The "Paris Review" Interviews* (2nd series). New York: Viking Press, 1963.

________. *Writers at Work: The "Paris Review" Interviews* (3rd series). New York: Viking Press, 1967.

________. *Writers at Work: The "Paris Review" Interviews* (4th series). New York: Viking Press, 1976.

Rohman, D. Gordon, and A. F. Wlecke. "Pre-Writing: The Construction and Application of Models for Concept Formation in Writing." U. S. Office of Education Cooperative Research Project, No. 2174. East Lansing, Mich.: Michigan State University, 1964.

Smith, Frank. *Understanding Reading.* New York: Holt, Rinehart, and Winston, 1971.

________. *Comprehension and Learning.* New York: Holt, Rinehart, and Winston, 1983.

Sommers, Nancy. "Revision Strategies of Student Writers and Experienced Adult Writers," *College Composition and Communication,* 31 (1980): 378–88.

Staton, Jana, Roger Shuy, Joy K. Peyton, and Leslie Reed. *Dialogue Journal Communication: Classroom, Linguisitc, Social, and Cognitive Views.* Norwood, N. J.: Ablex, 1988.

Stevenson, R. "Student Perspectives on Cognitively Challenging Curriculum," *Higher Order Thinking in High School Social Studies: An Analysis of Classrooms, Teachers, Students and Leadership.* F. Newmann, ed. Madison, Wisc.: The National Center on Effective Secondary Schools, 1988a.

________. "Student Perspectives on Engaging Curriculum," *Higher Order Thinking in High School Social Studies: An Analysis of Classrooms, Teachers, Students and Leadership.* F. Newmann, ed. Madison, Wisc.: The National Center on Effective Secondary Schools, 1988.

Williams, Joseph. "Rhetoric and Informal Reasoning: Disentangling Some Confounded Effects in Good Reasoning and Good Writing." *Informal Reasoning and Instruction.* David Perkins, Judith Segal, and James Voss, eds. Hillsdale, N. J.: Lawrence Erlbaum, in press.

Sheryl L. Finkle and Edward P. J. Corbett

11. *The Place of Classical Rhetoric in the Contemporary Writing Classroom*

We are willing to bet that having seen the title of this chapter and having continued to read into the first paragraph, you are a member of either an elite or an eccentric group of writing teachers. For many, classical rhetoric is a subject that is of no interest at all. They believe that its study consists solely of reading highbrow theoretical material full of highfalutin terms such as the *enthymeme* developed by antiquarian philosophers like Aristotle, dreary work that finally leaves a teacher on his or her own to determine what to do for Monday morning's assignment anyway. Part of our mission in writing about classical rhetoric is to dispel the notion that it is "merely" theoretical by focusing our attention primarily on the comprehensive system of instruction the ancient rhetoricians developed and discussing how the combination of activities employed in that system can be useful in the classroom today.

At the same time, we have no intention of dismissing ties between teaching practices and rhetorical theory. Some college researchers of composition delight in leveling indictments for "malpractice" against writing teachers because they believe that we composition instructors are defiantly ignorant of *all* rhetorical theory, classical or contemporary, and its importance in developing a writing curriculum. In fact, whether teachers choose to recognize someone else's ideas as our guide, whether we consciously promote our own ideas, or whether we teach what strikes our fancy with no conscious attention to what we do and why, we are always creating or using theory to make our decisions about writing practices. Another goal of this essay, as we show how certain predispositions of classical rhetoricians are essential to a proper understanding of their rhetorical teaching practices, is to make our readers conscious of how their own predispositions about writing instruction can influence and may have already influenced the effectiveness of certain practices that we have inherited from the ancients.

Researchers on college writing are also engaged in a debate about the extent to which ancient rhetorical theory and practice are at all compatible with contemporary rhetorical theory and its practice. Some researchers have said that classical rhetorical theory and practice are the sources of most of what is "wrong" with the teaching of writing in the contemporary classroom. For instance, they suggest that the classical rhetoricians, teaching their students to consistently include six parts in an oration and focusing mainly on persuasive discourse, more or less directly influenced teachers of rhetoric today to assign five-paragraph themes that persuade *or* inform *or* narrate *or* describe rather than to recognize the natural combinations of essay structures that comprise discourse today. They suggest that the classical rhetoricians, using preexisting texts as models of good writing, caused teachers of rhetoric today to ask students for error-free texts with ritualistic, if not clichéd, content. They suggest that the classical rhetoricians, asking students to consider the five canons of rhetoric (invention, arrangement, style, memory, and delivery) as they constructed texts, urged teachers of rhetoric today to train students in a mechanized ritual of finding a topic, narrowing its scope into a thesis, finding support for the claim, and writing down all of these ideas in tidy language. In general, some critics blame classical rhetoricians for making writing instruction in public schools nothing more than a prescription of meaningless exercises designed to produce in students the potential for producing certain types of texts correctly.

Critics of classical rhetoric fail to consider that if what writing teachers do at present is an unconscious adaptation or, in many cases, a perversion of classical theory and practice based on misconceptions, many of the criticisms leveled at classical rhetoric may not be as valid as they seem at first. Creating a skills-oriented and product-oriented program of teaching may be the result of doing what we have seen our own teachers do without considering how to orchestrate the individual lessons we remember within the context of a rhetorical approach to (or theory of) teaching writing, which many teachers have long forgotten involves teaching students how to make choices appropriate to specific contexts and audiences. It is, moreover, easier for us as teachers to adopt wholesale the approach our former teachers modelled as successful teaching than it is for us to attempt to isolate and respond to problems that our own students are having with our teaching approach by exercising different options.

In order for us to choose from the best theories and methods available to ensure our students' success in writing, teachers need to be aware of misconceptions about traditional theory and practices. We need to be aware of recent advances in the theory and practices of our profession. Teachers need constantly to test the validity of assumptions that other people make about students seeking alternative methods consistent with our objectives but that encourage more students to exercise and develop their writing and speaking abilities in a variety of ways while evidencing an enthusiasm for communicating and learning through writing and speaking. With more alternatives available to us, teachers will need to be cautious about assigning tasks that are at cross-purposes with our goals or that repeat one aspect of learning and leave others unattended. Through analyzing the misapplications of certain classical teaching devices, this chapter presents critical issues for teachers to consider as we attempt to reconstruct effective programs of writing instruction. Perhaps, through a better understanding of classical rhetoric, we can revitalize our contemporary composition teaching and revitalize the rhetoric of the ancients.

CORRECTING MISCONCEPTIONS OF CLASSICAL THEORIES OF LANGUAGE USE

When we speak of classical rhetoric, we are referring to theories, concepts, and practices that the Greeks and Romans developed about the composition or oral discourses and that remained in vogue from the fifth century B.C. until the nineteenth century. The most common misconception about this body of knowledge is that it comprises a single theory of writing. The Greeks and Romans held as many conflicting ideas about the teaching of public discourse as teachers do today. Classical rhetoric has been made to seem monolithic because some important texts have been lost, some theories have been privileged by receiving more commentary than others, and some of what was said about rhetoric was never recorded. Our understanding of classical theories, moreover, is impaired because through time much of what was once commonplace knowldege has changed. We have inherited various "interpretations" of the ancients' theories as researchers have struggled to reconstruct the relationship of competing ideologies in the context of their own predispositions about rhetoric.

From its inception, rhetorical education was meant to be practical. First of all, in the last quarter of the fifth century B.C., after the expulsion of the tyrants, citizens in the Greek cities of Sicily had to resort to rhetorical persuasion in the courtrooms in order to reestablish their title to ownership of property that had been taken from them during the period of the tyranny (Vickers 6). So Corax and Tisias formulated practical guidelines to help the citizens conduct their litigations in the courts. Second, in the political arena, the growth of democracy made learning how to speak effectively in the public forums advantageous for ordinary citizens. Rhetorical theory and rhetorical training developed as the need for rhetoric developed.

CLASSICAL RHETORIC AND THE FUNCTIONS OF LANGUAGE

One area of the study of writing that researchers contend was vastly unexplored in classical rhetorical theory concerns the functions that language might serve. Today, discourse is understood to include means of self-expression and means of knowing as well as means of persuading or informing others. Classical rhetoricians, most often represented by public figures such as Aristotle and Cicero, are assumed to be outmoded because they limited themselves to the study of argumentation. But claims against the validity of classical rhetorical theory in this area are unfounded for several reasons. Implicit in both Aristotle's and Plato's philosophies of rhetoric, though often discounted in modern interpretations, is the notion that rhetoric should advance inquiry as well as communicate knowledge. And Isocrates explicitly argued in his *Antidosis* that language plays a vital role in intellectual activity. He explained, "none of the things which are done with intelligence take place without the help of speech... in all our actions as well as in all our thoughts, speech is our guide" (quoted in Clark 54). If expository and argumentative writing dominate other forms of writing and all forms of speaking in the modern curriculum, then, it is not that classical rhetoricians privileged these forms of communication over others in their teaching. This emphasis probably evolved in response to the practices of communication that educators observed in society and business and assumed were essential to public education.

Despite the fact that rhetoricians focused their practical examples on courtroom argument, much of what they had to say about rhetoric is still applicable to other types of expression. Classical rhetoric need not be discarded simply because someone has pointed out its inconsistencies or deficiencies. It needs, instead, to be updated and applied in a wider variety of ways.

CORRECTING MISCONCEPTIONS OF CLASSICAL TEACHING PRACTICES

Just as we have had difficulty interpreting the theory that governed rhetorical education, we also have had difficulty understanding its methodology. Even though we know quite a bit about the curriculum they followed, we have no idea of what the ancient teachers said individually to students as they encouraged them to use what they had learned from precepts and imitation or what teachers did to intervene in students' writing or speaking to make it more effective. One cannot ignore the possible effects of very small classes on language learning. One can also not overlook the fact that rhetoric was the cornerstone of early education and that its study occupied most of the students' time in school, whereas rhetoric plays a limited and isolated role in the contemporary curriculum. In order to make decisions about what classical rhetoric has to offer us today, we need to know both what the ancients conceived of as effective practice and how what we often call *traditional* teaching practices may have distorted the intentions of the ancients. We briefly explore the classical practices as perceived in antiquity and discuss their contemporary misapplications so as to provide some common background before explaining more appropriate uses of these practices.

PRECEPTS

The means of teaching formal speaking and writing (as its importance increased) in classical times were precepts, imitation, and practice. Although contemporary educators might not consciously resort to these three means, they still educate students by exercising them in one or the other or a combination of these means, not simply because the means are "traditional," but because these are the natural and inescapable means of acquiring any physical or intellectual skill.

The first of these means, rhetorical precepts, which the Greeks called *techne* and the Romans called *ars,* were presented to students in the form of lectures or textbooks outlining the "rules" of rhetoric. The precepts that guided students in making judicious choices about composing and the observations that they made about how other writers exercised these choices were further explained by the teacher's explicit instructions or *praelectio.* From both lectures and reading, classical students learned that constructing effective discourses required attention to all five canons of rhetoric: invention, arrangement, style, memory, and delivery. They learned that their audiences expected a discourse to include six parts: the *exordium,* which tried to secure the audience's attention and good will; the *narratio,* which summarized the situation that prompted the discourse; the *partitio,* which outlined the main points of the argument to be made; the *confirmatio,* the main body of the discourse, which presented the arguments or proofs for the thesis; the *confutatio,* which attempted to refute opposing arguments; and the *peroratio,* which provided a recapitulation, a conclusion, and a final appeal to the audience. Students also learned that the arguments used in each part of the discourse must address the special interests of their audience. And students learned that because of the dispositions and limitations of that audience, perspicuity, elegance, forcefulness, and grace in the wording of their discourses were important. These basic precepts, then, were meant to answer common questions of ancient students, which roughly correspond to questions that students ask today, such as "What is my writing supposed to do?" "What is my writing supposed to look like?" "How can I make my writing understandable to my audience?"

Despite changes in our time from educating relatively few students in well-defined writing or speaking tasks required by their occupations to educating the masses in tasks representative of rising standards of literacy, rhetorical teaching techniques seem not to have altered radically. We recognize the classical precepts mentioned earlier because they are still reprinted in most contemporary textbooks and because in many classrooms, much time is invested in rhetorical education that centers around reciting this abstract advice to students. Some researchers trace this rule-bound and teacher-centered approach to education in antiquity. But ironically, Isocrates, the most successful ancient teacher of rhetoric, emphasized imitation and practice rather than precepts in teaching students to compose texts.

Undoubtedly, the later devaluation of writing *practice* in rhetorical education and subsequent shifts to lecturing about writing has resulted as much from conditions in the contemporary classroom as it has from teachers' own overzealous focus in precepts. Despite this fact, we must avoid mistakenly blaming our ancestors for our actions and resist the temptation to develop a kind of "circumstantial conscience." In other words, we would gladly provide our students with opportunities for diverse writing practice rather than tell them about the rules of writing if we only had the right class size for doing so or if students were only more motivated to learn.

IMITATION AND LANGUAGE EXERCISES

Isocrates, as we just mentioned, taught primarily through models and exercises. And other rhetoricians, in varying degrees, concurred with Isocrates that trial and error, prescribed exercises, and imitation were essential to language learning. Quintilian was much in favor of having students imitate and memorize "the best words, phrases and figures," which are "not sought for the occasion, but offer themselves spontaneously from a treasure house, as it were, within them" (quoted in Clark 170) because he was aware that the greater students' facility with language in general, the greater their capacity for thinking through the use of language. Exploring the various forms of language without regard for context was meant to be done in tandem with and not in place of composing and studying language in the context of whole discourses.

IMITATION OF STRUCTURE

Imitation, as we most often hear about it, was taught by presenting a careful analysis of the virtues of a work—including an explanation of how to achieve those virtues. Students were then asked to compose a similar essay with the same patterns as those in the model. In a lesson such as this, students reconstructed the thinking they had observed and matched it with suitable stylistic choices. Translation for the Romans provided another interesting way to view the function of figures and vocabulary in their own language, by comparing them with the function of figures and words in Greek. Students also paraphrased works by turning another's phrases into their own words or turning poetry to prose. And more advanced imitation exercises, called *emulation,* required students to write something on the same subject as a model author and to compare the points where either the student or the model had the superior turn of phrase. All these exercises called attention to the way in which words, phrases, sentences, and larger discourse structures were used. But they were not necessarily meant to reveal prescriptive recipes for writing.

Still, when those of us who teach writing today do not entirely overlook these practices, we misemploy imitation. The ancients realized that creating a text is a different operation than imitating one because composing for oneself requires more cognitive and social sophistication than imitation. Accordingly, practice in composing a whole discourse in all its complexity was included in the curriculum along with practice in imitation. But today imitation has sometimes been used as a substitute for composing rather than as an aid to it. Students perform better, of course, in certain aspects of this kind of writing because some of the choices involved in composing have been made for them. A teacher's pleasure, however, can soon turn to dismay if in the next writing assignment students are asked to produce an essay of another sort on a vastly different topic without the aid of a model. The anticipated "gains" that were evidenced in the imitation assignment most likely will have failed to "carry over." This effect is not unexpected because when students are not encouraged in models to use the structures they have imitated or observed in models in writing contexts of their own making, they seldom develop command of these structures; nor will they see the need for remembering them and keeping them in their repertoire of choices. Imitation lessons should support students who are striving to refine the processes and products of their own writing.

IMITATING STYLE

Teachers, too, can misuse imitation and other language activities, such as stylistic analyses, by employing them to teach correctness or a preferred style rather than constructing opportunities for students to experiment with language and to observe the variety of forms that language can take. Lessons that provide students with new ways of expressing themselves in their own discourses might become "meaningless exercises" simply because students are not encouraged to try new forms to help them develop ideas in relation to the needs and expectations of an audience or to the demands of a particular rhetorical context. Imitation lessons can teach students about figures, schemes, and structures in whole discourse that they have not previously encountered. If we believe that writing represents a mode of learning, we will recognize that such lessons give students not only new tools for language-building but also new structures for meaning-making. They can also heighten students' powers of observation about language by showing them how "seeing language itself" is sometimes as important as trying to "see through" language to find meaning. But, again, the activities can be only as useful as teachers allow them to be by using them properly and in ways relevant to our students' contemporary writing needs.

EXTENDING IMITATION TO PLAY WITH LANGUAGE

Once students have examined the implications of writing about something in different ways, we can then devote a regular part of class time to experimenting with language structures. For instance, students can be encouraged to play language games with other students when they peer-edit one another's papers. They might ask questions about a word choice, a sentence, a chunk, or a paragraph, suggesting a variety of options from which to choose. They might make remarks about why they handled a particular situation differently in their own papers or suggest another student's work that has been successful in achieving what is wanted in this paper. Students might eventually feel confident enough to submit writing problems to a peer group or to the whole class for a once-a-week consultation or help session.

Language options might be increased by having students seek out "new forms" and "new situations for language use." A good place to start is by having students collect samples of structures that interest or puzzle them in their outside reading or in reading each others' papers. They might share these with classmates as they comment on their writing, or they might share these in class discussions of what they have accomplished in their study of writing over a certain period of time. Through such activities, students not only learn something about the function of language in texts but also define a context for the discussion of writing in their classroom. They can discuss the universal nature of "writing problems," and they can learn the value of collaboration in overcoming their individual language blocks and mazes. They can also learn to discuss writing positively in terms of discoveries and accomplishments. Writing may no longer seem a solitary, defensive act but rather a means of establishing an identity within a community.

PRACTICE-WRITING ASSIGNMENTS

For the Greek and Roman schoolboys, a large part of language instruction consisted of exhaustive practice in composing. The first writing assignments, called the *progymnasmata,* were collected in the *Rhetorica ad Alexandrium* in the fourth century B.C., but Hermogenes and Aphthonius were the major progenitors of these lessons. The *progymnasmata* gave grammar school boys patterns to follow in producting compositions through a graded series in which each assignment built on the previous one and added something to it. Hermogenes' program, as Donald Leman Clark describes it, included twelve lessons divided among the three types of rhetoric that Aristotle had described: judicial (for blaming or praising), deliberative (for inciting others to action), and epideictic (for ceremonial speaking). Teachers played an all-important role in working with students on ways to produce meaningful yet well-articulated texts. Unfortunately, those words and deeds in the classroom that probably had the most influence on the students' motivation and progress are lost.

In the advanced grades or the *toga viriles,* the writing and speaking exercises took two forms. The *melete* (Greek) or *declamatio* (Latin) could be *suasoriae,* advice-giving texts, or *controversiae,* arguments pro or con. Because students had limited experiences from which to write, the *suasoria* were based on *prosopopoeiae* (speeches whose words were written by the student as though he were a famous historical figure). These exercises had the same advantages as role-playing exercises today and were difficult for the same reasons. They gave students practice in writing from a particular perspective, but students were challenged because they not only had to assume the character of the speaker but also had to adapt their orations to the fictitious audience and the fictitious setting.

The *controversiae* were more popular with students because they could invent in these essays fantastic circumstances, things that intrigued them to write about. These assignments encouraged students to play out ideas they were interested in, much as journal assignments do today. But the *controversiae* carried with them added constraints of writing polished prose.

A more complex variation of the *controversiae* was a moot-court argument in which a student argued a case using real facts from a pending appeal. This assignment was similar to contemporary assignments, such as those given in college technical writing classes that ask students to assume a professional role in their writing. The assignment carries with it all the complexities of assuming control over situations that the student might know about but has not previously participated in.

The ancient rhetoricians' priorities of instruction in assigning essays and assessing them seem to be nearly the reverse of those of many writing teachers today. Invention is a province of rhetorical training ignored for at least two centuries before regaining prominence in the writing curriculum of the past decade or so. But the Greeks and Romans regarded it as the first priority in composition instruction. Moreover, the Greek concept of *stasis* (the Roman *status*), which roughly translates into a means of finding the "issues" involved in a topic, was employed to help students discover what they wanted to discuss in the composition. The ancient rhetoricians felt that this type of inquiry must logically precede the kind of discovery involved in what Aristotle described as the search for the "available means of persuasion." Only when we know what we want to accomplish in the speech, they argued, can we proceed to create a favorable impression of our ideas, arouse assent, allay dissent, and so on, as Aristotle would have us do.

In some contemporary writing classrooms, the teaching of grammar is the main focus of writing instruction. Practice in composing essays plays a secondary role, if it receives much attention at all. Compositions are often conceived of as single-product "tests" of grammatical competence rather than as multidraft learning tools. Grammar was not taught *instead of* composing in the ancient rhetoric classrooms but was taught *through* the teacher's commentary on style, clarity, and appropriateness in student writing and reading. Rhetoricians, on the other hand, were more interested in familiarizing their students with concepts of style than with the niceties of grammar. They concerned themselves with the selection of words (diction or *electio verborum*), the arrangement of words in a sentence (*compositio verborum*), and the virtues of clarity or plain meaning, embellishment through the use of schemes and tropes, and the register or the formality of language in the context of the content, purpose, occasion, and audience for a particular composition. Even though many teachers attend to these elements of prose, we often address them in abstract ways by teaching general precepts about them rather than by discussing them in the context of a student's writing before the work is graded.

What then is the usefulness of such writing assignments as the *progymnasmata* or the *suasoria* or the *controversiae?* First, they reflect several principles that are important in assignment-making. Assignments in the *progymnasmata* were designed to build one on another, suggesting to students that everything they wrote was related to everything else they wrote in some way and reminding teachers that these assignments were supposed to encourage development of writing. Second, the *suasoriae* (advice-giving texts) and the *controversiae* (formal arguments) advance two other features of assignment-making that are relevant today. The *suasoriae* provided students with contexts for writing and gave them practice in making appeals to real audiences to achieve some purpose. Because the background for these assignments was historical material, the students had some sense of how the audience responded previously and were able to anticipate how an audience might respond to their own appeals. Similarly, purpose and context were clearly defined aspects to be addressed in the composition. Thus, responding to a rhetorical context and defined audiences were important features of learning in the students' rhetorical educations.

Frequently, assignments in the contemporary classroom are chosen because they are favorites of a teacher, because students like them, because they yield interesting products, or because they simply produce better reading for the teacher than other types of assignments. Sometimes they are chosen for unarticulated reasons. Assignments that are given without regard for their relationship to one another fail to give students a sense of relevance in their work. Moreover, students frequently choose to do what they can already do well. And while writing assignments that allow them to do just that are probably not harmful to students, they do not exercise the students' abilities in a variety of types of discourse. This kind of assignment-making might convince students that all writing is to be approached in the same way, leaving the language of the text as devoid of the influence of certain aspects of the rhetorical situation as other carelessly given assignments. It can also confuse students when they are required to perform other writing tasks that may not allow them to write in familiar ways.

What we are striving for are assignments that have a logical developmental relationship to one another, such as those of the ancients, but that reflect more contemporary notions of what writing development means. Such development might be perceived taxonomically (e.g., Alexander Bain's progression of difficulty in various discursive modes) or functionally (e.g., James Britton's taxonomy of audience and purpose as related to the functions of discourse).

Teachers' goals for student writing should be clear from the onset of composing. They should comprise the content of student and teacher commentary on the drafts of papers, and they should include those aspects of writing assessed most rigorously when the final draft is presented.

We find no evidence to suggest that students in antiquity were highly motivated to write simply because the rhetorical situations were provided for them, but at least essays arising from these situations did not ask students to speculate about abstract concepts such as, "What Freedom Means to Me." Instead, they encouraged students to think of their composing as a kind of problem-solving process, a human drama in which they could participate. In this process, real-life decisions were more closely associated with decisions that students made in the classroom. Studies such as those of Britton, James Moffett, and others suggest that considerations of audience and purpose are frequently overlooked in assignment-making today. Assignments that allow students to write to real-life audiences and opportunities for students to test out one another's intentions against their actual achievements are sorely needed.

In order to provide as much information as a situation calls for or as an audience might require, writers must be able to "play out" ideas in a variety of ways and, usually, in more detail than they are generally able to do. The ancient *controversiae* allowed students to write on subjects that were interesting enough to compel them to think harder and achieve more in terms of subject development. The kind of writing that is ungraded or that rewards development more than correctness is necessary to encourage students to take chances in their thinking. Invention techniques such as Richard Larson's problem-solving heuristic, Kenneth Burke's pentad, Richard Young, Alton Becker, and Kenneth Pike's tagmemic system and its adaptation by Janice Lauer, which have surfaced in the past decade; and the multiple variations on Aristotle's topics from classical theory provide several structured techniques that stimulate students' thinking about subjects.

Finally, the way that students were advanced through the grades or forms of education in ancient Greece and Rome has some implications for modern rhetorical education. Students did not receive individual grades on each piece of writing as students do today. Nor did groups of students pass on to subsequent grades together. Early schools allowed individuals to progress at their own rate. Moreover, the classical instructors never expected two students to achieve exactly the same proficiency with an assignment. We are not optimistic or idealistic enough to believe that teachers should drop all grading in their writing classes. And we are painfully aware that individual instruction is difficult to facilitate in ridiculously overcrowded classes sanctioned by a system that promotes "mass production" and "standardization" of literacy skills. But teachers should be aware of activities, such as peer-editing, that can enhance students' abilities to deal with texts and encourage useful dialogue among students while freeing teachers from the burden of responding to every word each student writes.

THE RENAISSANCE COMMONPLACE BOOK— A CONTEMPORARY STUDENT'S WRITING JOURNAL

Perhaps the most intriguing classical teaching device is the commonplace book, which had its roots in rhetorical concepts of the Greeks and Romans but did not find its way into rhetorical education until the Renaissance. Commonplaces can be traced to two polar definitions of Arstotle's *topoi.* One use of the term *commonplace* derives from Aristotle's mention of the common topics as categories from which came definitions, divisions, and causes that can be applied to any subject to show where arguments can be found. These common topics seldom, if ever, comprised headings in commonplace books, however. Instead, they were considered to be analytic devices, related to the first stages of invention.

The second notion of the commonplace provides for an abundance of arguments about a subject and roughly corresponds to what Aristotle started to describe as specific topics. Under a variety of topic headings, Renaissance schoolboys recorded maxims, allusions, and quotations that helped to "make their case" in an oration in a variety of ways. Sister Marie Lechner points out in her *Renaissance Concepts of the Commonplace* that we cannot claim any direct development of these commonplace books in the Renaissance from the specific topics because Aristotle did not define those topics very completely.

A third historically related definition of commonplace is linked to the subject topics in the commonplace books in yet another way. Student essays, as well as public orations, needed to achieve a certain level of adornment as well as apt argumentation. Using a commonplace entry as a "speech within a speech" allowed the writer or speaker to amplify or malign a certain idea or person with a combination of common, acceptable, eloquent, and familiar phrases. Snippets in the commonplace book were simply transplanted to a certain section of a theme to produce the desired effect of making a point seem more or less important through the invocation of eloquent statements of others.

Commonplace books have been used only rarely in the contemporary classroom, and then they have been employed only to aid invention in the limited sense of developing arguments about an existing issue, not in generating topics or issues for writing or for work with other aspects of writing like style and organization. Students generally record information that their teacher has given them about "places" to find information and then gather details that they organize topically much as schoolboys did in the Renaissance. Because one concern in contemporary composition instruction is teaching students to find issues that interest them, what students today need from a commonplace book is a common space to jot down ideas and to list reasons why they believe these ideas are significant enough to them to write about. If they have a few developmental points in mind that they want to make, students can include those remarks in their explorations of the subject.

But the commonplace book serves students best as a place to do problem-finding, something that precedes what we typically call prewriting and that encourages students to explore a wide variety of issues before they settle on one. Used in this way, the commonplace book will allow students to write first impressions, feelings, responses, ravings, confusions, or disappointments about subjects while they are "hot" items in their minds. We want students to develop a pool of issues that they can explore in early drafts and prewriting and will be compelled to work out in their essays.

Larson's system of prewriting, for instance, helps students to explore their ideas about a subject and to structure their essays. Specifically, Larson asks students to conceive of their topic as a problem that needs to be solved. To introduce their issue to the audience (and themselves), students are asked to define as clearly as they can what the problem is and state why the problem is a problem. Then the students list the goals for solving the problem and rank them according to their priority in a good solution. The students write about as many viable solutions as they can, complicating their descriptions by weighing the advantages against the disadvantages of each solution. Finally, the students describe the best solution to the problem, taking into account the goals to be served. Even though Larson's heuristic can be applied in most writing situations and generates the most information of the heuristics without being overly complex, we still recommend providing students with *several* other techniques so that they can choose the ones that they feel most comfortable using.

Contemporary use of the commonplace book for purposes other than invention is virtually unexplored. What we would like to see in student writing is enrichment. Students, we believe, can develop an enriched command of language in two ways: by observation and by experimentation. The commonplace book can be useful for language development in both of these areas through a number of activities.

Imitation exercises, including language-option games in which students play with sentences, chunks, or words to give them different meanings in a particular context, and short imitations of writers working on similar problems might also consititute a section of the commonplace book. Students might, in addition, keep something similar to a process journal in one section of the commonplace book, where they record difficulties encountered while composing so that they can discuss them with other students or with the teacher at a later time. These records can sometimes be a useful index of problem patterns for teachers, helping them to plan activities that address a student's needs.

Additionally, teachers might ask students a number of questions about their writing processes for each assignment that could yield important information about planning further assignments and completing them successfully. We offer some samples as a starting point:

- When did you do most of the writing?
- Where did you do your writing for this assignment?
- How did you begin to think about this assignment?
- How would you paraphrase the assignment if you had to describe it to a friend who missed class?
- What was the most difficult part of this writing task?
- How would you compare your process for writing this assignment with the one that preceded it?

Finally, in another section, students might collect information they see about writing in the newspaper, magazines, or other classes that could be used for discussions about what writing does for us. They might test what other people say about writing against their own views as writers so that they come to see themselves as members of a community of literate individuals who are empowered through their language abilities.

A carefully planned commonplace book can be a powerful tool for building coherence among various other activities that we have described for the writing classroom. In this single book, what the teacher says about invention can be placed side-by-side with experiments in using heuristics and the very beginnings of the students' own essays. In another section of the same work, students will have information about and experiments with form and style. In yet another section, the work will talk about writing processes. And still other sections can address the ways in which writing can work for people.

The commonplace book can become, then, a student "work" book in which students can do some of the work of writing, and the writing that they do can be made to work for them. The commonplace book can bring different aspects of writing together for the student, much as textbooks are meant to do, but the advantage of the commonplace book is that it is student-generated, built from the needs and concerns of students about their own writing experiences.

Rhetorical education has been misconceived by its own masters and mistreated by outsiders who did not understand the extent of its value for at least two centuries. "Faults" in the foundation of composition teaching today cannot be blamed on once-prevailing features of its original surface which have been misshapened over time nor on those who reside in the now corrupted environment. But it is our responsibility as caretakers of this province to preserve what can be revived and made useful in the new climate and to cultivate new features that will enhance the land as it stands now, not only making it more attractive but also more productive and enduring.

Works Cited

Ad Herennium. Harry Caplan, trans. Loeb Classical Library. Cambridge, Mass.: Harvard University Press, 1954.

Aristotle. *The Rhetoric and Poetics of Aristotle.* W. Rhys Roberts and Ingram Bywater, trans. New York: Random House, 1954.

Bain, Alexander. *English Composition and Rhetoric.* New York: D. Appleton and Co., 1866.

Brinsley, John. *Ludus literarius: Or the Grammar Schoole.* E. T. Campagnac, ed. Liverpool: University of Liverpool Press, 1917.

Britton, James, et al. *The Development of Writing Abilities 11–18.* London: Macmillan, 1975.

Burke, Kenneth. *A Grammar of Motives.* Berkeley: University of California Press, 1969.

Clark, Donald Lemen. *John Milton at St. Paul's School: A Study of Ancient Rhetoric in English Renaissance Education.* Morningside Heights, N. Y.: Columbia University Press, 1948.

———. *Rhetoric in Greco-Roman Education.* Morningside Heights, N. Y.: Columbia University Press, 1957.

Hoole, Charles. *A New Discovery of the Old Art of Teaching Schoole in Four Small Treatises.* E. T. Campagnac, ed. Liverpool: University of Liverpool Press, 1913.

Isocrates. Antidosis. George Norton, trans. 2 vols. Loeb Classical Library. Cambridge, Mass.: Harvard University Press, 1929.

Knoblauch, C. H., and Lil Brannon. *Rhetorical Traditions and the Teaching of Writing.* Upper Montclair, N. J.: Boynton-Cook, 1984.

Larson, Richard. "Discovery Through Questioning: A Plan for Teaching Rhetorical Invention." *College English* 30 (November 1968): 126–34.

———. "Problem-Solving, Composing, and Liberal Education." *College English* 33 (March 1972): 628–35.

Lauer, Janice M., et al. *Four Worlds of Writing.* New York: Harper and Row, 1981.

Lechner, Sister Joan Marie. *Renaissance Concepts of the Commonplaces: A Historical Investigation of the General and Universal Ideas Used in all Argumentation and Persuasion with Special Emphasis on the Educational and Literary Tradition of the Sixteenth and Seventeenth Centuries.* New York: Pageant Press, 1962.

Marrou, H. I. *A History of Education in Antiquity.* George Lamb, trans. A Mentor Book. New York: New American Library, 1964.

Moffett, James. *Teaching the Universe of Discourse.* Boston: Houghton-Mifflin, 1968.

Price, Gayle B. "A Case for the Modern Commonplace Book." *Rhetoric and Composition: A Sourcebook for Teachers and Writers.* Richard L. Graves, ed. Upper Montclair, N. J.: Boynton-Cook, 1984.

Quintilian. *Institutio Oratoria.* H. E. Butler, trans. 3 vols. Loeb Classical Library. Cambridge, Mass.: Harvard University Press, 1920–22.

Vickers, Brian. *In Defense of Rhetoric.* Oxford: Clarendon Press, 1988.

Young, Richard, Alton Becker, and Kenneth Pike. *Rhetoric: Discovery and Change.* New York: Harcourt, Brace, and World, 1970.

Andrea A. Lunsford and Cheryl Glenn

12. *Rhetorical Theory and the Teaching of Writing*

RHETORIC AND THE DYNAMIC ELEMENTS OF WRITTEN COMMUNICATION*

For some 2,500 years, speakers and writers have relied—often unknowingly—on rhetorical theory to achieve successful persuasion and communication or to gain cooperation. "Rhetorical theory?"—it sounds formidable, perhaps even beside the point. Yet every teacher and every student works out of rhetorical theory, a conceptual framework that guides us in the dynamic process of making meaning, sustains our classroom writing practices, and informs our textbooks.

Long the staple of communication theory, *the "communication triangle,"* comprising *sender, receiver,* and *message,* has expanded to incorporate *universe* (or *context*), the fourth component of this rhetorical set of interrelationships. These four elements of meaning not only guide teachers in their teaching choices but also guide writers in their writing choices, choices based on (1) their own values; (2) those of their receivers; (3) the possible range of messages; and (4) the nature of the universe, of reality.

Aristotle may have been the first to separate the rhetorical elements (the persuasive appeals) of communication when he wrote that the true constituents of the art of rhetoric are *ethos,* the appeals exerted by the speaker (the sender); *pathos,* the appeals to the emotions or values of the audience (the receiver); and *logos,* the appeals to

* We thank Gerald Nelms for helping with the citations and bibliography. We are also grateful to Jon Olson and Jamie Barlowe Kayes, whose sensible suggestions and supportive criticism helped us rewrite parts of the manuscript.

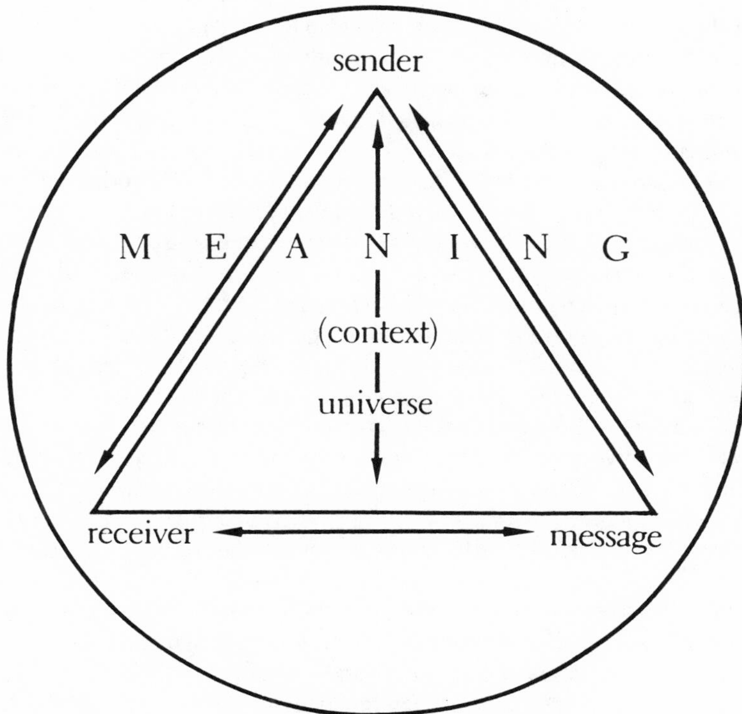

Figure 12.1

reason of the message itself—with all appeals reflecting or affecting the *universe* (*Rhetoric,* I.2.1356c). And his definition of *rhetoric* as "the faculty of observing in any given case the available means of persuasion" (I.2.1355b) has undergirded all rhetorical theory thenceforth, providing scholars, critics, and rhetoricians a dependable and expandable base for their own contributions to rhetorical theory and practice.

In his landmark *Theory of Discourse* (1971), James Kinneavy relates Aristotle's rhetorical triangle to fields other than rhetoric (such as literary theory, anthropology, communication, and semiotics), showing, in each case, just how *any* communication can emphasize one particular element of the triangle. As with Aristotle, who demonstrates three purposeful discourses, Kinneavy locates the variable aims of discourse in its emphatic triangulation of author, audience, universe, or in its reflexive emphasis on itself, the text.

Kinneavy refers to the work of literary theorist M. H. Abrams (310–48), whose *The Mirror and the Lamp* posits the four elements in the total situation of a work of art: the *work,* the artistic product itself; the *artist,* who produced the work; the *universe,* the subject of the work itself or from which the work is derived; and the *audience* to whom the work is addressed or made available (6–7). Although a work of artistic literature itself always implicitly assumes an author, an audience, a universe, the four coordinates of the work vary in significance according to the theory in which they occur: mimetic theories emphasize art's imitation of the *universe;* pragmatic theories propound art's effect on the *audience,* on getting things done; expressive theories center on the *artist* as cause and criterion of art; and objective theories deal with the *work of art* itself, in parts and in the mutual relations of its parts.

Kinneavy also refers to the work of anthropological linguists, who, similar to literary theorists, evaluate language in terms of its aims: as verbal gesture, *interjectional;* as imitation of reality, *representational;* as a pragmatic symbol for getting things done, *ultilitarian;* and as expression of the sender, poetic or *play* (51–52). The communication theorists, too, refer to language aims: informative, exploratory, instrumental, and emotive—aims that stress the importance of one rhetorical element (53–54). Communications call the elements *encoder, decoder, signal,* and *reality,* and they connect informative communication with the signal or text; exploratory with reality or the universe; instrumental with the decoder or the audience; and emotive with the encoder or the author.

Eminent rhetorician Kenneth Burke extended the grammar of rhetoric to encompass five elements, expanding the rhetorical triangle to a pentad: agent (who?), action (what?), scene (where and when?), purpose (why?), and agency (how?) (*A Grammar of Motives*). Not intended as a heuristic, an aid to discovery or invention, Burke's pentad nonetheless supplies writers and readers with a method for establishing the focus of a written or spoken text. His theory of dramatism, focusing as it does on the ratios between the elements in the pentad, calls attention to the ways these representative terms are linked. Dramatism is a theory of action that breathes life into a text, humanizing the action. When a person's acts are to be interpreted in terms of the scene in which he or she is acting (as in *Robinson Crusoe, Lord of the Flies,* or *Riddley Walker,* for example), his or her behavior falls under the heading of a "scene-act ratio." In *Lord of the Flies,* both Ralph and Jack, leaders of opposing factions, "act" in reaction to the "scene": they are stranded on a desert island without the traditional protection of society. Yet, within the scene-act ratio, falls a range of behavior that must again be evaluated according to the "agent-act ratio"—what is the correspondence between a person's character and action and between the action and the circumstances? Well-adjusted, optimistic, and athletic Ralph "naturally" acts out the desire for civilization, while Jack, the cruel and ugly bully, acts out the feral desire for mastery by intimidation and violence. Other dynamic relationships, other ratios, disclose still other features of human relations, behavior, and motives. Yet no matter how we look at texts, no matter which theorist's game we play, we always seem to swing around the poles of the original rhetorical triangle.

Like Burke, Wayne Booth also expands the notion of the rhetorical triangle. Burke uses his pentad retrospectively to analyze the motives of language (human) actions—texts or speeches—while Booth stresses the persuasive potential of his triangulated proofs: *ethos,* which is situated in the sender; *pathos,* in the receiver; and *logos,* in the text itself (*Modern Dogma and the Rhetoric of Assent* 144–64). Both their analytical frameworks can be used two ways: (1) as systems or frames on which to build a text; and (2) as systems of analysis for already-completed texts. Booth's rhetorical triangle provides a framework that can be used to analyze a text, for it is the dynamic interaction of *ethos, pathos,* and *logos* that creates that text. To understand the *meaning* of an already-completed text, however, Booth would examine the content, analyze the audience that is implied in the text, and recover the attitudes expressed by the implied author. The total act of communication must be examined in order to recover the ethos/character of the speaker, authorial attitude and intention, and voice—vital elements, resonant with attitude, that create a text. Burke, too, realized the importance of "attitude" and often talked of adding it to his dramatistic pentad (thereby transforming it into a hexad).

In "The Rhetorical Stance," Booth's message to teachers, he posits a concept of rhetoric that can support an undergraduate curriculum:

> The common ingredient that I find in all of the writing I admire . . . is something that I shall reluctantly call the rhetorical stance, a stance which depends on discovering and maintaining in any writing situation a proper balance among the three elements that are at work in any communicative effort: the available arguments about the subject itself, the interests and peculiarities of the audience, and the voice, the implied character, of the speaker. (27)

Like Aristotle, Booth posits a carefully balanced tripartite division of rhetorical appeals. Ever mindful of the audience being addressed, Booth would have us—as writers—strike such a balance to have a clear relationship with our reader(s) and our texts. As readers, Booth would have us keep this triangulation in mind, too, searching for and analyzing ethical, emotional, and logical appeals as we read. Otherwise, he warns, our reading of the text will be at best insensitive, at worst inaccurate. In *Lord of the Flies,* we analyze Ralph's and Jack's speeches for persuasive appeals, just as we analyze the appeals imbricating the omniscient author's narrative. Similar to Aristotle, who believed the ethical appeal to be the most effective, Booth wants speakers and writers—teachers and students alike—to examine their assumptions and to inspect the reasons for their strong commitments. Booth would like to reintroduce into education a strong concept of *ethos,* the dynamic start of persuasive communication: in balancing these three elements, the *logos* may determine how far we extend our *ethos* or what *ethos* we use or how much *pathos.* Booth goes on to say that "it is this balance, this rhetorical stance, difficult as it is to describe, that is our main goal as teachers of rhetoric" (27).

The traditional, stable, tricornered dynamics of written communication have been recently expanded. Gone is the notion of one speaker, one listener, one message—one voice. Instead, such univocal discourse has been replaced with many speakers, many listeners, many messages. In most communications, people are both speakers *and* listeners, or there is a multitude of listeners for one speaker; and the message is constantly affected by and adjusted to both speakers and listeners. To complicate communication even further, each listener interprets each speaker differently, even if only one speaker exists. Thus, just as the speaker and listener cannot be univocal, neither can the interpretation. Although the resulting icon is no longer the "rhetorical triangle," the triangular dynamics remain, for the figure becomes one of equilateral triangles with varying but concentric orientations. The familiar triangle has been embellished, but the original three key terms—speaker, listener, subject—remain.

WHAT RESEARCH TELLS US ABOUT THE ELEMENTS OF WRITTEN COMMUNICATION

The revival of rhetorical theory witnessed during the last twenty-five years has reacquainted teachers with the primary elements of the rhetorical tradition—ethos/ audience; logos/text—and with the way those elements have been played out in the canon of rhetoric. Although they might not be familiar with the actual names, most teachers are familiar with concepts forming the canons of rhetoric: invention, arrangement, style, memory, and delivery. While this formulation is in some sense reductive, it nevertheless provides a useful framework for investigating the recent contributions of rhetorical theory to the teaching of writing. Close attention to the *writer* during this time has resulted in much important work that attempts essentially to answer this twofold question: where do a writer's ideas come from and how are such ideas formulated into writing? Such a question demands a new focus on *invention,* the first canon of rhetoric, and has led in two provocative and profitable directions. The first, represented in the work of Richard Young, Janice Lauer, and Richard Larson (to name only a very few) aims at deriving heuristic procedures or systematic strategies that will aid students in discovering and generating ideas about which they might write. Such strategies may be as simple as prompting students to generate ideas about a subject by asking—who, what, when, where, why, and how—the traditional "journalistic formula" mentioned above. Or they can be as complex as the nine-cell matrix presented in Young, Becker, and Pike's *Rhetoric: Discovery and Change.* Essentially, this heuristic asks student writers to look at any subject from nine different perspectives. For example, a student writing about a campus strike might look at it first as a "happening" frozen in time and space, or as the result of a complex set of causes, or as a *cause* of some other effects, or as one tiny part of a larger economic pattern. Looking at the subject in such different ways "loosens up" mental muscles and jogs writers out of unidimensional or tunnel-vision views of a subject.

We see this interest in procedural heuristics as related theoretically to the work of researchers interested in cognition. Linda Flower and coauthor John Hayes are best known for their studies of writers' talk-aloud protocols, tape-recorded documents that catch a writer's *thoughts* about writing while the writing is actually in progress. As any methodology is bound to be, such methodology is flawed, but it *has* provided a fascinating "window on writers' minds," to use Flower's descriptive phrase. Stephen Witte has recently built on the work of Flower and Hayes in order to study what he calls a writer's "pretext," a writer's "trial locution that is produced in the mind, stored in the writer's memory, and sometimes manipulated mentally prior to being transcribed as written text" (397). Other researchers have attempted to map the relationship of affective factors to a writer's "invention": John Daly, in terms of writing apprehension, and Mike Rose, in terms of writer's block. All of this research aims to help teachers understand the rich, diverse, complex, and largely *invisible* processes student writers go through in writing.

But a renewed interest in student writers has led in another powerful direction as well, notably in the work of Ken Macrorie and, more pervasively, of Peter Elbow. Elbow is interested in how writers establish unique voices, in how they realize individual selves in discourse, and his work with students presents dramatic evidence of such activity. In a series of very influential books (*Writing without Teachers, Writing with Power, Embracing Contraries*), Elbow has focused on how writers come to know themselves—and then share those selves with others.

The researchers and teachers we have been surveying here differ in many ways, but their work is all aimed primarily at that point of the rhetorical triangle that focuses on the writer and his or her powers of invention. They want to know what makes writers tick—and how teachers can help writers "tick" most effectively.

If we shift the focus of our discussion from writer to *text,* we also find that rhetorical theory has much to offer the teacher of writing. Students are often puzzled when teachers do not "get the meaning" they intend. Rhetorical theory helps us explain why such miscommunication takes place and suggests powerful ways to avoid it. One of the simplest to use with students is I. A. Richard's own version of the rhetorical triangle:

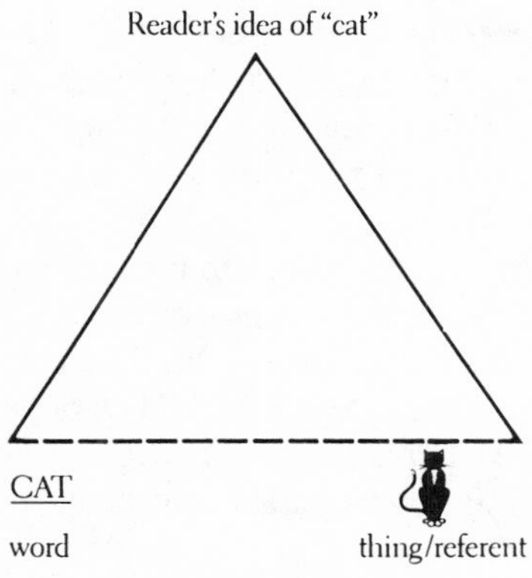

Figure 12.2

Richards argues that no direct relationship exists between a word—a set of black marks on a page—and its referent in the world (*The Meaning of Meaning* 1–13). That is to say, the meaning of *cat* is not inherent in the little squiggles we call letters nor in the furry, purry pet we might have. Rather, meaning arises in the perceivers—in people—as they filter the linguistic signal *cat* through all their experience with both word and thing. So *cat* might well mean one thing to someone who adores cats and something quite different to someone who was, as a child, badly scratched by a cat.

Richards uses another principle to help us understand how we derive meaning from tests. He calls this principle *interinanimation of words,* which simply means that any one word is strongly affected by other words around it (*Philosophy of Rhetoric* 47–66). The word *love,* for instance, suggests one meaning when connected to the words *grandparent* and *grandchild,* another when connected to *husband* and *wife,* and yet another when connected to a business tycoon and his or her self-image. Students can put Richard's principle to use by examining a text closely for the ways its words interinanimate one another. And teachers can use the principle of interinanimation to show students that we are all very much *what we say,* that our words work together (interinanimate) to create the people we are, with our individual values, prejudices, and so on.

Three other concepts used by modern rhetorical theorists may help students and teachers get inside the intricacies of any text. Richard Weaver provides one set, what he calls *ultimate* or *God terms* and *Devil terms,* to indicate those words or concepts that represent something we will make sacrifices for (87–112). In the 1950s, Weaver hypothesized that *Americanism, progress,* and *science* served as God terms, large concepts that most people held very dear. He went on to suggest that God or Devil terms establish hierarchical relationships in texts—that is, that many other related terms usually clustered under them. Identifying such central terms and then mapping ralated clusters of terms can help students get at complex meanings in texts.

Burke suggests that we look at a text (or any discourse, spoken or written) as a *terministic screen* ("Terministic Screen" 59 ff). If we think of a text as a very fine-meshed screen, with every point connected to every other point, what Burke has in mind becomes apparent. The "screen" of the text directs our attention in certain ways, selecting some points for emphasis, deflecting others. And the screen is made up not of wire, but of words or *terms.* Burke challenges us to trace all the minute interstitial connections among terms in any text/screen as a means of constructing meaning.

One other key principle deserves our attention in discussing rhetorical theory and texts: intertextuality, which refers to a principle very similar to those we have been discussing. Most simply, intertextuality denotes the great conversation among texts, the way texts refer or allude to one another, build on or parody one another, revolve around one another. The Mel Brooks movie *Young Frankenstein,* for instance, is part of an elaborate and extensive conversation stretching back through countless other movies to Mary Shelley's novel (with its subtitle *The Modern Prometheus*) to many poems and plays and mythical accounts of Prometheus, to the creation of Adam in the Bible—or *forward* to the contemporary debate over genetic engineering and our ability to create life. Introducing students to this principle of intertextuality allows them to enter this great conversation and provides them with an effective method for probing textual meaning.

The theorists we have been discussing offer ways to see the "big picture" of a text; they deal with the macrostructure element of the second canon of rhetoric, the *arrangement* of argument. But rhetorical theory offers help on the microstructures of the "little picture" as well. This tradition of research, which focuses on organization, on the relationship between form and function, is extensive and complex. Here we will cite two rhetoricians whose work seems most helpful for the teaching of writing. Many readers of this book already might be familiar with the first, Francis Christensen. In a series of essays, Christensen demonstrated a way to map sentences and paragraphs according to levels of generality and modification. *Periodic* sentences and paragraphs are those that delay or postpone announcing the general main clause/topic until the very end, leading into the topic with supporting or modifying details ("A Generative Rhetoric of the Sentence" 155–56). This kind of structure forces a reader to hold the subject in mind until the very end and keeps syntactic tension high. In the hands of skilled writers, periodic structures can keep readers alert for what is to come and make the main idea, when it finally does appear, all the more impressive.

Although structures using various degrees of periodicity can be very effective in challenging and interesting readers, they do not constitute the most freqently used pattern in modern English. Rather, the *cumulative* structure, which adds details after the main clause or announcement of the topic, is the more dominant. Christensen writes: "The main clause, which may or may not have a sentence modifier before it, advances the discussion; but the additions move backwards, as in this clause, to modify the statement of the main clause or more often to explicate it or exemplify it, so that the sentence has a flowing and ebbing movement, advancing to a new position and then pausing to consolidate it, leaping and lingering as the popular ballad does" (156). Because the main clause/topic is presented at or near the beginning of the sentence/paragraph, cumulative structures do not require readers to hold the subject in suspense until the end. In one sense, then, these structures may be easier to read than periodic ones, yet the skillful writer can position the most important piece of information at the end. As with all sentence patterns, however, the cumulative sentence can be used effectively or, as in the following example, ineffectively: "The cumulative sentence in unskilled hands is unsteady, allowing a writer to ramble on, adding modifier after modifier, until the reader is almost overwhelmed, because the writer's central idea is lost."

Using exclusively periodic or cumulative structures, of course, would be monotonous. And so the best writers mingle structures—short and long, periodic and cumulative—although never forgetting that the most important ideas naturally deserve the most prominent positions. Our own students can easily test the structures of others' as well as their own texts, relating purpose to structure, and can learn to balance their own prose with purposeful and effective movement between general and specific information.

More recently, Richard Coe has elaborated and extended the work of Christensen, moving toward what he calls a *grammar of passages*. In his monograph by the same name, Coe takes the traditional syntactic relationships between form and function—coordinate, subordinate, and superordinate—and subdivides them further: (1) coordination: contrasting, contradicting, conjoining, and repeating on the same level of generality; (2) subordination: defining, exemplifying, giving reasons, deducing (deductive conclusion), explaining (making plain by restating more specifically), qualifying; and (3) superordination: drawing conclusion, generalizing (making an inductive inference), commenting on a previously stated proposition (32–33). Then Coe goes on to develop a system of mapping these relationships. This syntactical system has been tested extensively with student writers, in classes ranging from ESL to technical writing, to basic writing, to advanced composition, with dramatic results. Students learn to "map" their own texts and thereby have a means of deciding whether those texts are coherent, whether they "make sense."

But what of the third angle of the rhetorical triangle—that pointing to *audience* and *context?* Does rhetorical theory offer any insights into these crucial elements in communication? Of course. As a discipline, rhetoric has always been intensely interested in the effects a writer's intentions, words, texts, have *on people* in varying situations. That is to say, taking a "rhetorical stance" always places us in a full context. In this regard, rhetorical theory has helped us learn about the psychology of readers (or listeners, interpreters, responders), from Aristotle's discussion of how different types of people react to different subjects and Plato's elegant oration on souls, to contemporary persuasion theorists (Petty, Brock, and Ostrom) on the one hand and reader-oriented researchers and critics (Rosenblatt, Bleich, and Iser) on the other.

What this research tells us as teachers of writing is simply this: the processes of reading and responding to texts are at least as complex as those of writing a text; that all readers build up frameworks (called schemata), which they use to make sense as they read; that such frameworks are affected both by everything we already know and by what we are (gender, for example, exerts powerful influence on patterns of interpretation and response). As teachers, we must help students understand and theorize about their own such patterns. Doing so leads to the second major point we want to make here. That is, we can often understand our own patterns of response by seeing them *in context,* as related to others' responses and as part of a large social process aimed at negotiating and constructing meaning. If intertextuality is a coin, this is its flip side—interreaderability—the fully contextualized, multiple voices out of which we forge an understanding of texts.

PEDAGOGICAL IMPLICATIONS OF A WRITTEN COMMUNICATION

A rhetoric of written communication demands a dynamic balancing of speaker, listener, subject (of *ethos, pathos, logos*). And when a teacher introduces these elements into the writing classroom, he or she can expect learning to emerge. The interdependency of these elements creates galvanic tension, in terms not only of the rhetorical elements themselves, but also of the students, teacher, and texts.

The pedagogical implications for teachers are manifold, most prominent being that they must learn to share authority, thereby enabling students to experience, create, and evaluate their own and others' texts. One of the best ways teachers can share responsibility for learning is to provide "demonstrations," occasions for active learning for their students. In the terms of education researcher Frank Smith, demonstrations provide students with opportunities to become so engaged that they really teach themselves; they forget that they are learning and take an active role in their own learning.

In fact, writing teachers can most easily provide students with demonstrations by adjusting writing assignments, making them (to use an overused term) "relevant" to the students' lives. Often, meaningful writing assignments are merely those that provide students with information on their intended audience, their purpose for writing, and the context of the communication—information that encourages students to harness the dynamics of the rhetorical triangle. Other teachers provide demonstrations by building their syllabi on a theme, such as "education" (cf. Bartholomae and Petrosky; Lunsford). A teacher in an open admissions college provided his students with demonstrations by building a syllabus on "work." Urging his students to meet in small groups, to speak out, to read and respond to one another's writing, to expect concrete details and supporting observations, this teacher watched as his class of low-paid, blue-collar manual workers reinvented their daily lives, sharing their experiences, critically analyzing their situations, and writing persuasively and feelingly about their lives. No longer was learning the retrieval and transmission of static information—from the teacher's head to the students'. Rather, learning became the dynamic interactions of the students, a demonstration of their abilities to discover and create, construe and communicate their own knowledge. Once they realized their own rhetorical stance, the values and attitudes of their intended audience, and the importance of their message, their rhetorical triangles were balanced. In this case, choice of writing assignments indicated the teacher's willingness to share responsibility for classroom learning.

Hence, such a classroom transforms itself from uni- to polyvocal. The original rhetorical triangle, weighted fully on the teacher/speaker side, becomes a series of phase-shift rotations, rhetorical triangles that constantly achieve, lose, and reestablish rhetorical balance. Each shift, a fusion of rhetoric and dialectic, is determined by whose paper is being featured, who is serving as author, who is serving as audience, and how the in-draft text is being affected and effected by the speaker and audience. And ultimately, that original triangle, in recreating itself, begins to round out and resemble an expanded circular universe of discourse.

To make the polyvocal, rhetorical classroom "work," students, too, must learn to share responsibility for their learning, and to rely no longer solely on their teacher for grades, knowledge, approval, or ego gratification. What might be initially perceived as instability will soon be seen for what it is—dynamics. Once students begin to take advantage of these classroom dynamics—teacher and students alike working as sharers and evaluators—they will realize the potential for their own written communication. No longer will they be content to serve as repositories for their teacher's knowledge, to write *for* and *to* only their teachers, to remain silent. Yet often and understandably, just transferring their allegiance from their teacher to their peers is difficult, accustomed as they are to years of passive learning. Inured as teachers are to years of one-way teaching and nearly total responsibility for learning (and teaching), many find relief in newly shared allegiance. Students need to know that in the rhetorical classroom, their teachers are willing to share their work, their responsibility, even their authority.

In the rhetorical writing classroom, students broaden their intended audience from the teacher-evaluator to include their peers, carefully considering the responses and evaluations of those peers, perhaps more than they did those of their teachers. Many students choose to respond orally and in writing to classroom, in-draft texts and to participate in the final evaluation of themselves and their peers. Peers create an actual audience and often a reason for writing, for they provide response—what Elbow calls "the main experience that makes people want to write more" (130). In *Writing without Teachers,* Elbow writes about one student's thrill of working with her peers: "Her words got through to the readers. She sent words out into the darkness and heard someone shout back. This made her want to do it again, and this is probably the most powerful thing that makes people improve their writing" (130).

When students are involved in one another's writings, serving as senders and receivers of communication, as questioners of purpose, as judges of *ethos, pathos,* and *logos,* as refiners of style and tone, when they are respectfully attentive of one another's *author*-ity, when students have the opportunity to question responses to their drafts *as they draft,* when they coach as they are being coached, then they are indeed sharing the responsibility for their own learning and incorporating in their learning the dynamics of rhetorical theory.

The implications for a rhetoric of written communication go beyond those for the teacher and students, however, to affect the very physical structure of the classroom itself. Always, or so it seems, students have sat in neat rows of nailed-down desks, discouraged from making so much as eye contact with their peers, asked to write in solitude. But as teachers and students begin to use rhetorical theory, begin to see that senders need the responses of receivers, that the universe, the "out there," plays an integral part in communication, and that messages are colored by all the elements in the rhetorical triangle, they will be unable to work in the traditional classroom environment. They will want tables or moveable desks so they can sit and work together. They will want to talk on the phone or through their computers both during and after school. They need to be together. And they need time.

Gone should be the days when students are asked to complete their writing in forty-eight minutes or to evaluate the work of their groups in forty-eight minutes. Gone should be the days when one draft—the first and final—is handed in for an unchangeable grade. Many schools, in fact, are moving toward the portfolio method of evaluation, which encourages students to gather their best revisions for one end-of-the-term grade.[1] Thoughtful writing and thoughtful responding take time, time foı planning, thinking, drafting, responding, revising, and polishing. Hence, classrooms themselves must be designed in response to the evolution of classroom practices as well as classroom schedules.

ISSUES RAISED BY A RHETORIC OF WRITTEN COMMUNICATION

Teachers and students committed to examining the dynamic relationship among writers, audiences, texts, and contexts will face a number of important issues, foremost among them the complex question of ethics and language use. If we are not so much what we *eat* as what we say or write, if as Jacques Derrida claims, we don't write language so much as language *writes us,* then words can never be "mere" words again. Instead words are, to use Burke's term, symbolic *acts* (*Language as Symbolic Action*); as Weaver says, a speaker's words have *consequences,* and these consequences affect other people, texts, and contexts (221 ff). As language users, we thus must be responsible for our words, must take the responsibility for examining our own and others' language and seeing how well, how truly, it represents the speaker. We can do so playfully, through parody or spoofing, or we can do so most seriously, as in an analysis of the consequences of political doublespeak. But we—teachers and students alike—must carry out such analyses consistently and rigorously.

Once students grasp this principle of analytic responsibility, they become rhetors. They see writing and reading not as boring school-bound drills or as ways of packaging static information, but as ways of creating and recreating themselves through and with others, as a student reported during a recent evaluation of one of our courses:

> When we first started this class, I couldn't *imagine* what you meant by our being rhetoricians, getting rhetorical stances of our own. What's all this, I thought? You're the teacher. You know a whole lot of stuff, and you better just *tell* it to us. Now I know that you really do know a lot of stuff, more even than I thought. But that's not what matters. What matters is what I know. And now I know that I'm making what I know in language, forming, transforming, and reforming myself with other people. What I know is we are all of us learners in progress. Even you! So—*wish me luck.*

Teachers, of course, are the ones who develop and nurture such an atmosphere, who set the terms within which an ethos of the classroom emerges. Building such an atmosphere implies that the teacher becomes a member/participant of the class, providing questions, tasks, and situations that will allow the class to experience what it means not to *reveal* knowledge but to *construct* it, to be learners-in-progress. This role is a demanding one, far more so than traditional teacherly roles have been.

In the final analysis, a rhetorical perspective on the teaching of writing pushes us outside our private selves, beyond our solitary teacherly or writerly desks, to a realization of the ways in which we all use language to create—or destroy—communities, societies, worlds. The writing classroom is one such world. Rhetorical theory provides us, together with our students, with the means of making that world, one that is rich in diversity, complex in meaning, and full of all the life our blended voices can give it.

Note

1. The portfolio method of assessment has been most thoroughly documented and argued for by Peter Elbow of University of Massachusetts–Amherst. The largest school with plans to adopt a portfolio method of assessment is University of Minnesota, which, beginning in 1990, plans to use portfolios for evaluation in introductory composition as well as for promotion.

Works Cited

Abrams, M. H. *The Mirror and the Lamp: Romantic Theory and the Critical Tradition.* New York: Oxford University Press, 1953.

Aristotle. *The Rhetoric and the Poetics of Aristotle.* W. Rhys Roberts, trans. New York: Modern Library, 1984.

Bartholomae, David, and Anthony Petrosky. *Facts, Artifacts, and Counterfacts: Theory and Method for a Reading and Writing Course.* Upper Montclair, N. J.: Boynton Cook, 1986.

Bleich, David. *Subjective Criticism.* Baltimore, Md.: John Hopkins University Press, 1978.

———. *Readings and Feelings: An Introduction to Subjective Criticism.* Urbana, Ill.: National Council of Teachers of English, 1975.

———. "The Subjective Character of Critical Interpretation." *College English* 36 (1975): 739–55.

Booth, Wayne C. *Modern Dogma and the Rhetoric of Assent.* Chicago: University of Chicago Press, 1974.

———. "The Rhetorical Stance." *Now Don't Try to Reason with Me: Essays and Ironics for a Credulous Age.* Chicago: University of Chicago Press, 1970.

Bruffee, Kenneth. "Collaborative Learning and the 'Conversation of Mankind.'" *College English* 46 (1984): 635–52.

———. "The Brooklyn Plan: Attaining Intellectual Growth through Peer-Group Tutoring." *Liberal Education* 64 (1978): 447–69.

———. "Collaborative Learning: Some Practical Models." *College English* 34 (1973): 634–43.

Burke, Kenneth. *A Grammar of Motives,* Cleveland: World, 1962.

———. *A Rhetoric Motives.* Cleveland: World, 1962.

———. "Terministic Screens." *Language as Symbolic Action.* Berkeley: University of California Press, 1966.

Christensen, Francis, "A Generative Rhetoric of the Sentence." 14 (1963): 155–61.

———. "A Generative Rhetoric of the Paragraph." *College Composition and Communication* 16 (1968):144–56.

Coe, Richard. *A Grammar of Passages.* Carbondale: Southern Illinois University Press, 1987.

Daly, John. "The Effects of Writing Apprehension on Message Encoding." *Journalism Quarterly* 54 (1977): 566–72.

———. "Writing Apprehension and Writing Competency." *Journal of Educational Research* 72 (1978): 10–14

Derrida, Jacques. *Of Grammatology.* Gayatri Chakrovorty Spivak, trans. Baltimore, Md.: Johns Hopkins University Press, 1974.

Ede, Lisa S., and Andrea A. Lunsford. "Collaborative Learning: Lessons from the World of Work." *Writing Program Administration* 9 (1986): 17–26.

———. "Let Them Write—Together." *English Quarterly* 18 (1985: 119–27.

———. "Why Write . . . Together?" *Rhetoric Review* 1 (1983): 150–57.

Elbow, Peter. *Embracing Contraries.* New York: Oxford University Press, 1986.

———. *Writing with Power.* New York: Oxford University Press, 1981.

———. *Writing without Teachers.* New York: Oxford University Press, 1973.

Flower, Linda, and John R. Hayes. "Uncovering Cognitive Processes in Writing: An Introduction to Protocol Analysis." *Research on Writing.* P. Mosenthal, S. Walmsley, and L. Tamor, eds. London: Longmans, 1982. 207–20.

Haring-Smith, Tori, ed. *A Guide to Writing Programs, Writing Centers, Peer-Tutoring Programs, and Writing Across the Curriculum.* Glenview, Ill.: Scott, 1985.

Iser, Wolfgang. *The Act of Reading: A Theory of Aesthetic Response.* Baltimore, Md.: Johns Hopkins University Press, 1974.

———. *The Implied Reader.* Baltimore, Md.: Johns Hopkins University Press, 1975.

Kinneavy, James L. *A Theory of Discourse.* New York: Norton, 1971.

Larson, Richard L. "Discovery through Questioning: A Plan for Teaching Rhetorical Invention." *College English* 30 (1968): 126–34.

Lauer, Janice. "Heuristics and Composition." *College Composition and Communication* 21 (1970): 396–404.

Lunsford, Andrea A. "Assignments for Basic Writers: Unresolved Issues and Needed Research." *Journal of Basic Writing* 5 (1986): 87–99.

Miller, Susan. "The Student's Reader is Always a Fiction." *Journal of Advanced Composition* 5 (1984): 15–29.

Morgan, Meg, Nancy Allen, Teresa Moore, Dianne Atkinson, and Craig Snow. "Collaborative Writing in the Classroom." *The Bulletin* (September 1987): 20–26.

Ogden, C. K., and I. A. Richards. *The Meaning of Meaning: A Study of the Influences of Language upon Thought and of the Science of Symbolism.* New York: Harcourt, 1936.

Petty, Richard E., and Thomas M. Ostrom, and Timothy Brock, eds. *Cognitive Responses in Persuasion.* Hillsdale, N. J.: Earlbaum, 1981.

Richards, I. A. *The Philosophy of Rhetoric.* New York: Oxford University Press, 1936.

Rose, Mike. *Writer's Block: The Cognitive Dimension.* Carbondale: Southern Illinois University Press, 1984.

Rosenblatt, Louise. *Literature as Exploration.* 3d ed. New York: Barnes and Noble, 1976.

———. *The Reader, the Text, the Poem: The Transactional Theory of the Literary Work.* Carbondale: Southern Illinois University Press, 1978.

Smith, Frank. "Research Update: Demonstrations, Engagements, and Sensitivity—A Revised Approach to Language Learning." *Language Arts* 68 (1981): 103–12.

Weaver, Richard M. *Language Is Sermonic: Richard M. Weaver on the Nature of Rhetoric.* Richard L. Johannesen, Rennard Strickland, and Ralph T. Eubanks, eds. Baton Rouge: Louisiana State University Press, 1970.

Witte, Stephen. "Pre-Text and Composing." *College Composition and Communication* 38 (1987): 397–425.

Young, Richard E., Alton L. Becker, and Kenneth L. Pike. *Rhetoric: Discovery and Change.* New York: Harcourt Brace, 1970.

Cynthia L. Selfe

13. English Teachers and the Humanization of Computers: Networking Communities of Readers and Writers

The move to integrate computers into English courriculum, a task that members of our profession have just begun to undertake during the last several years, has encouraged many teachers to rethink and then revise the theoretical and pedagogical premises upon which they base their classes, their research, and their curricula. In this sense, computers have been an exciting catalyst for some of the most productive work now happening in the field of English composition. Computer networks, for example, have given teachers new ways to invite readers and writers in different geographic areas to exchange texts and ideas (Ludtke), to work effectively with students outside of traditional classroom settings (Hiltz; Spitzer), and to encourage collaboration among students (Selfe and Wahlstrom, "An Emerging Rhetoric").

However, as many teachers can also attest, the rapid growth of computers in our profession has led to challenging problems as well. In our rush to buy equipment, establish computer-supported writing laboratories, and teach computer-supported writing classes, we have often been in too much of a hurry. We have not made time to share our pedagogical experiences, to discuss how the integration of computers might change the way we design our courses, teach them, and evaluate their success. Given this lack of shared knowledge, then, we all have to admit to shooting, or teaching, "from the hip" at times in our computer-supported writing classes.

Although such teaching glows with a pioneering spirit that can inject vigor and excitement into the classroom, it remains atheoretical, untested, unexamined, and less than systematic. The way we have set up our computer-supported writing classrooms, the strategies we have used to teach within these facilities, and the ways in which our colleges and universities have prepared prospective English teachers to enter computer-supported classrooms have all grown out of isolated experiments and informal observations. In the next five years, we shall face a most important challenge: that of moving beyond initial exploratory work with computers to projects that provide documented pedagogical strategies; systematic, theoretically based inquiry; and sound, accessible approaches to teacher education.

One of the most promising approaches for beginning this journey involves the use of computer networks and computer-based networking strategies. With these computer tools, English teachers can create curricula that incorporate process-based approaches to composition and that encourage the vision of writing and reading as socially constructed acts that involve making meaning in concert with other human beings in light of personal experiences.

To help readers understand why and then how computer networks and computer-based networking strategies can help English teachers, this chapter addresses both the theory and practice of using computer networks in composition classrooms. The first half of the chapter suggests how computer-based networking strategies can help solve problems of English composition instruction. It discusses networking within the framework of currently accepted theory and research in literacy that stresses process-based writing and reading instruction in richly contextual classroom settings that value social and linguistic interaction. The second half provides readers with five practical suggestions about how to proceed with the task of integrating computer networks or networking strategies into their own academic sites.

THE VALUE OF COMPUTER NETWORKS: PROCESS-BASED COMPOSITION AND THE SOCIAL VIEW OF LANGUAGE PRODUCTION

To understand why computer networks and networking strategies can be so valuable in writing- and reading-intensive classrooms, teachers need only to examine briefly the current state of literacy studies. Over the last two decades, our understanding of writing and reading processes and the social contexts in which these processes occur has changed dramatically and has encouraged us to see writing- and reading-intensive classrooms from new perspectives.

One major change in the way we now think of literacy studies involves our understanding of the dynamic processes by which meaning is constructed. We have come to value a process-based approach to literacy in which attention is paid to the complexly recursive processes by which students compose text and to the ways in which human beings read and make meaning from texts. English composition teachers, for instance, are no longer satisfied with evaluating the end products of a writing task; rather they feel an obligation to teach students a range of rhetorical and cognitive strategies that they can draw on in solving writing problems of various kinds (Emig; Flower and Hayes; Pianko). In a similar movement, teachers of literature and reading no longer talk of a single interpretation of text in the style of new critics but rather work with students as they make their own meaning from texts by interpreting the content of the printed page in light of their purposes, their personal experiences, and their needs (Berthoff; Bleich; Tierney and Pearson).

Our profession has also begun to see the importance of the social context in which literate individuals create meaning through reading and writing. We now think of communication as happening within the context of discourse communities that have their own rhetorical and text-based conventions (Berkenkotter; Fish; Swales). We talk to students of the importance of analyzing a range of audiences and using discourse conventions accepted by the readers who will be using the texts. Given this notion of text as socially and historically influenced (Bizzell; Bartholomae; Bruffee), we also talk to students about the relationships among texts, how one writer and piece of discourse comes to affect other writers and other texts in a complex social dialogue (Bazerman; Porter).

Viewing language production and activity within the larger context of a social perspective has grown out of our profession's realization that knowledge and texts are not generated in a vacuum, that, as Kenneth Bruffee notes, "reality, knowledge, thought, facts, texts, selves" are "community-generated and community-maintained linguistic entities" (774). This realization dramatically affects our understanding of linguistic activities as they occur in reading- and writing-intensive classrooms. We now teach our students, as Janet Eldred notes, that "humans develop by hearing, speaking and using a variety of social voices. They become individual by selecting the discourses in which they will participate" (207). The upshot of this thinking about writing as a social activity is a rediscovered appreciation, on the part of English teachers and English educators, of pedagogical approaches that involve collaborative writing, group work, the formation of discourse communities within and outside of English classrooms, writing-across-the-curriculum efforts, and dialogic exchanges.

This understanding of reading and writing as process-based social acts of making meaning in concert with other human beings both past and present clarifies the justification for using computer networks or computer-based networking strategies in English classrooms. English teachers and teacher educators can now see computers in two complementary lights: first, as personal tools that facilitate an author's process-based approach to discourse production, and, second, as social tools that link readers and writers in rich electronically based conversations.

First, we can see how networks and networking strategies, as with all computer-based activities, support a process-based approach to composition. Although studies disagree about the extent to which computers affect writers of varying backgrounds, ages, and genders (Hawisher, "Research Update"; Hawisher, "Studies in Word

Processing"), our profession now has evidence that the use of computers can facilitate invention by encouraging the generation of ideas (Burns), creating a more positive attitude toward writing tasks (Bridwell, Sirc, and Brooke; Kurth; Rodrigues), and increasing fluency (Collier; Etchison; Kaplan); enhance drafting and revision by removing the drudgery of repetitive text production (Collins and Sommers; Daiute; Miller); and improve editing by providing a means of checking certain spelling and style conventions (Kiefer and Smith; Reid and Findlay).

More specifically, we have evidence that computer networks and computer-based networking strategies can help teachers emphasize collaborative exchanges and activities among writers (Bernhardt and Appleby; Daiute; Selfe and Wahlstrom, "An Emerging Rhetoric"; Spitzer). One recent study, for instance, indicates that the conversations occurring on computer-based conferences encourage groups to function in a more egalitarian and democratic manner because they encourage more active participation by more group members (Kiesler, et al.) and may remove some of the hierarchical social cues that constrain face-to-face encounters.

Other studies suggest that computer networks and computer-based networking activities can help to increase the social/rhetorical interaction and exchange among children (Daiute) and college students in classrooms (Selfe and Wahlstrom, "An Emerging Rhetoric"); to establish new discourse communities whose formation has been hindered by a lack of a common forum or meeting place (Bernhardt and Appleby; Selfe and Eilola; Spitzer); to encourage "conversations" among students and teachers from disparate geographical and cultural backgrounds (Fersko-Weiss; Ludtke); and to instill an immediacy and wider sense of perspective to written dialogues and exchanges (Selfe and Eilola; Spitzer).

If computers are valuable as personal tools that facilitate a process-based approach to composition and as social networking tools that encourage dialogic exchanges and enhance the successive refinement of ideas and concepts within a socially-based framework, how then can teachers and teacher educators best go about integrating computers into English studies? First, we must understand computer networks; then, we must plan carefully for them.

UNDERSTANDING COMPUTER NETWORKS AND NETWORKING STRATEGIES

For most teachers at the secondary and elementary levels, the phrase *computer network* refers to a series of personal computers hooked together electronically, either with a network server (a device that allows each computer on the network to access a common storage place for documents and files) or on computer networks (which provide a common forum or electronic meeting place for writers). In networked environments, students can store their papers, exchange them with other members of peer-critique groups, establish electronic mailboxes, hold dialogues or conversations with teachers and professional writers, revise a common text, or establish a public conference on vaious topics of interest.

Networks can link local sites (a personal computer in one room with a personal computer in another room, or a computer in an elementary school building with computers in the adjoining high school building), or they can link more distant sites via telephone communication technology (tying a computer in a junior high English classroom into BITNET, an electronic conferencing and mail system, and then into a computer in the next state, the other side of the country, or half a world away). Networks—depending on their architecture, sophistication, and design—allow asynchronous communication (think of our current postal system; one must receive a communication and open it before responding to it—no interruptions, strict turn taking) or synchronous communication (conversation that occurs in real time complete with the ability to interrupt speakers/writers as they communicate).[1]

Given these capabilities of networks, teachers who have access to appropriate computer hardware and software, and the professional education needed to use such equipment effectively,[2] can establish electronic webs that support student-to-student, student-to-teacher, and author-to-reader conversations. Within these dialogic exchanges of written information, individual scholars are encouraged to become actively engaged in making meaning within socially based contexts.[3]

PLANNING FOR COMPUTER NETWORKS

Computer networks and computer-based networking strategies are not automatically effective. Such networks and strategies, if planned carelessly, are prone to all the same problems and challenges outlined earlier in this chapter: users must still acquire computer-based literacy skills as well as the traditional literacy skills connected with reading and writing; the dangers of abusing techno/power remains; and poor pedagogical approaches are just as ineffective on a computer network as they are in a traditional classroom.

Teachers and teacher educators who are deliberate in their planning of computer resources, who want to use computers to reinvigorate their curricula in positive ways might want to consider the following suggestions as they plan to establish and then use networks and networking strategies.

Suggestion 1: Start with teachers. Provide computer education and network access to teachers first. Then think about networking students.

Computer networks and human networking strategies that are designed to share access to technology and invite egalitarian involvement of writers and readers can help teachers avoid the destructive competitiveness between techno/crats and techno/peasants withing an institution. With sound training, teachers can learn to use computers as a means of creating new language and discourse communities that might not otherwise come together. None of this worthwhile activity will take place, however, until teachers themselves experience the advantages of communicating on computer networks.

For teachers, computer education works best when it is adequately funded and supported by school administrators; available at convenient times (summers, evenings, weekends, breaks) and in convenient places (in a functioning classroom or computer lab within a school, or at a site nearby); when it is affordable (tuition free or tuition subsidized); when it is tailored carefully to practical concerns; and when it accommodates individuals with a range of technological experience.

For faculty who do not yet use computers, such education might begin with basic computer literacy. Several schools have already established training groups that pay particular attention to the special pedagogical needs of English teachers who want to begin using computers.[3] These groups generally focus on the uses of stand-alone computers that use a word-processing package to support process-based writing and reading activities and that prepare teachers to experiment with computer use in their own classrooms.

Although few of these basic training programs teach educators to use computer networks, they do illustrate how stand-alone computers can be used to generate, modify, and exchange texts among networks of readers and writers within a classroom or among several classrooms. Most training programs for English educators involve teachers in using microcomputers to support collaborative group writing tasks, to provide critiques of others' written efforts, and to support multiple revisions of a text.

For faculty who already use stand-alone computers, providing training on, and access to, active local, national, and international computer networks that connect teachers with similar interests is often the best way to demonstrate, in a practical fashion, the benefits of computer networks. On these networks, teachers learn, through firsthand experience, what is involved in holding electronic conferences with colleagues, exchanging papers and publications electronically, and holding on-line discussions of topics that interest members of the community. Involvement with such activities allows teachers the background experience necessary to structure effective networking activities for their own students.

Suggestion 2: Take plenty of time to plan. Articulate the goals you have as teachers of English, and keep these goals in the foreground of your thinking about computer networks and computer-based networking strategies.

After undertaking a program of professional, in-service education, teachers will come to understand and appreciate the complex web of concerns that surround computer networks. The next step for a single teacher or a group of teachers interested in tying computers, computer networks, and computer-based networking strategies more effectively into an English curriculum is to focus not on technology, but on literacy and the teaching of literacy. Before teachers can begin to make decisions about what features a computer network might need to include, they need to articulate for themselves the philosophical and theoretical bases on which their curriculum is founded. These assumptions, these pedagogical roots, will shape an effective use of computer networks or networking strategies.

Although the process by which such assumptions are identified is a lengthy one and one not often amenable to a quick-fix mentality, the time invested in these activities provides teachers with the basis for making a consistent set of informed decisions about any large-scale curricular change. Teachers may want to begin the process of identifying their pedagogical assumptions by meeting as a group or in a series of faculty meetings designed to answer questions such as the following:

1. What are our students' special literacy needs?
2. What assumptions about writing and reading can we draw from our own experiences as literate humans?
3. What assumptions about teaching writing and reading can we draw from our experiences as classroom teachers?
4. What have we learned from our reading and research that will help us develop sound strategies for teaching with computers?

For some faculties, this process of identifying pedagogical assumptions might be facilitated by an outside consultant knowledgeable in both literacy studies and computers; for other faculties, expertise in these areas already might be available on-site. By considering the answers to these questions, teachers can reach consensus about the instructional goals they hold in common as a faculty and that drive the teaching of literacy within their curriculum. A group of teachers might find, for example, that they place a high value on process-based instruction in reading and writing, have a strong commitment to teaching students to shape prose for particular audiences, and share a desire to help students develop critical reading skills and collaborative strategies.

These assumptions, then, shape instructional goals, which, in turn, help teachers sketch the parameters of an effective computer network or a computer-based networking activity: one that will support process-based writing and reading instruction with an easy-to-learn word processor; one that will allow writers and readers to communicate with a variety of audiences; and one that will facilitate the exchange of prose, critical reading activities, and collaborative ventures in learning.

Suggestion 3: Choose a networking approach. Identify what kind of networking activities will work best in your classroom or school context, given your instructional goals and institutional constraints.

Once teachers have educated themselves in connection with computer networks and identified the instructional goals that will inform their networking activities, they can decide on the networking approach that will best help them achieve those goals within the constraints of their institutional context.

Basically, the teacher who wants to use networking has three choices: *Local area networks (LANs)* link faculty and student computer users within the same institution.

These networks, often used to tie together computers and computer users on a university campus or within a computer lab at the secondary and elementary levels, are formed by cabling personal computers or workstations to one another and purchasing software that will allow these machines to exchange information—retrieving and storing documents in a central storage device. Once the hardware and software for a LAN is purchased, teachers and students can exchange any kinds of materials—drafts of papers, newspaper copy, letters, play scripts—on the LAN without incurring additional costs for time spent on the network. *State/National/International networks* link individuals at one site with individuals at other geographically distant sites via modems and telephone lines. Generally, hooking into one of these national networks requires participants to purchase a modem and subscribe to the network. In addition, participants who use the network to exchange communications are often charged according to the amount of time they spend using the system to transmit text. Examples of such networks are BITNET, HumaNET, NETI, BreadNET, and EDUCOM. Local-area computer networks can be hooked up to these larger state/national/international networks so that every participant on a LAN can also take part in wider conversations and exchanges. *Computer-based networking strategies* use computers to support the formation of information-exchange networks among groups of individuals. Teachers and students can use computers to generate information, draft documents, manipulate information and redraft documents, facilitate the exchange of documents, enhance collaborative efforts, and provide the means of distributing information. Although the computer supports these activities, the networks themselves are not electronic; they are human. The cost of such systems, relative to the two networking options is minimal: one computer, floppy disks, paper, a printer and/or a large screen projection system.

Each of these approaches has elements that recommend it, but only individual English teachers can know which will work best within a given educational site or reading- or writing-intensive classroom. Among the factors that should and will influence any decisions to integrate computer networks or networking strategies into English curricula are the following considerations: budgetary constraints, existing computer facilities, availability of technical support, teacher training and experience with technology; administrative support, student population, community support, and motivation.

Suggestion 4: Get help. Establishing a local-area computer network or hooking into a larger computer network generally requires technical expertise. Get technical assistance to make computer hardware do what you want it to do.

Those educators responsible for establishing local-area computer networks or hooking into larger state/national/international networks face technical difficulties beyond the expertise of most humanists. Not all networks are created equal; some will accommodate the hardware and software present in a school, others will not; some are amenable to modification that will make them easier to use, others are not; most require initial programming, equipment maintenance, and frequent attention from hardware and software experts. Without such attention, networks are "down," or not functioning, more than they are "up," or serving the purpose for which they are intended.

The best solution is to employ a team of hardware-software experts who can help create the kind of network English teachers want to establish. These experts can help teachers tie a school's computers into existing local, national, or international networks through modems or cable systems, can modify a commercial network program to fit the needs of a specific school setting, and can teach faculty how to perform network maintenance tasks.

The right team of technical assistants, for instance, can use the instructional goals articulated by an English faculty to help a school tailor a local area (LAN) network to its own community purposes. A school could, in this way, create a network that includes an electronic school bulletin board; an electronic mailbox for every student and teacher; an electronic conference or discussion area, where students can discuss controversial topics; an electronic polling place where students and faculty can vote on matters of concern to the school community; separate electronic suggestion boxes for teachers and students; a teachers-only corner for communication among the faculty; a "make-up work" section where assignments for ill students are posted; and an electronic school newspaper. Once such a network system is created, much of it can be maintained by students or faculty with minimal training, and there is no cost for on-line exchanges because the school owns the hardware and network software.

Schools that have limited budgets or only want to test the waters of networking may want to hire a team of technical experts to tie individual classroom computers into existing commercial networks that are prestructured at the national or international levels. Generally the exchange of dialogue and information on such networks —among them *BITNET, Participate, Humanet, Educom,* and others—is paid for by users according to the amount of time that a communication takes. Teachers and students on *BreadNet,* for example, send their written work—letters, essays, critiques —to other schools and students across the country. Because teachers plan carefully for the exchanges and encourage students to spend minimal time actually transmitting information, the costs of using modems and long-distance telephone lines to exchange such information can be lower than $500 per year (Holvig).

Suggestion 5: For students, remember that the use of a computer network or computer-based networking strategies both complicates and invigorates the business of acquiring literacy skills.

Traditionally, literacy studies address both reading and writing, and concern themselves with the ways in which human beings make meaning from printed texts by interpreting content in light of their own purposes and needs. Acquiring literacy skills within a computer-based classroom is quite another thing. Computer users must learn a whole new and distinct set of "grammatical" conventions involving virtual texts

(texts existing only in the memory of a computer) rather than printed texts, screens rather than pages, and network directories rather than postal systems (Selfe, "Redefining Literacy").

Even this brief list of differences illustrates the challenges inherent in literacy demands when they are based on a computer network. In English programs that require students to use computers or computer networks as they write or read, the demands of computer-based literacy (knowledge of a word-processing package, knowledge of a computer network, knowledge associated with a keyboard and a printer) are layered over the tasks of reading and writing. This multilayered literacy might explain why some students have a harder time reading and manipulating on-line computer texts (Hass and Hayes; Gould and Grichowsky; Wright and Lickorish) and writing with computers (Selfe, "Electronic Pen") than they do when reading and composing hard-copy texts.

Hence, when English teachers use computer networks as teaching and learning tools, we must also work to identify strategies tht help students deal with multilayered literacy demands engendered by computers. Teachers might have to help students develop, for instance, different methods for reading texts on a computer screen to supplement the instruction they received in reading hard-copy texts. Similarly, teachers may have to show students how to move about in a virtual (on-line) text more efficiently: how to use color to mark the organizational levels of an on-line text, how to use intratextual markers to locate information without scrolling, or how to use hyper text strategies to layer and access information more effectively. Certainly, we must recognize the increasingly complicated demands that exchanging information via computer networks place on our students and discuss among ourselves the changing nature of literacy within the computer-supported reading and writing environments that we create.

Fortunately, computer networks and computer-based networking strategies, because they do encourage the formation of intellectual communities and facilitate the exchange of information among students, can also help students teach each other how to develop and use effective computer-based literacy skills. Students linked by computers commonly exchange information about the reading, writing, and learning strategies they find most useful on computers. Students who use computer-based networking strategies within a classroom can observe firsthand how other students manipulate on-line text, read such texts, and deal with the computer's effect on their composing processes (Selfe and Wahlstrom, "An Emerging Rhetoric").

This exchange of information among users is a common characteristic of classrooms that are computer supported—either through a computer network or through computer-based networking strategies and frequently engenders a workshop atmosphere within the writing- or reading-intensive classroom (Selfe and Wahlstrom, "Lessons for Teachers"). In fact, the primary value of networks seems to rest in their ability to connect writers and readers to each other, thus stimulating the exchange of information and knowledge.

Teachers who have worked in computer-supported classrooms know the impossibility of giving a traditional lecture or having a teacher-centered class. The excitement and enthusiasm with which students approach computer-based communication tasks is impossible to control within a traditional classroom format. When young writers are empowered by computers, when their sense of adventure, play, and intellectual curiosity are engaged, they take off after literacy at warp speed. Teachers, in such classrooms, are left shaking their heads and chasing after students who quickly learn to use the electronic medium to generate, manipulate, and exchange information in ways that teachers never considered possible.

A FEW FINAL WORDS

We are teachers of English first and computer specialists second. This point is important for English teachers because we cannot allow our concern for the machine and its workings to eclipse our concern for students and colleagues.

Should this situation occur, we would be making what the American Baseball League or the National Baseball League would consider a bad trade: forgetting what we know about teaching writing and reading—the uniquely human of activities—in exchange for acquiring knowledge about technology. This last challenge, I believe, addresses not only the central humanistic contribution of our discipline, but also ironically the success of all future efforts to integrate computers effectively into English classrooms and programs. If we, as humanities scholars, cannot approach the machine in a humane manner that serves to link human beings in a complex network of communication and exchange, how can we hope to influence like-minded approaches to technology in the fields of math, engineering, or computer science?

Our job, then, is to teach people in ways that celebrate the diversity of the human spirit. Computer support for English programs will succeed when we identify for the profession our own uniquely humanistic vision of computer technology and its ability to support the networking of individuals.

Notes

1. For a more complete discussion of synchronous computer networks, see *The ENFI Newsletter* (T. Batson, ed.) published at Gallaudet University. For further information about asynchronous networks, see the March 1986 issue of IEEE Transactions on Professional Communication, *PC-29* (1), edited by V. Arms.

2. The responsibility for ongoing professional development, as so many teacher educators have pointed out, must be shared by teacher-education institutions, school administrators, and teachers. Although teachers must provide the personal motivation and enthusiasm for such development, they cannot be expected to design their own curricula and fund their own participation. Support for professional development—monetary, curricular, and emotional—must be provided by school administrators and teacher-education institutions.
3. Not all teachers and not all schools have computer networks available to them. Fortunately, many of network-based activities described in this paper can be completed in a modified form on stand-alone machines and exchanged via floppy disk. Under such conditions, although the computers are not networked electronically, the users themselves do form a human network that shares texts in a computer-supported writers' environment.
4. The National Council of Teachers of English (NCTE) is currently involved in publishing a description of thirteen preservice, in-service, and professional development programs that help English teachers learn to integrate computers into their curriculum.

Works Cited

Arms, Valarie, ed. *IEEE Transactions on Professional Communication* PC-29.1 (1986).

Bartholomae, David. "Inventing the University." *Journal of Basic Writing* 5 (1986): 4–23.

Barret, M. *Women's Oppression Today.* London: Verso, 1980.

Bazerman, Charles. "A Relationship Between Reading and Writing: The Conversational Model." *College English* 41 (1980): 656–61.

Bernhardt, Steven, and Bruce Appleby. "Collaboration in Professional Writing with the Computer." *Computers and Composition* 3.1 (1985): 29–42.

Berthoff, Ann. *Forming/Thinking/Writing.* Montclair, N. J.: Boyton-Cook, 1981.

Berkenkotter, Carol, Thomas Huckin, and John Ackerman. "Conventions, Conversations, and the Writer: Case Study of a Student in a Rhetoric Ph.D. Program." *Research in the Teaching of English* 22.1 (1988): 9–44.

Bizzell, Patricia. "College Composition: Initiation into the Academic Discourse Community." *Curriculum Inquiry* 12 (1982): 197–207.

Bleich, David. "Cognitive Stereoscopy and the Study of Language and Literature." *Convergences: Transactions in Reading and Writing.* Bruce Peterson, ed. Urbana, Ill.: National Council of Teachers of English, 1986. 99–114.

Bridwell, Lillian, Geoffrey Sirc, and Robert Brooke. "Revising and Computing: Case Studies of Student Writers." *The Acquisition of Written Language: Revision and Response.* Sarah Freedman, ed. Norwood, N. J.: Ablex, 1985.

Bruffee, Kenneth. "Social Construction, Language, and the Authority of Knowledge: A Bibliographical Essay." *College English* 48 (1986): 773–90.

Burns, Hugh. *Stimulating Rhetorical Invention in English Composition through Computer-Assisted Instruction.* Urbana, Ill.: ERIC Document Reproduction Service, 1979, ERIC ED 188 245.

Collier, Richard. "The Word Processor and Revision Strategies." *College Composition and Communication* 35 (1983): 149–55.

Collins, James, and Elizabeth Sommers. "Microcomputers and Writing." *Computers and Composition* 2.4 (1985): 27–35.

Daiute, Colette. "Issues in Using Computers to Socialize the Writing Process." *Education Communication and Technical Journal* 33.1 (1985): 41–50.

Dowling, Colette. *The Techno/Peasant Survival Manual.* New York: Bantam Books, 1980.

Eisenstein, Zillah R. "Developing a Theory of Capitalist Patriarachy and Socialist Feminism." *Capitalist Patriarchy and the Case for Socialist Feminism.* Z. R. Eisenstein, ed. New York: Monthly Review Press, 1979.

Eldred, Janet. "Computers, Composition Pedagogy, and the Social View." *Critical Perspectives on Computers and Composition Instruction.* Gail Hawisher and Cynthia Selfe, eds. *New York: Teachers College Press, 1989.*

Emig, Janet. *The Composing Processes of Twelfth Graders.* Urbana, Ill.: National Council of Teachers of English, 1971.

Etchison, Craig. *A Comparative Study of Quality and Syntax of Compositions by First-Year College Students Using Handwriting and Word Processing.* Unpublished ms. Indiana University of Pennsylvania, Indiana, Penn., 1986.

Fersko-Weiss, Harry. "Electronic Mail: The Emerging Connection." *Personal Computing* (1985): 71–79.

Fish, Stanley. *Is There a Text in the Class? The Authority of Interpretive Communication.* Cambridge, Mass.: Harvard University Press, 1980.

Flower, Linda, and John Hayes. "Problem-Solving Strategies and the Writing Process." *College English* 39.4 (1977): 449–61.

Gould, John D., and N. Grichowsky. "Doing the Same Work with Hard Copy and with Cathode-Ray Tube Computer Terminals." *Human Factors* 26.3 (1984): 323–37.

Haas, Christina, and John Hayes. "What Did I Just Say? Reading Problems with the Machine." *Research in the Teaching of English* 20.1 (1986) :22–35.

Hawisher, Gail. "Studies in Word Processing." *Computers and Composition* 4.1 (1986): 6–31.

————. "Research Update: Writing and Word Processing." *Computers and Composition* 5.2 (1988): 7–27.

Hiltz, Roxanne. "The 'Virtual Classroom': Using Computer-Mediated Communication for University Teaching." *Journal of Communication* 36.2 (1986): 95–104.

Holvig, Kenneth. "Voices Across the Wires through Breadnet and Clarknet." Paper presented at the Annual Meeting of the National Council of Teachers of English. Los Angeles, Calif., 1987.

Kaplan, Howard. "Computers and Composition: Improving Students' Written Performance." *Dissertation Abstracts International* 47 (1986): 776A. University of Massachusetts.

Kiefer, Kathleen, and Charles Smith. "Improving Students' Revision and Editing: The Writer's Workbench System." *The Computer in Composition Instruction: A Writer's Tool.* William Wresch, ed. Urbana, Ill.: National Council of Teachers of English, 1984.

Kiesler, Sara, J. Siegel, and T. McGuire. "Social Psychological Aspects of Computer-Mediated Communication." *American Psychologist* 39 (1984): 1123–34.

King, Barbara, Jane Birnbaum, and Jane Wageman. "Word Processing and the Basic College Writer." *The Written Word and the Word Processor.* T. Martinez, ed. Philadelphia, Penn.: Delaware Valley Writing Council, 1984.

Kurth, Ruth. "Using Word Processing to Enhance Revision Strategies during Student Composing." Paper presented at the Annual Meeting of the American Educational Research Association. San Francisco, Calif., 1986.

Larsen, Richard. "The One-Computer Classroom." *Computers and Composition* 4.1 (1986): 46–60.

Ludtke, Melissa. "Great Human Power or Magic: An Innovative Program Sparks the Writing of America's Children." *Time* (14 September 1987): 76.

Miller, S. "Plugging Your Pencil into the Wall: An Investigation of Word Processing and Writing Skills at the Middle School Level." *DAI* 46 (1984): 1827A.

Ohmann, Richard. "Literacy, Technology, and Monopoly Capital." *College English* 47.6 (1985): 675–89.

Peterson, Bruce, ed. *Convergences: Transactions in Reading and Writing.* Urbana, Ill.: National Council of Teachers of English, 1986.

Pianko, Sharon. "A Description of the Composing Processes of College Freshman Writers." *Research in the Teaching of English* 13.1 (1979): 5–22.

Porter, James. "Intertextuality and the Discourse Community." *Rhetoric Review* 5 (1986): 34–47.

Reid, Stephen, and Gilbert Findlay. "Writer's Workbench Analysis of Holistically Scored Essays." *Computers and Composition* 3.2 (1986): 6–32.

Rodrigues, Dawn. "Computers and Basic Writers." *College Composition and Communication* 36 (1985): 336–39.

Selfe, Cynthia. "Computers in English Departments: The Rhetoric of Techo-Power." Paper presented at the annual conference of the Association of Departments of English. Annapolis, Md., 1987.

———. "The Electronic Pen: Computers and the Composing Process." *Writing On-Line: Using Computers in the Teaching of Writing.* J. Collins and E. Sommers, eds. New York: Boynton Cook, 1985.

———. "Redefining Literacy: The Multi-Layered Grammars of Computers." Paper presented at the annual Conference on College and Communication. Atlanta, Ga., 1987.

Selfe, Cynthia, and J. Eilola. "The Tie that Binds: Building Discourse Communities and Group Cohesion through Computer Conferences." *Collegiate Microcomputer* 6.4 (1988): 339–48.

Selfe, Cynthia, and Billie Wahlstrom. *Computer-Supported Writing Classes: Lessons for Teachers.* Unpublished ms. Michigan Technological University. Houghton, Mich., 1988.

———. "An Emerging Rhetoric of Collaboration: Computers and the Composing Process." *Collegiate Microcomputer* 4.4 (1986): 289–95.

Sommers, Elizabeth, and James Collins. "Microcomputers and Writing." *Computers and Composition* 2.4 (1985): 27–35.

Spitzer, Michael. "Computer Conferencing: An Emerging Technology." *Critical Perspectives on Computers and Composition Instruction.* Gail E. Hawisher and Cynthia L. Selfe, eds. New York: Teachers College Press, 1989.

Swales, John. "Approaching the Concept of Discourse Communities." Paper presented at the Conference on College Composition and Communication. Atlanta, Ga., 1987.

Tierney, Robert, and P. David Pearson. "Toward a Composing Model of Reading." *Language Arts* 60 (1983): 568–80.

Vogel, Lise L. *Marxism and the Oppression of Women: Toward a Unitary Theory.* New Brunswick, N. J.: Rutgers University Press, 1983.

Weizenbaum, Joseph. "Not Without Us: A Challenge to Computer Professionals to Bring the Present Insanity to a Halt." *Fellowship* (1986): 8–10.

Wright, P., and A. Lickorish. "Proofreading Texts on Screen and Paper." *Behavior and Information Technology* 2.3 (1983): 227–35.

IV

The Learning of Language: Teachers and Their Students

Dennis Baron

14. *Watching Our Grammar: The English Language for English Teachers*

You taught me language, and my only benefit is that I learn'd how to curse.
—William Shakespeare, *The Tempest*

The study of the English language is an essential and unquestioned part of every level of the American educational system. It is taken for granted that without formal instruction, the language Americans so carefully guard and cultivate would languish or worse yet that it would deteriorate into unrecognizable grunts and scrawls. In fact, many language critics assume English to be in such desperate straits that they pessimistically conclude that the educational system can do little to save it.

Unfortunately, most English teachers believe in this myth of language decay and become frustrated when attempts to alter their students' language fail. While most of the students to whom we teach English already know how to speak it quite well before they are of school age, we assume that their English is either not very good to begin with, or if in some few cases it is good, then we try to make it better. But we are wrong to view the situation of language so bleakly.

The assumption that English is in a period of decline is contradicted by the undiminished energy with which our language is spreading across the globe as the essential international tongue, by the continued high level of literary activity of the speakers and writers of English, and by the undeniably strong creative energy evidenced in the new words and expressions which daily enrich our speech. If, in the face of this evidence, we approach the instruction in English of speakers of English entirely from a compensatory or remedial viewpoint, we limit our effectiveness, reinforce negative attitudes toward the study of the language both by those who are born to it and those who are adopting it, and create linguistic insufficiencies where none might have existed before.

Despite its present position in the curriculum, the centrality of English is a recent phenomenon in the history of education. Although English grammar and spelling began to displace the classical languages for students in the less academic tracks in eighteenth-century schools, English language and literature did not become a universal subject until well into the nineteenth century. From the complaints lodged against our schools, and from the uninterrupted string of diatribes against the misuse of English that have appeared over the past two centuries, the spread of English education clearly has reinforced rather than stemmed our fear of linguistic barbarism.

One reason why language instruction is felt to be central to the educational mission, yet perceived to be inefficient, if not a virtual failure, is an educational philosophy that characterizes the teacher as an expert imparting knowledge to the student-novice, undercut by an educational practice that impedes teacher expertise, effectively limiting how much teachers may actually learn about the language they must teach. This is not the most appropriate model for English language instruction, and it puts teachers in an unfair position. In learning to speak their language before coming to school, students have already become experts at the practice of English, mastering a much more complex form of verbal behavior than that required by any reading or writing task we are likely to set before them. Moreover, while our students are skilled in oral communication (their reading and writing is something else again), English teachers do not generally qualify as academic experts in the English language for, although the curriculum emphasizes the importance of our literary training, it does not prepare us to teach langauge as a subject.

While it is one of our most important tasks, English teachers are at a definite disadvantage when it comes to teaching about language. We are well-trained in literature and pedagogy, but not in the history and structure of our tongue, standard or otherwise. Furthermore, we are generally drawn to the profession of English by an interest in literature, discovering only when it is too late that much of our class time is consumed by teaching students who can already speak, read, and write English how to speak, read, and write English.

The undergraduate English major has always stressed literature at the expense of language study—in their ineffectual and increasingly outmoded display of modernism and relevance, few liberal arts curricula now require any sort of philology course (fewer still offer an undergraduate or even a graduate English language track). The present English *teaching* major does little to remedy the situation, generally requiring one or sometimes two courses, perhaps history of the English language or descriptive English grammar, merely to satisfy state certification requirements. Changes in teacher education programs that will require prospective teachers to take straight liberal arts subject majors could further limit the exposure of teaching candidates to English language studies. On the other hand, such changes present an opportunity to make language courses a more integral part of the English major.

The English professional associations, recognizing that literature is after all a very particular use of language, have always tried to balance language and literature. To cite a recent example, in their suggestions for revising the English curriculum, both the National Council of Teachers (NCTE) and the Modern Language Association (MLA) stress the need to educate English majors and prospective English teachers in the history and structure of the language, dialect variation and its relation to language change, the process of language standardization, and the differences between spoken and written language. Yet despite the publicity generated by the so-called literacy crisis of the past few years, official government agencies such as the National Endowment for the Humanities (NEH) remain leery of encouraging curriculum revisions for high schools and colleges that seek to introduce students and teachers to the power of their own language, promoting instead a core *literature* curriculum whose essential texts educators and school boards will never be able to agree on.

For the federal government, then, as for most specialists and nonspecialists, the study of English is the study of literature; everything else is either secondary or derivative. Perhaps it is time to question the assumption that both teachers and students generally prefer literature to any of the language-related aspects of the English classroom. And perhaps it is time to introduce into the high school English language curriculum some of the descriptive and historical linguistics that English teachers currently do learn as part of their subject preparation. After all, teachers do not learn what they do not teach. And secondary school students are ready to study language not as a deadly set of prescriptions that they can never remember, let alone obey, but as a social phenomenon in a constant state of change. They are remarkably sensitive to linguistic nuances and language change, and they take great pride in demonstrating their verbal agility in nonacademic situations. Why not have them engage in ethnographic research and study language change in their own community? High school language curricula and textbooks have generally emphasized terminology, parsing, and corrective or prescriptive lingusitics, exercises that are most aptly described as *grammar-grinding.* But if students study language as they do literature, as a living phenomenon that stretches their imagination, challenges them to think independently, and has a significant impact on their future, they too will be able to make the subject their own, once and for all.

GRAMMAR GRINDERS

The image of the English teacher as an overly fussy usage purist or grammar grinder should give way to something much more positive. We can do this through a language curriculum more in line with current scholarship in the historical, social, and psychological functions of language and the practical ways in which we use language, and it uses us.

The avoidance of English linguistics is nothing new. Before the nineteenth century, language study generally meant second language study: the classical languages, or perhaps French or another modern European tongue. But the eighteenth century was a period when great attention was being paid to the structure of English, and, toward the end of that century, English grammar had firmly established itself as an academic subject. In the nineteenth century, English grammar became a hot potato in the American educational curriculum. Colleges did not want to deal with it because they felt it was too basic. Grade schools shunned it because they thought it too hard. And both high school administrators and teachers' associations initially resisted state mandates to teach grammar because the teachers felt unqualified to teach it. Early grammar textbooks, explicitly acknowledging the unpreparedness of student and instructor alike for this new and challenging subject, were designed to be self-teaching: the English teacher needed only to stay one page ahead of his or her pupils to be a language expert. The grammar text of today is not much different from its precursors in this self-teaching philosophy, and the expertise thus acquired remains both precarious and facile.

If *grammar* has become a bugbear for generations of students, it is because far too many teachers, feeling their own inadequacy to handle the subject, become tied to automatized textbooks and worksheets that try to teach the subject for them and that minimize the opportunity for students to ask the unanswerable questions that teachers sometimes dread. Add to this the negative implications of grammar as a corrective rather than a descriptive tool: it is difficult for students and teachers to take kindly to a subject that takes as its fundamental goal the alteration of something so personal as language behavior.

Language is one of the traits that makes us human, and because our language ability is so directly tied to our self-esteem, it is difficult for students to be placed in a situation, as they invariably are in English class, where their language is always on trial, always subject to the severe judgment of the teacher, the textbook, and the class. I believe that because language is always fair game for the teacher's correction in English class, even when the topic of discussion is literature or something not even remotely related to grammar and usage, students are reluctant to put their language on the line. Their responses in English discussions are often more tentative than they are in the classrooms of other disciplines, and students show their reluctance to assert themselves by engaging in language behavior designed to lower their visibility and minimize the consequences of incorrect behavior. As a result, students in English classes are more likely than students in other disciplines to preface their questions with such self-effacing disclaimers as, "I know this is a dumb question, but..." and their inquiries with similarly self-deprecatory remarks such as, "This is probably wrong, but. . . ." I do not think math teachers, who teach a course generally assumed to provoke even higher anxiety than grammar, are as likely to hear, "I know this is wrong, $6x10^{-23}$," nor are history teachers as likely to encounter "This is a dumb question, but when did the Civil War end?" We must own up to the fact that the teaching of English to speakers of

English has promoted much of the linguistic insecurity and fear of grammar that we observe today.

Complicating matters, too, and contributing to the wariness of language study shown by some federal agencies is the fact that language, like literature, has been affected by shifting and sometimes distracting theoretical concerns. The most striking of these, lately, have been the movements in the 1940s and 1950s to base classroom language instruction on structuralist linguistics, the counterswing, in the 1960s and 1970s, which sought to introduce transformational-generative grammar into the secondary school classroom, and the back-to-basics reaction of the 1980s that calls for a return to paradigm drill and sentence parsing.

The failure of movements in linguistics to apply theory on a basic level is no surprise because neither structural nor transformational theory are designed to answer the basic requirements of school grammar: how to make students critically aware of the structures and functions of their language and how to empower students so that they can get English to do what they want it to do more effectively. But parsing and "What's wrong with this sentence?" exercises is not the answer either, for these techniques come from the area of second language acquisition—even there they are viewed as questionable techniques—and have only a limited significance to the teaching of English to speakers of English.

ENGLISH FOR ENGLISH TEACHERS

Although neither English majors nor English teachers are sufficiently trained in the English language, our society expects its English teachers to be experts on language as well as literature, and school boards and curriculum supervisors see to it that despite our inadequate preparation, our lesson plans are full of vocabulary, spelling, punctuation, usage, grammar, reading comprehension, and composition as well as the great books. We may pepper our conversation with literary allusions, but people do not want to know from us whether Hamlet was really mad or whom Shakespeare was addressing in the sonnets; they want us to tell them where to put their commas. The driving need of Americans to be correct in matters of language has foced English teachers to function as experts in the English language, answering polite inquiries about spelling, punctuation, and usage, telling petitioners if *whom* is dead and just what the subjunctive is anyway. Even if we do answer such inquiries, our questioners do not listen, and they resent us on top of it. We may see ourselves as guardians of Shakespeare and Hemingway, Austen and Dickinson, but the stereotype of the English teacher is more often that of syntax snob and pedant, the revealer and reviler of mistakes, than that of literary aesthete, selflessly exposing students to the best that has been thought and writ.

Inadequately trained, but presumed nonetheless to be experts on language, English teachers are generally set up as arbiters of linguistic correctness and taste by the usage-anxious public. We are expected to authorize pronunciation, correcting students' mistakes and modifying their accents. This is a throwback to the days when prospective teachers were excluded from the profession (at least in large, urban school systems) if their speech revealed the barest trace of religious, ethnic, or geographic origin, and those who made it to the classroom were forced to speak in an accent natural to no one but the teaching cadre itself.

Although we are trained in literature, we are expected by society to become language guardians, protecting English from external invasion or internal rot. Many people consider any sort of language change to be a change for the worse. The introduction of a newly coined or foreign word; the spread of a slang or dialect term; the use of a noun as a verb—all of these contribute to a popular conception that the English language is losing precision, that it is coming under mob rule.

Language change always produces some reaction: we have been hearing laments over the death of English since writers started commenting on the language in the sixteenth century. Many features of Modern English usage and vocabulary were objected to by experts when they were first noticed: common words such as *presidential, physicist, reliable, telegraph, ice cream,* even *mob* itself, were angrily denounced in their day. Other features of the English language went unchallenged for centuries before someone decided to put a stop to them: no one lodged objections to the passive voice, now the bane of teachers and editors, until the early part of the twentieth century, when commentators started blaming the passive for being a wordy, weak, and deceptive syntactic structure.

One striking example illustrates the absurdity and lexical paralysis that usage controversy can induce. In 1912, two well-respected usage experts hotly disputed the correctness of the phrases *a quarter to* and *a quarter of* in reference to the telling of time. One, Josephine Turck Baker, insisted that *a quarter to seven* literally meant six-fifteen, because *a quarter to* really meant 'one quarter of an hour toward, or in the direction of, on the clock dial.' For her, only *a quarter of seven* was correct, standard English. But the other expert, Frank Vizetelly, insisted that *a quarter of seven* literally means 'seven divided by four, or one and three quarters.' For him, only *a quarter to seven* was acceptable. Neither suggested *a quarter till,* presumably because both felt it was a dialect term. But what is the poor English speaker to do in the face of such contradictory "expert" instruction? Better to say *six forty-five* and have done with it, a more appropriate solution anyway now that digital time telling is fast replacing the analog variety.

Just how much English teachers should attempt to modify their students' English is a controversial matter, for language is a subject that is easily politicized. In the early 1970s, the movement to defend students' right to their own language sharply divided the teaching profession. While many language experts caution teachers to leave the language alone, a teacher's reluctance to impose standards of language correctness is seen by the public not as a concession to linguistic sophistication—as in the time-telling example above, it is a mistake to hold language to a strict, literal interpretation, although in other instances literality can be very important—but as an admission of ignorance, and that, in turn, might have a disastrous effect on our employment status. Ironically, teachers who accept or actively embrace the role of English monitors develop a reputation for unwarranted interference with other people's language and are shunned. People may want to be told what is right, rather than figure it out for themselves, but they also resent the person who tells them. Announcing to someone I have just met that I teach English draws one of two responses: fear or a collusive sort of camaraderie. I'm either told, "English was my worst subject; I'd better watch my grammar," which severely limits further conversation, or I'm asked to agree with my interlocutor that English is certainly in a bad way, a position which contradicts all that scholars know about language use and change.

Furthermore, although people claim they wish to adhere to the standards of language, they are strangely unwilling to accept the facts of English that they seek to master. Thus, a teacher's efforts to alter a student's language might backfire: for some students, an effort to be "correct" (in other words, to please the teacher) results in a new error; for others, the fear of making yet another in an endless string of mistakes leads to silence. Yet students are also uncomfortable with uncertainty. If we tell them several right, or acceptable, ways of using or analyzing a piece of language exist, we should be prepared for resistance and anxiety. Concerned above all with acquiring and maintaining Standard English, both the public and the educational establishment resist the notion that *standard* is an imprecise term when applied to a system as complex and contextually dependent as language.

It is certainly not my intention to require prospective English teachers to complete a language major in addition to a literature major. While such a double major might indeed produce an ideal high school English teacher, it is to say the lease impractical, for besides language and literature, an English teacher must study the fundamental theories of reading and composition and master their instruction as well. However, the language component of our teacher preparation programs needs much reform and some expansion. If English teachers must act as language experts, English educators must find a way to provide that expertise. Just as teachers will read literary texts that have no direct application to the high school classroom, teachers must learn more about the English language than they will be asked to teach to their students. The knowledge thus acquired, however, will form the tangible basis of the English teacher's language expertise, enabling him or her to make informed, professional judgments and recommendations about English, while awakening students' interest in the power and beauty of language.

The following suggestions regarding what English teachers need to master about language is not intended as either an exhaustive or an ideal curriculum. I make no recommendation here as to the number of courses needed, or the amount of time to be spent on a topic in any given course, although the way most English majors are currently structured, as a rule, more will be better than less. It is simply one of several possible lists that contain a sound balance between factual content and theoretical interpretation, between the study of the nature of language and its function in literary and socioeconomic contexts, covering some of the linguistic skills and expertise all English teachers should acquire.

Ideally, a language sequence should provide students with "What every English teacher ought to know about the English language." Such linguistic knowledge, although much of it might not translate directly into lesson plans, will aid teachers to understand, analyze, and develop the linguistic abilities their students bring to school, linguistic abilities that we all agree require careful development by instructors who know what they are doing.

STANDARD ENGLISH

Standard English is a term that is loosely thrown about in educational circles, particularly when language deficiency is being discussed. But it is a term that is at best unconstitutionally vague, and at worst it functions as a test, a shibboleth used to exclude individuals and groups from the ranks of the linguistic elect.

While much of our grammatical terminology dates back to the earliest grammars of the classical languages, the now-pervasive phrase *Standard English,* referring to the prestige literary dialect of spoken or written English, is fairly new. The word *standard* as a measurement of correctness or perfection first appears in the fifteenth century, but it is not connected with language until the eighteenth, when it is applied to Greek and French, languages whose reputed superiority was frequently held up for users of English to envy.

Standard is not joined to English until the late nineteenth century. It appears in the title of T. Kington Oliphant's historical study, *The Source of Standard English,* in 1873. Expressions such as *the King's English, the King's language,* and *received English* do occur before that, giving evidence for our early and ongoing concern with correct, good, or approved English. However, the association of the term *standard* with precisely defined and regulated weights and measures, as well as with monetary systems, creates the modern illusion that Standard English has scientific validity, that it can be defined and replicated, like the standard meter or kilogram, and that it has the same currency for everyone.

We commonly suppose, for one thing, that a standard of usage exists which we all agree upon, a standard that may be described with some precision, reduced to a few simple rules, and imposed on the entire nation, if not the whole English-speaking world. As a concession to the varieties of English used in such diverse areas as Australia, Canada, Great Britian, India, Ireland, New Zealand, Nigeria, and the United States, we commonly—although sometimes reluctantly—acknowledge the existence of regional or national spoken and written standards. But whether we are dealing with standards or Standard, we are invariably thwarted by the problem of definition.

Try as we do, we have yet to achieve anything even closely approximating an exhaustive description of the varieties of English, or to arrive at an understanding of the complex nature of language standards and the degree of variability permissible within what we broadly term acceptable English. Put simply, our grammars and dictionaries are all open-ended. No matter how many correct ways of saying things we manage to collect, there are many we have missed, and more still that have yet to be invented.

Nor can we agree on how such acceptable language use is to be enforced. Despite numerous proposals over the past 400 years, no English-speaking country has chartered an English Language Academy to monitor the course of the language, nor has language legislation been particularly successful. Neither the United States nor the United Kingdom has an officially sanctioned dictionary or grammar, and neither has an official language law, despite attempts to impose one on the national level in this country. Although students and teachers alike complain that English spelling is irrational and difficult to learn, and nominate our orthography as the one aspect of the language they would change if they could, the American public has traditionally resisted spelling reform. When in 1906 President Theodore Roosevelt, by executive order, demanded the adoption of simplified spelling by the Government Printing Office (GPO), the GPO refused to comply, and the public outcry was so great that Roosevelt quickly abandoned his big stick approach to the English language.

Lacking official guidance, then, what we mean by Standard English, beyond our identification of it with a vague, consensual prestige norm, is never precisely clear. Instead, it is generally easier for us to say what is *not* standard, for example, errors in subject-verb agreement (*they was*) or in the concord of pronouns with their referents (*everyone . . . their*). We further assume that students of English, native speakers as well as second language learners, will make such errors given half a chance, and that these errors may be avoided by offering models of good usage to be imitated or sentences containing errors for correction.

Such assumptions will not profit us: the listing of standard deviations, even in combination with a catalogue of the supposed rules of correctness, is not an efficient way of getting at good English, for as the linguist and usage critic Bergen Evans maintains in *Comfortable Words* (1961), "There is no simple rule about English that does not have so many exceptions that it would be folly to rely on it" (8). To deny the existence of acceptable variation in English even in so apparently standard an area as subject-verb agreement is impossible. In British English, collective nouns such as *government* and *corporation* are treated as plurals, while Americans employ them in the singular. Even within America there is disagreement over the status of *data,* scrupulously construed as a plural by number-crunching researchers unwilling to seem ignorant of Latin, but more comfortably treated as a singular among the general population.

Even so stigmatized a word as *ain't* has its defenders, particularly among the most conservative of usage critics, who at one time maintained that *ain't I?* is preferable to *aren't I?* Its acceptance in informal, standard speech in England earlier in this century and in the American South is in sharp contrast to the general perception of *ain't* as the most despised word in the English language. When *Webster's Third New International*

Dictionary was published in 1961, a critical outcry resulted over the editors' comment that some educated speakers do use the word without apologizing for it.

In fact, complaints against variant pronunciation, morphology, syntax, or diction frequently signal that the offending form is either threatening to become standard, or has already become so. The adverb *hopefully* has been used in written English as a sentence modifier, as in *Hopefully, this won't last too long,* since the 1960s. Once established, the construction spread to the point where it is now virtualy universal in American English. The general outcry among usage commentators against this innovation is looked on with astonishment by the rest of the population—including the vast majority of English teachers, who have never heard of the controversy and assume the form to be perfectly acceptable.

Standard English is no less real for being vague or subjective. However, it must be studied not as a set of correct sentences but as a social phenomenon of language. It consists of shifting attitudes of different social groups toward changing usages in a variety of language contexts. Imprecise as this characterization of Standard English sounds, it removes our attention from a rigid, monolithic view of language as it must be, and directs our focus more appropriately to the close examination of language as it is and as it can be.

THE FACTS AND CONTEXTS OF ENGLISH

Prospective English teachers must learn the facts of spoken and written English and master the terminology required to describe language, particularly written language. Such knowledge is essential in order to deal with students' writing and with literary texts. They must learn the terminology of a variety of schools of linguistic thought—traditional, structural, and transformational—and understand the various approaches to grammar instruction that have come to be termed *school grammar.* But more important, they must develop a philosophy of language instruction that focuses students' attention on the description of the various kinds of spoken and written language with which they come in contact and varieties of English, old and new, they might not have yet encountered.

Although the relativism of linguistic usage has always been anathema to purists, who prefer to rely on logic and their own inner vision for their judgments, and a more general educational relativism has lately come under some attack from the back-to-basics camp, language must be studied from a relative and comparative rather than an absolute point of view. We want students to master a certain amount of subject matter while at the same time learning how to think for themselves, how to solve language problems while developing and refining a sense of critical judgment. The difficulty is to convince students—and their teachers—to accept the uncertainties that language so often poses. We must abandon our predilection for unequivocal judgments of right and wrong in favor of the examination of the practical requirements of the various contexts in which language is used and rated.

English teachers and their students already know—at least implicitly—that in addition to varying degrees of formality, each speaking or writing situation requires certain things of language users. It is appropriate to interrupt a speaker in certain conversational contexts, for example, or even in certain more formal situations such as a classroom lecture or demonstration, while interrupting a public speech, a newscast, a judge, a drill sergeant, or a terrorist might meet with less approval. Slang and familiarity are required in certain social gatherings, and in certain writing situations, while they are taboo in others. In many contexts, a range of linguistic behavior is permitted, or even encouraged.

When a speaker or writer is placed in a new situation and does not know the rules of language etiquette or the particular standards demanded by the group or the context, difficulties might arise ranging from mild embarrassment to complete failure to communicate. Most people eventually adapt to such new linguistic environments, while others retreat from the challenge in fear, dismay, or anger. Although the choice of behavior might have more to do with personality than with the structure of language, teachers—and their students—must recognize that language poses some problems that have simple, singular answers, but it also poses many others—and these are the most interesting of its problems—for which a few right answers, any number of wrong answers, some daring answers, some preferable answers, and many possible answers might be found.

LANGUAGE THEORY

Because no description of language can exist outside a theoretical framework, teachers must also become familiar with the major concepts of general linguisitics, notions of linguistic universals, language families, language development in humans, and the controversy over communicative development in animals.

More specifically, prospective English teachers should understand the history and structure of the English language, the processes of linguistic change, the social and geographical varieties of English, and the processes whereby standards of English have arisen. They must know where English comes from, what groups and languages have contributed to its vocabulary, syntax, and pronunciation, what changes in its form and in its status have affected the language, how it has competed against other languages on the international scene, and what the many inadvertent and conscious attempts to alter its course have accomplished. They should understand the relationship between inflection and syntactic variation, the process of sound change, and the ways in which new words enter the linguistic mainstream. One of the key problems with which they will have to grapple, both in their studies and in the classroom, is the sociolinguistic evidence that some varieties of American English seem to be drifting farther apart rather than coming closer together. This centrifugal phenomenon, seen as a tendency for American society to become more fragmented along racial and ethnic lines, has important implications both for language change and language instruction.

English teachers must become comfortable with the four major aspects of grammatical study: phonology, syntax, semantics, and pragmatics, and the notions of prescriptive and descriptive linguistics. They should be able to put traditional, structural, transformational and functional linguistics into perspective, recognizing the similarities as well as the differences between these views of language structure, and understanding how they might or might not be applicable to classroom needs.

Teachers should recognize the difference between *linguistic theory,* which is meant to describe language as it occurs, and *school grammar,* which is intended primarily to teach students about language and its use. And they should develop an approach to the teaching of English that allows students to apply their expertise to new situations and to gain more facility with linguistic analysis and language use. Students will learn more about the subtle effects of language by investigating language in a social and historical context than they will through drill and rote learning, which will only affect their temporary, short-term memory. Topics such as school jargon, nicknames, the language peculiarities of friends and relatives, the hidden messages of advertising and song lyrics, the language dynamics of the classroom, and male/female language will involve them in projects that require the development and mastery of terminology, sets of data, and analytic techniques. These fieldwork topics have the additional advantage of removing the teacher from the authoritarian role of language judge, placing him or her in a better position to aid and abet language learning, rather than impose or smother it.

LANGUAGE FUNCTION

English teachers must learn how language is acquired by the human infant and how it develops during an individual's lifetime. They should be familiar with certain kinds of language pathology—for example, dyslexia—but they must also learn that certain linguistic features that have often been classified as pathological, for example regional accent, are actually normal variations that do not require formal intervention.

They must become aware of the differences between spoken and written English, and the complex and shifting sets of factors that determine ideas of correctness in each. Because their students and the general public will expect them to answer the kinds of questions received by grammar hotlines, they must become familiar with the history and present status of usage controversies, disputed spellings, variation in punctuation, and ideas about language reform, and they must be prepared to make recommendations. They should also know something about the development of English dictionaries, and the major differences among them, and they should be aware of the strengths and weaknesses of the major English language reference tools: dictionaries, grammars, usage guides, thesauruses, histories of the language, and commentaries on the language.

In order to emphasize a number of key points, I have left unexpanded several important topics in this catalogue of language subjects to be included in the basic education of the English teacher. Among them are etymology, metaphor, semiotics, literary stylistics, the idealization of the plain style and ordinary language by writers and critics, language as a tool of persuasion and propaganda, the controversial question of bilingualism, and the assumption that language reflects, in addition to psychological and sociological attitudes, both political organization and national culture.

ENGLISH FOR ENGLISH SPEAKERS

In 1921, Oxford philologist Henry Cecil Wyld lamented that while everyone has something to say about the English language, most of what people think about their language is downright wrong. Although Wyld's comment is an exaggeration, of course, much myth and misinformation circulates about language. For example, there is the myth, recounted as the absolute truth in the television series. "The Story of English," which states that certain residents of the islands off the Carolina coast speak English exactly the way it was spoken in Shakespeare's day. Of course such a linguistic fountain of youth cannot exist, for languages never stop changing, and while some elements of a region's speech may appear old fashioned to outsiders, other elements are distinctly advanced in comparison to neighboring areas. In addition to such folklore, much of what we think about language goes into the formation of language standards, and even if Wyld disapproved of public linguistic opinion, we must still take it into account, for it has a significant impact on language use. We constantly modify our speech and writing to match what we think others expect of us, and we also react against those expectations to assert our individuality through language.

If books and newspapers are any indication, popular interest in the English language remains intense. Journalistic writers about English attract faithful and vigilant followings for their regular columns and books. The publishers of dictionaries, thesauruses, and usage guides compete frantically for market share. And the abovementioned public television series on the English language reached a sizable audience and spawned a lavishly illustrated, best-selling book.

Yet Wyld was right about one thing: despite our persistent interest in things linguistic, too many of us resist the notion that a considerable body of well-ascertained facts about language exists and that a knowledge of linguistics can illuminate the language questions which concern teachers, writers, editors, and the general public. Acquiring this knowledge will allow instructors to become the experts we expect them to be. It will allow them to train students in a new kind of language awareness and sensitivity and perhaps to produce an American public whose linguistic knowledge more accurately reflects the state of linguistic scholarship and more closely matches the language requirements of the educational system and of everyday life.

What proves most daunting to English teachers as we contemplate our language chores are the groans from students at the mention of *grammar.* Although no dictonary, no matter how recent or unabridged, records the fact, for many of us *grammar* has become a dirty word, one that signals not the broad, fascinating study of language and its structures, but the dry-as-dust drilling of *dos* and *don'ts.* While we continually strive to bring literature alive for our students, too many generations of English teachers have allowed language study to become a dead and deadly issue. Clearly this need not be the case, for while students may show resistance to grammar lessons, they are as interested in language as any segment of the American public and are as sensitive to language as any group in our society. A discussion of school or campus slang draws excited participation from a class. High school students are aware that "grown ups" use language somewhat differently from them and that babies are linguistically creative, saying things like *goed* and *ated.* But they also know that their younger cousins and siblings too have a dialect or jargon of their own that high schoolers find difficult to penetrate and that makes them feel their age. Students are extremely sensitive to notions of correctness, not only when it comes to Standard English, but also within the speech communities of their peers. Although they may find the notions difficult to articulate, because many of them lack an appropriate metalanguage for precise description, they can comment astutely on their own dialects and those of "outsiders" and, in private, can do some pretty fair imitations of the speech of their teachers. Students are linguistically competitive as well: the participants in our regional spelling bee have the intensity of coaching and the partisan support of parental cheering sections that we have come to expect from grudge football games.

A language curriculum in the schools that builds on student interest and ability is most likely to succeed where others, concentrating on the negative aspects of correction and remediation, or the boredom of rote learning, have failed. To implement such a curriculum, however, requires some rethinking of the basic problem of teaching English to speakers of English.

Language instruction does have practical advantages for students, who already know that certain types of behavior, linguistic and otherwise, are required for academic, business, and professional success. But teaching students about the English language in order to get them better jobs, or to improve their speech and writing, is a bit like promising them that algebra will help balance their checkbooks once they enter the world of work is simply not true. Study after study has shown that grammar drill does not result in better writing, and pronunciation drill makes students self-conscious and reluctant to speak. We must teach language not as something students are bound to do wrong, if given half a chance, but as a vital symbolic system, one that helps us survive on this planet, one that, according to many theorists, is a distinguishing characteristic of the human species, and one that is a complex and little-understood subject in which students are predisposed to be interested. Teaching about language in this way, not as a rigid set of standards to be defended at all costs, but as a flexible and ever-expanding body of knowledge worthy of its own study, just as we teach literature, all but guarantees a successful set of lessons. Approaching language with a positive rather than a negative view of students' abilities saves us from the Henry Higgins trap. Higgins, in Shaw's *Pygmalion* and its later musical adaptation, *My Fair Lady,* is based on Henry Sweet, a prominent British linguist of the early twentieth century. Higgins's claim to fame in the play is his ability to perform a language transplant, turning a cockney match girl into an aristocratic debutante with whom he then falls in love. Shaw took the idea from the myth about the sculptor and King of Cyprus, Pygmalion, who falls in love with an ivory statue he carved. In answer to his prayer, Aphrodite brings the statue, Galatea, to life. The Pygmalion effect, as it is called, is often applied to education: it states that students will perform as well or as badly as the instructor expects them to. The analogy of Pygmalion/Henry Higgins to teaching needs expansion, though, when the issue is one of language. The statue we bring to life is not the student, but the subject (even in the myth, it took divine interference to enliven the statue created by the human). We can teach students about language, but we can perform no dialect transplants. The kind of content proposed here can help us put life into our subject, turning language from a cold and deadly study into one that our students live and breathe every day.

Works Cited

Baker, Josephine Truck. *Correct English: How to Use It.* Baltimore, Md.: Sadler-Rowe, 1907.

Baron, Dennis. *Declining Grammar and Other Essays on the English Vocabulary.* Urbana, Ill.: National Council of Teachers of English, 1989.

———. *Grammar and Gender.* New Haven, Conn.: Yale University Press, 1986.

———. *Going Native: The Regeneration of Saxon English. Publication of the American Dialect Society,* no. 69. University, Ala.: University of Alabama Press, 1982a.

———. *Grammar and Good Taste: Reforming the American Language.* New Haven, Conn.: Yale University Press, 1982b.

Evans, Bergen. *Comfortable Words.* New York: Random House, 1961.

Kington-Oliphant, T. L. *The Sources of Standard English.* London: 1873.

Vizetelly, Frank. *Desk-Book of Errors in English.* New York: Funk and Wagnalls, 1907.

Wyld, Henry Cecil. *English Philology in English Universities.* Oxford: Clarendon Press, 1921.

Anna O. Soter

15. The English Teacher and the Non-English-Speaking Student: Facing the Multicultural/ Multilingual Challenge

American schools have large percentages of minority students and do not know how to teach them those abilities that are usually grouped under the heading of English. If such students are classified as ESL (English as a Second Language), they may be provided with intensive English instruction by an ESL teacher for a relatively brief period in their school lives. Once they leave the ESL teacher, they enter the mainstream English classroom and must cope as best they can with their regular English classes.

This chapter describes the nature of the challenge with which we are faced, the complexity of the students with whom we are concerned, and examines the requirements in English and language arts curricula, along with ways in which these requirements conflict with what ESL learners can realistically do. It then turns to the contributions of second language research: what it means to be communicatively competent for the ESL student in secondary school English classes; the roles and relationships of ESL and regular classroom English teachers; and the implications and applications these factors have for the field of English education as a whole.

THE NATURE OF THE CHALLENGE

Virginia Allen quoted the latest census figures as showing more than eight million school-aged children living in homes in which the language is other than

English (61). Paul Ammon cites demographic figures that project, by the year 2000, nearly three-and-one-half million ESL children between ages five and fourteen enrolling in the elementary schools and subsequently secondary schools in the country (65). Many of the ESL students will spend most, if not all, of their time in the regular English classroom with some ESL instructional support for recent arrivals but little, if any, for those born in the United States. These children are also likely to spend much of their school time in lower-level groupings within grades and will have their limited proficiency in writing and reading English perceived as indifference or as demonstrating an inability to learn. Adding to the problem of such large numbers of children whose native language is not English or solely English is that they are often grouped with those whose family life is deprived of emotional, social, or intellectual nourishment. Terms and phrases, such as *disadvantaged, limited English proficient* (LEP) or *at-risk* are often used to characterize these students. Jack Richards argues that such students are also perceived as "culturally deprived" so that school failure to recognize difference rather than deficit results in the "generation of such concepts as cultural deprivation, restricted language development, and even cognitive deficiency, . . . symptomatic of analyses that fail to recognize the real ingredients of the child's experiences" (74).

In a recent editorial, Mary Healy cites John Ogbu who argues that the way minorities perform in school requires more than just linguistic or cultural information:

> . . . while cultural, language and opportunity barriers are very important for all minorities, the main factor differentiating the more successful from the less successful minorities appears to be the nature of the history, subordination and exploitation of the minorities and the nature of the minorities' own instrumental and expressive responses to their treatment, which enter into the process of their schooling. In other words, school performance is not due only to what is done to or for the minorities; it is also due to the fact that the nature of the minorities interpretations and responses make them more or less accomplices to their own school success or failure. There are thus three sources contributing to the school failure of the minorities who are not doing well in school, namely, society, school and community. (quoted in Healy 68)

Furthermore, English teacher educators have not faced the challenge of preparing regular classroom English teachers to accommodate and assist children from diverse cultural and linguistic backgrounds. In the May 1980 issue of *English Education,* Chester Laine and Edward Fagan observed that graduates of English education courses feel they are inadequately prepared to teach students classified as "slow learners" or as "culturally different" (204). What is significant to us is that these descriptions are coupled.

A reading of the *National Council of Teachers of English (NCTE) 1986 Guidelines for English/Language Arts Teacher Preparation* shows that only one item directly addresses students from diverse cultural and linguistic backgrounds. Pedagogically, teachers of English and language arts must be able to "use a variety of effective instructional strategies appropriate to diverse cultural groups and individual learning styles" (11) and must have "a respect for the individual language and dialect of each student" (14). Translating these principles into practice in English teacher education programs requires including courses in language acquisition, educational anthropology, applied linguistics and courses such as sociolinguistics and psycholinguistics. Current programs already might contain courses in which individual topics address social and cultural differences among students, but one or two topics are hardly sufficient to prepare teachers to carry out even the minimal requirements proposed in the *NCTE Guidelines.* English teacher educators are not entirely responsible for the limited inclusion of courses in anthropology and sociology in their programs. By the time students meet state certification requirements such courses add a considerable number of hours beyond a fourth or fifth year already facing teacher education candidates. Neither the community nor the prospective candidates themselves at this time may be prepared to meet the additional costs involved. Nevertheless, the most vigorous efforts to aid teachers in working effectively with culturally and linguistically diverse students must be made in teacher education for several reasons. First, professors, rather than school teachers, have immediate access to recent research developments in language and literacy acquisition. Second, teachers in the field have full daily schedules both in and out of school that do not permit a well-developed self-education effort. Third, in-service workshops, unless part of an ongoing program in faculty development, cannot offer comprehensive and continuous information and practical experience that a fully developed course on a college campus is able to offer. Finally, the current situation in schools clearly suggests that if teacher preparation programs limit or ignore the problem of culturally and linguistically diverse student populations, we can hardly expect the schools to do otherwise.

The Students

Because the term *multicultural* is broad enough to be a catchall for any student from any culture, we need to define its limits. Similarly, the phrase minority groups is so broad as to encompass immigrants, inner-city groups, black groups, native American groups, and diverse socioeconomic groups not part of the white middle-class. This chapter is primarily concerned with students whose parents were born outside of the United States or who themselves were born outside of the United States and for whom the mother tongue is either the native language (i.e., dominant in their home in the United States) or equally used with English as the second language. This group can best be described as including those described as minority immigrants who, by having English as a second language and by belonging to that specific group, are at an educational as well as social disadvantage. However, what will be said about second language learning and the acquisition of a second literacy also may be applied in principle to any student whose mother tongue is not English. I do not focus on all students who are often included in the term *minority* (e.g., black students) although at times reference will also be made to this group where appropriate.

Many English teachers have had students from culturally diverse backgrounds in their classrooms. In composition courses in colleges, the so-called basic writer is often, although not exclusively, a writer who is black, or from an inner-city migrant background. Additionally, although students from inner-city migrant backgrounds actually might have been born in the United States, the native language of the home is not necessarily "literate" English. Parents who may have arrived as children themselves or as young adults often speak of a "fossilized" form of English which gets them by in their daily working and social lives. Jack Richards describes the form as having linguistic features derived from limited exposure to English and that become fixed through lack of reinforcement from native speakers (68–72).

Why focus on these students? In part, because they form such a large proportion of the students to whom Allen refers in her article and thus deserve attention because of their obvious impact on classroom effectiveness. Furthermore, they also highlight a question that remains unanswered in second language acquisition research but that has powerful implications for the effectiveness of ESL programs in secondary and elementary schools. That is, how long does it take to acquire a second language with a level of proficiency that permits successful functioning as a fully literate member of the adopted culture?

Much of what will be said about the kind of student described here is somewhat speculative. Research on second language learners has used the ESL classroom as a research laboratory rather than following ESL students in the regular English classroom. Additionally, where children and adolescents have been the focus of research, they have either been studied in bilingual programs (Spanish or French) or in what are termed "immersion" programs in Canada and in some few U. S. school districts. As yet, little is known of ESL students' literacy performance in the regular English classroom or how we can help such students achieve proficiency levels required for successful academic performance.

School Language and Literacy Requirements

When we talk about school-level proficiency in language use, we are not only concerned with grammatical aspects (such as parts of speech, word order, spelling, etc.,) but also with semantic properties of the language and with discourse properties (both pragmatic and rhetorical) in written and spoken language. High school students need a sophisticated command over the more sophisticated aspects of language use that often are not required outside of school and draw heavily on the written mode.

Indeed, as some second language researchers have found in their research, the more proficient in social communicative skills ESL students are, the less likely they are to be as proficient in the communicative skills required for success in academic contexts (Saville-Troike 215–17). This may seem paradoxical and, initially, somewhat surprising but, on further reflection, is consistent with the kinds of skills required predominantly in both domains. Social skills develop in highly contextualized situations and are dependent on constant interaction with others. Academic skills develop in very narrow contexts and, some would argue, in decontextualized contexts (i.e., written language creates its own contexts).

Within the academic context, learning is largely a dyadic interaction between student and teacher and, within that, a solo act. The language required is a Standard English—not "native" even to many native speakers—a formal genre, using relatively unfamiliar vocabulary that is often highly specialized. According to James Britton, the primary "audience" is a "default" audience or a pseudoaudience such as the teacher as examiner (132) whose purpose is to test whether students have understood concepts and learned the material.

SELECTED SECOND LANGUAGE ACQUISITION RESEARCH: ITS RELEVANCE TO ENGLISH TEACHERS

Because the primary concern of English teachers is to help students develop literacy skills, I shall concentrate on some of the major factors that affect the acquisition of reading and writing in students who are ESL learners. Included in this discussion is the role of the native language; problems in language learning; the acquisition of grammatical rules; input and language learning; affective factors; the role of cognitive styles; the meaning of biliterary and cultural factors involved in second language learning.

I also discuss how English teachers can benefit from such knowledge in assisting their second language learners to become confident readers and writers of English and argue why such knowledge is vital. What follows is a necessarily reduced and highly selective summary of what we know about factors involved in acquiring a second language.

Role of the Native Language. Cross-linguistic research has revealed that the native language plays a role in the rate at which learners restructure the rules derived from the native language and move through successive states of second language acquisition. The greatest difficulties in acquiring a second language occur when linguistic aspects are considerably similar. The first language also appears to influence the acquisition of the second language in additional ways: through the transfer of native forms into English; and through the students' competence in the native language. That is, proficiency in the native language appears to coincide with relative achievement in English (Saville-Troike 214). However, most striking is the extent to which individual differences exist among nonnative subjects. Thus, great diversity can also occur among children who share the same mother tongue (Saville-Troike 214).

Another problem is that different linguistic forms require different lengths of time to be acquired—that is, the rate of acquiring negation might differ substantially from that of acquiring prepositions depending on the student's language background and other variables. This applies at whatever age the second language learner begins the acquisition of the target language. Theresa Pica found that Spanish and Italian speakers often remain at the preverbal stage in their acquisition of English negation, unlike Japanese, German, and Norweigan (693). In the former languages, negation is expressed before the verb and in English use often appears as "I no go." In the latter, negation occurs after the verb and does not resemble a transitional stage in the acquisition of English negation.

Research on *interlanguage phenomena* indicates that second language learners transfer various forms and linguistic strategies known in the native language to their communicative attempts in the second language (Schachter and Rutherford 303). This strategy was traditionally negatively regarded as *interference* by linguists. Subsequently, *transfer,* as the phenomenon is now known, came to be regarded as a natural artifact of learning and acquiring a second language and, as such, must be accounted for in the development of the target language.

For our purposes, five of the seven factors found by Jack Richards and Gloria Sampson that might influence and characterize second language learner systems are particularly relevant. These are language transfer (as described above); intralingual interference—a process during which the learner makes generalizations based on partial exposure to the second language and makes errors; sociolinguistic situation (setting for language use); modality (whether learners are producing the language or receiving it (for example, spelling pronunciations and confusions between written and spoken styles); and age, which might affect the processing strategies used in acquiring the language because age also influences memory and the number of abstract concepts that can be handled simultaneously at any one time (5–18). Acquiring the more complex syntactic patterns more typical of written language might take even longer than we have previously thought. These factors may help teachers identify writers' strategies and errors with greater understanding and accuracy, and point to the usefulness in adopting rhetorical models as a means of helping students understand the operations of second language discourse—both orally and textually.

Acquisition of Grammatical Rules. Current research concerning successive language acquisition (i.e., acquiring a second language after having developed basic linguistic skills in the first) stresses that the grammatical knowledge undergirding language ability and proficiency is acquired quite unconsciously (Gathercole 415). Similarly, we know from first language acquisition research that children adopt the basic linguistic and pragmatic patterns of their native language in an unconscious, informal way. Therefore, an additional objective in language teaching in schools should be to develop *metalinguistic skills* (i.e., knowing language about language). For example, describing the grammatical function of words in a sentence is essentially a metalinguistic skill. Although metalinguistic skill is somewhat dependent on linguistic proficiency, they are not one and the same thing.

Input and Language Acquisition/Learning. Both the linguistic and pragmatic input received and the way in which second language learners interact with this input are important determinants of acquisition (Long; Pica, Young, and Doughty). Thus, mere quantity of contact with English-speaking students has little affect on second language learning, but the degree of active participation in communicating with English-speaking peers is a significant factor (Johnson; Strong).

Unlike day-to-day communication with peers, academic success requires competence in using and understanding language in context-reduced situations where students cannot rely on nonverbal (i.e., paralinguistic) elements of communication. This kind of competence is most likely achieved through writing (Saville-Troike 216–7). Among the conclusions Muriel Saville-Troike draws from her study of nineteen elementary children representing seven languages and ranging from Grades two through six are (1) vocabulary knowledge is the most important aspect of oral language proficiency for academic achievement; (2) spoken practice in English may not be necessary for the development of English proficiency and may retard it—that is, an emphasis on interpersonal communication may inhibit academic achievement; (3) mastery of English grammatical structures is more closely related to native language background than to an ability to use English for academic purposes; (4) most children who achieved best in the content areas, as measured by tests in English, were those who had the opportunity to discuss the concepts in their native language (216).

Affective Factors. Motivation to learn a second language is an important determinant in second language acquisition and appears to be enhanced by decreasing the social distance between learners and members of the target language group (Schumann 15–18). In addition, Michael Strong suggests that personality and attitudes may contribute to differential academic success in second language learning by children (255).

Role of Cognitive Styles and Individual Learning Styles. Cognitive styles as they relate to second language learning were first defined by James Cummins through field dependence and field independence—that is, contrasting tendencies to rely on either external or internal frames of reference in perceiving, organizing, analyzing, or recalling information and experience (197–205). Field-dependent persons tend to rely more on others, to be more skilled in interpersonal relations, and to derive their identity from others around them. Field independent persons, in contrast, tend to be more independent, competitive, and self-reliant (Hansen 311). Cultural factors and social factors may influence the degree to which individuals exhibit field dependence and independence.

A favoring of field independence appears to be somewhat necessary for successful academic performance—a finding that accords with Saville-Troike's arguments that ESL children who exhibit greater sociability and risk-taking in informal, oral communicative situations do not necessarily perform well in the academic domain (216). Thus, teachers should not be misled into thinking that the outwardly more verbal child is actually more linguistically competent (for academic purposes) than the child who is less eager to "practice" his or her English language use with peers and in classroom discussions. Saville-Troike and others also found that native language cognitive-academic proficiency appears to be reflected in the written products of the second language writer (217). These findings suggest that more attention be paid to early practice in writing and reading tasks for ESL students.

Biliteracy and Potential Advantages. Some research with older students indicates that reading and writing programs based on biliteracy enable them to perform well in both languages (Duran 49). Increasing support is emerging for allowing ESL children to write and read in their native language because they seem to develop control over the written medium without the additional stress of understanding the language of expression.

Little research, if any, has investigated what effect no exposure to literature of their own background culture has on the reading interests and ability of ESL students in secondary schools. Yet recent schema-related research highlights the significance of background knowledge as an influence on the ability to fully comprehend text. Furthermore, the teaching of literature in the secondary school has traditionally assumed shared cultural knowledge although ESL students do not necessarily share that common context, nor do they share common responses to literary texts (Graham 505).

Cultural Factors in Learning a Second Language

Research by sociolinguists and anthropologists such as Gordon Wells, Sarah Michaels, and Shirley Brice-Heath confirms that language learning is essentially cultural learning which varies from one sociocultural group to the next. Stephen Boggs examined school failure in Hawaiian children and concluded that much of this failure can be attributed to differences in both verbal and social behavior at home in contrast to that expected and experienced at school (167). A relevant example relates to the different functions that the same type of questioning has in the home and school, that is, direct questioning. For the teacher, such a questioning style occurs for the purpose of recitation of information. For Hawaiian parents, the function is to elicit incriminating information that will be the source of subsequent punishment. Understandably, these children either avoid direct questioning by adults or answer only as briefly as possible (Boggs 166). Boggs argues that we need congruence between home and school verbal interaction with children from diverse linguistic and cultural backgrounds in order for them to engage in the social and academic routines of schooling that lead to achievement rather than to failure (167).

An additional and significant factor that determines school performance among ESL students relates to learning styles, which may differ as a result of the cultural backgrounds of learners. Joy Reid's study, which involved more than 1,000 ESL students and identified their perceptual learning style differences, found that these differed significantly from the perceptions held by native English speakers (96–101). Differences occurred among Koreans, Chinese, and Arabic students who preferred visual presentations in contrast to native speakers of English who preferred verbal presentations. All ESL students showed strong preferences for tactile learning whereas the native English speakers did not. Others have suggested that variables such as sex, length of residence, length of time studying English in the United States, and age are also related to differences in learning styles. Both elementary and secondary school students revealed different patterns of mental abilities, for example, visual, spatial, abstract, and numerical, depending on their sociocultural backgrounds (Reid 90).

According to Reid, ESL instructors often use methods and materials that have been developed with the learning needs of native speakers of English in mind (91). Although learning styles cannot obviously be rapidly changed, sensitivity to them and to their sociocultural diversity may enable teachers to select materials and to develop more effective teaching approaches.

Thus, learning a second language for academic performance is not simply the easy task of learning the grammatical rules of that language. Participation in an ESL class or even in an intensive-language group for several months will not prepare the ESL student for competent performance in school. The process is an ongoing one, requiring continued support from regular classroom teachers who are sympathetic to the ESL student and who understand the tremendous diversity of variables affecting second language acquisition.

I have focused on the language learning process as it relates to school performance because this process forms the foundation for understanding what is involved in learning literacy as a second discourse system. Although I have separated language and literacy in the discussion so far, the two are mutually interrelated in the context of schooling. In the next section of this chapter, I discuss factors that affect reading and writing in a second language.

LEARNING LITERACY AS A SECOND DISCOURSE SYSTEM

As noted in an earlier section, research in second language acquisition indicates that children will be more successful in learning literacy skills if they are already literate in their native language. Having acquired literacy in the native language, the student has already gained the necessary strategies for negotiating meaning in print. This distinction between strategies and the actual learning of the language is important. Although language and its obvious role in reading and writing is central to these two activities, it is not the sole component in achieving success in those same activities. In addition to knowing the language, one must also know literate behaviors, that is, how to approach print (e.g., directionality is an important print component and varies among cultures.) Robert Kaplan argues that paragraphing as a discourse convention also appears to vary across cultures (286).

Factors Affecting Second Language Literacy Learning

Among factors that might affect becoming literate in a second language are the significance of literacy in the home; whether parents are literate; the proximity of the home-discourse system to that used in the school; the relationship of background knowledge to comprehension, shared values and attitudes, types of discourse and their related conventional systems; and content knowledge. None of these factors has been investigated with ESL students in regular classrooms over short or long periods of time, but research in native language literacy acquisition strongly indicates that we must take these factors into account.

Additionally, research in literacy acquisition has also investigated differences between speech and written discourse, and related differences in cognitive styles. These are discussed briefly in the following section in terms of how this research is relevant to second language literacy acquisition. Also discussed is the development of writing in a second language and factors that positively and negatively affect this development.

Research in early literacy acquisition in the United States indicates that the process involves a shift from the physical world of experience to a symbolic representation of that world, much as Vygotsky described in the development of symbolism in children (105–16). However, in these early stages of differentiation between print symbolism and gestural symbolism, the difference lies only in the fact that print symbolism fixes on the page what is still mutable in the gestural dimension. As the child continues to develop and becomes acquainted with more complex concepts, the print world becomes the communicative vehicle most capable of symbolically representing those more complex concepts.

Even in the earliest phases of literacy acquisition, children are developing an awareness that representing information in print necessitates acquiring different symbolic systems from those they habitually use in speech and gesture. Research in early child literacy development shows that when children grow up in a print-rich environment and have opportunities to read and write before attending school, they are capable of developing this awareness, a consequence of the innate development of symbolic representation (Goodman 315).

In the early days of literacy research, scholars such as Jack Goody and Ian Watt, David Olson, and Walter Ong investigated differences between oral and literate cognitive styles in orally-based and literacy-based cultures. Initially, we assumed that literacy had significant, isolatable effects on the way we think. Some of the common assumptions were that literacy creates the capacity to think analytically, to be rational, to think logically. However, cognitive psychologists such as Scribner and Cole suggest that the differences in thinking styles are school-related rather than literacy-related (254). In other words, the nonliterate person is neither illogical nor irrational nor nonanalytical so much as one who possesses a logic and reasoning that are qualitatively different.

Subsequently, anthropologists, discourse analysts, and sociolinguists argue that literacy involves the learning of a different system of discourse, not only the organization of ideas but also their linguistic expression. Consequently, the closer the styles of home-school discourse patterns and the closer to the written discourse styles that the home-oral style approximates, the less problematic is the transition, or, one could argue, the translation process.

This leads to the central point I want to make about the acquisition of literacy in a second language. In thinking about second language literacy learning in formal contexts (e.g., in schools and colleges), we have frequently done so in a decontextualized way. That is, we have not taken into account what factors are involved in the acquisition of literacy and then examined these in light of simultaneously acquiring a second language.

Despite the often rigidly sequenced instructional pattern for ESL students (listening/speaking; reading/writing) researchers such as Sarah Hudelson confirm that ESL learners are able to read English before they have complete oral control of the language and can write before they have complete control over English (231). Hudelson's findings suggest that ESL children, if given opportunities for reading and writing, can extend their literate proficiency in English although the rate of acquiring proficiency varies on an individual basis (231).

Individual rates in development of proficiency cannot be overlooked. According to Virginia Collier's study of 1,548 (Limited English Proficiency) students, those from middle- to lower-middle-income groups of immigrants with upwardly mobile aspirations require between two and eight years to reach the national grade level norms of native speakers (617). The range in years is related to years of residency and age at arrival—the youngest (between ages five and seven on arrival) students somewhere in the middle, the preadolescent students (between ages eight and eleven on arrival) between two to five years for native-speaker grade-level proficiency, and the oldest students (between ages twelve and fifteen on arrival) as long as six to eight years to reach native-speaker grade-level proficiency (Collier 631–36).

Collier argues that six to eight years of residence might be needed to attain national averages for native speaker achievement across all subject areas (637). Suggested alternatives are instructing students in their native language in content area classes while they are mastering English or offering content area ESL classes taught at the level of English proficiency exhibited by students in their early years of ESL (Collier 637).

Significant implications for secondary English teachers from Collier's work are that we cannot assume that one or two years of intensive ESL-related instruction prepares students for complex expository writing or difficult comprehension tasks, such as analysis, synthesis, and evaluation.

Knowledge of Discourse Conventions in Written Language

As literate native English speakers much of what we take for granted about English expository and narrative discourse must be made explicit for the nonnative English speaker. What makes a story, for example, a "good" story versus a "poor" story is culturally determined. Assumptions about sharing similar understandings of "plot," "point of view," "figurative language," "character development," and so on in literature study and writing are ill-founded (Soter; Indrasuta). Students bring with them a culturally bound awareness of text and of story. Notions of plot vary among cultures as do stylistic elements such as the function of repetition, the degree of personal tone and involvement by the writer, and ways in which we address our potential audiences. Unfortunately, research in this domain of second language and literacy acquisition is still very limited, but pedagogical implications from the early research are quite clear: we do not share similar assumptions about text, and both teachers and students labor under unnecessary misapprehensions unless this factor is acknowledged.

The impact of using literature representative of other cultural groups (non-American) is not yet known. However, given that background knowledge is one of the single most powerful factors affecting comprehension in reading, unless we provide ESL and other minority students with the opportunity to respond to literature drawn from their own cultural contexts, we deny them the full engagement that can come with literary experiences.

Much of this is common sense but has only begun to be validated by empirical research. Researchers who have explored reading and writing connections argue that reading and writing are closely connected activities. One pedagogical application of these findings is the movement toward a curriculum that uses literature as a basis for not only reading but also writing. Implicit in this movement is acknowledgment that just as one must have constant exposure to discourse conventions related to spoken communication, so must one have constant exposure to discourse conventions related to written communication. One implication for the second language reader and writer is that literacy is most effectively acquired when print models of language use abound. Retaining students in "basic" classes, which focus on drill and routines of grammatical and lower-level rhetorical rules, does not provide them with the models of written language prized by schools.

Writing in a Second Language

The second language writer (and, perhaps, speakers of nonstandard dialects such as Black English) is not only faced with the task of learning the second language (English) but also with ways of manipulating that language into discourse patterns recognizable and acceptable to the literate native speaker.

The complexity of the processes involved in acquiring sophisticated writing skills is demonstrated in the illustrated model of writing development in Figure 15.1. The model is representative of school/academic writing and is, therefore, possibly more complex than it might be if we were representing writing required in daily life (e.g., personal letters, diaries, journals, greeting cards, shopping lists, etc.).

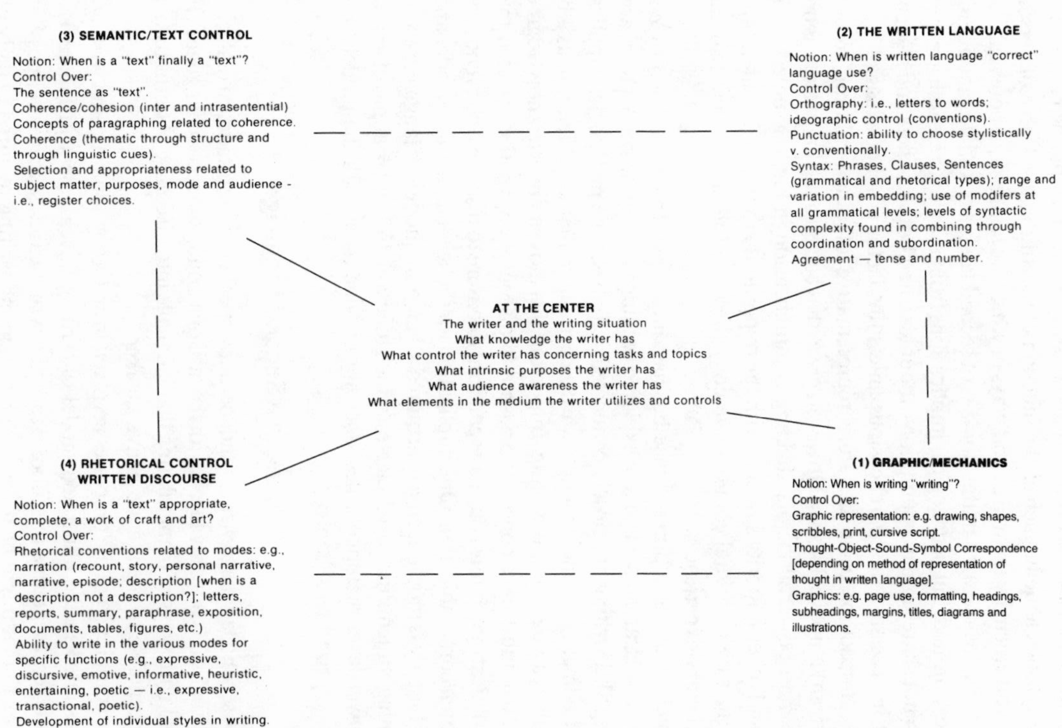

Figure 15.1: A Model for Describing Development in Writing

ESL writers may already know how to write in their first language and therefore will be familiar with conventions such as directionality, cohesion, or those governing coherence in their native written discourse. This means that a teacher can use the students' text-building knowledge and text-building strategies.

Because language is one of the features of text and appears to be developed in relation to its use in diverse cultures, language and text are closely related. That is, the English language may be well-suited to the creation of expository text of the kind we are familiar with whereas the students' native language may not help here. In this situation, the teacher must be sensitive to problems such students may face that are unique to their linguistic/discourse experiences.

Figure 15.1 indicates that writers must also know sociolinguistically related conventions, that is, those related to audience (e.g., status, age, interest groups) or those to purpose and choice of appropriate discourse forms (e.g., for persuasion, some forms are more suitable than others, such as argumentation, advertising, or satire). Within the sociolinguistic domain, writers need to know how to modify their message according to those whom they wish to influence or affect. Consequent linguistic choices are related not only to that audience but also to the form selected (e.g., different functions of persuasion).

The fact that second language learners may already have gained some knowledge in their native culture should be a useful starting point for teachers to help them become aware of different forms for similar (although not necessarily identical) discourse in the target culture. We can, therefore, build on the communicative strategies and patterns of the first language more effectively if we acknowledge their existence and their influence. Too often, we make the unconscious assumption that second language learners come to us knowing nothing of communicative strategies simply because they are unfamiliar with those of English.

WHAT DOES IT ALL MEAN AND HOW DO WE APPLY IT?

I have not by any means touched on all aspects related to the development of literacy skills by ESL students. However, what I have attempted to do in this chapter is to indicate how complex that process is and to argue that at least two challenges emerge for ESL and regular classroom teachers and for teacher educators:

1. Greater collaboration is necessary between ESL and regular classroom English teachers, who must focus on teaching discourse knowledge and on providing appropriate discourse experiences.
2. English teacher preparation programs need courses in second language acquisition that include cultural and social factors related to literacy development. Additionally, more visionary in-service experiences and opportunities are needed to enable classroom teachers and ESL teachers to share mutual knowledge and experiences concerning ESL students.

In this concluding section, I summarize the discussion of the preceding pages with a description of what is required to be communicatively competent and how this applies to the ESL student. It is followed by a brief discussion of how teachers and teacher educators may implement some of the principles and findings described in relation to second language learners in their classrooms.

Developing Competence in School Language Use

I have argued that acquiring and learning English in the school context is a very different activity from that of learning English for common social and work-related purposes. Recognition that learning English is not a simplistic, grammatical process is increasingly seen in second language research. Consider, for example, the varity of distinctions made by the English teaching field: English as a Foreign Language; English for Special Purposes; English as a Second Language; and English for Academic Purposes. The awareness that learning English is not a uniphenomological act is relatively new in the domain of second language research and instruction. It enjoys an extremely limited awareness in the mainstream elementary and secondary school context where it is most needed.

Additionally, students' performance profiles in tests of English achievement are shown to be significantly related not only to linguistic proficiency but also to social, cultural and affective factors (Goldman 4–5). Cultural bias in testing with respect to ESL learners is not a new issue but is seriously overlooked in mainstream, standardized testing, which does not account for factors affecting the performance of ESL students in such testing.

In school, language becomes a tool for learning and, in the secondary school, both language and the concepts it describes become increasingly complex. Not surprisingly, then ESL students who have not achieved a level of linguistic proficiency that matches grade level performance for native speakers fall behind in the subjects that are largely dependent on language (e.g., history, economics, geography, English, natural sciences). Two primary factors appear to operate in the school setting: (1) the social component interacts and influences the linguistic constraints and demands made of language use in a school setting and, (2) certain language forms become prevalent in a school setting for both native and nonnative speakers. In this setting, students need to master a level of linguistic and metalinguistic proficiency that enable them to conceptualize in specific ways about specific kinds of knowledge and information, to draw abstract generalizations, and to express complex relationships in speaking and writing (Swain). Thus, the task of developing communicative competence for an ESL student in schools is a comprehensive one.

The Role of Teachers and Teacher Educators

Although language study is asserted as significant, teachers are still not required to take a relevant sequence of courses in applied linguistics or even in traditional grammar. The current emphasis on using language and experiencing it in a variety of contexts is not sufficient for students to become metalinguistically competent or to understand explicitly how they need to manipulate language for particular purposes and audiences. Aspiring teachers in undergraduate and graduate courses in English education programs appear to be unfamiliar with ways in which language can be perceived and described (Laine and Fagan).

How can teachers develop students' understanding of their own language processes unless they can describe how students acquire language? To enable them to do so means that English teachers need some training in discourse analysis to guide students in perceiving and identifying links in language use in the context of speaking, listening, reading, writing. Unless English education programs recognize the urgent need to adequately equip English teachers with knowledge about the social and cognitive aspects of language use, teacher candidates will continue to feel inadequately prepared in their academic specialization.

A call for action might include urging English certification programs in colleges to hold a joint conference with public schools and focus on issues in multicultural and multiethnic education for secondary students. Because ESL teachers and regular classroom teachers often work under the same roof, if not side-by-side, collaboration between them could be fostered through a call for papers that focus on the shared tasks of ESL and regular classroom teachers. ESL teachers typically go to their own conferences and English teachers typically go to their conferences but rarely, if ever, do they meet at a professional level to discuss the common challenge described in this chapter.

Finally, teacher educators in English education must necessarily provide the role models for the transformation desired in the field of English teaching. Their courses should reflect an awareness of and attention to the problems of multicultural classrooms that many English education majors will face. Materials and methods of English teacher educators must become multiculturally and multilinguistically sensitive if program graduates are to learn how to integrate students from diverse cultural and linguistic backgrounds into the regular classroom activities.

Works Cited

Allen, Virginia. "Developing Contexts to Support Second Language Acquisition." *Language Arts* 63.2 (1986): 61–67.

Ammon, Paul. "Helping Children Learn to Write in English as a Second Language: Some Observations and Some Hypotheses." *The Acquisition of Written Language.* Sarah W. Freedman, ed. Norwood, N. J.: Ablex, 1985. 65–84.

Boggs, Stephen. *Speaking, Relating and Learning: A Study of Hawaiian Children at Home and at School.* Norwood, N. J.: Albex, 1985.

Britton, James, et al. *The Development of Writing Abilities (11–18).* London: Macmillan, 1975.

Collier, Virginia, P. "Age and Rate of Acquisition of Second Language for Academic Purposes." *TESOL Quarterly* 21.4 (1987): 617–42.

Cummins, James. "Cognitive/Academic Language Proficiency, Linguistic Interdependence, The Optional Age Question, And Some Other Matters." *Working Pages on Bilingualism* 19 (1979): 197–205.

________. "Empowering Minority Students: A Framework for Intervention." *Harvard Educational Review* 56 (1986): 18–36.

Duran, Richard. "Factors Affecting Development of Second Language Literacy." *Becoming Literate In English As a Second Language.* Susan Goldman and Henry Triska, eds. Norwood, N. J.: Albex, 1987. 33–56.

Fagan, Edward, and Chester H. Laine. "The Preparation of English Teachers: Has It Been a Decade of Change?" *English Education* 11.4(1980): 199–208.

Gass, Susan, and Carol Madden. Introduction. *Input in Second Language Acquisition.* Susan Gass and Carol Madden, eds. Rowley, Mass.: Newbury House, 1985. 3–12.

Gathercole, Virginia. "Some Myths You May Have Heard About First Language Acquisition." *TESOL Quarterly* 22.3 (1988): 407–436.

Goldman, Susan R. "Contextual Issues in the Study of Second Language Literacy." *Becoming Literate In English As a Second Language.* Susan Goldman and Henry Trueba, eds. Norwood, N. J.: Albex, 1987. 1–8.

Goodman, Yetta. "The Development of Initial Literacy." *Perspectives On Literacy.* Eugene Kintgen, Barry Knoll, and Mike Rose, eds. Carbondale: Southern Illinois University Press, 1988. 312–20.

Goody, Jack, and Ian Watt. "The Consequences of Literacy." *Comparative Studies in Society and History* 5 (1963): 304–45.

Graham, Janet G. "English Language Proficiency and the Prediction of Academic Success. *TESOL Quarterly* 21.3 (1987): 505–22.

Hansen, Lynne. "Field Dependence-Independence and Language Testing: Evidence from Six Pacific Island Cultures." *TESOL Quarterly* 18.2 (1984): 311–24.

Healy, Mary A. K. "Editorial Comment." *English Education* 20.2 (1988): 67–70.

Heath, Shirley Brice. *Ways With Words.* Cambridge, Mass.: Harvard University Press, 1983.

Hudelson, Sarah. "Kan Yu Ret an Rayt En Ingles: Children Become Literate in English." *TESOL Quarterly* 18.2 (1984): 221–38.

Indrasuta, Chantanee. "Narrative Styles in the Writing of Thai and American Students." *Writing Across Languages and Cultures.* Alan C. Purves, ed. San Francisco, Calif.: Sage, 1988. 206–26.

Kaplan, Robert. "Contrastive Rhetoric and Second Language Learning: Notes Toward a Theory of Contrastive Rhetoric." *Writing Across Languages and Cultures: Issues in Contrastive Rhetoric.* Alan C. Purves, ed. Newbury Park, Calif.: Sage, 1988. 275–304.

Laine, Chester H., and Edward R. Fagen. "The Preparation of English Teachers: Has It Been a Decade of Change?" *English Education* 11.4 (1980): 199–208.

Long, Michael. "Input and Second Language Acquisition Theory." *Input in Second Language Acquisition.* Susan Gass and Carol Madden, eds. Rowley, Mass.: Newbury House, 1985. 377–93.

Michaels, Sarah. "Sharing Time: Children's Narrative Styles and Differential Access to Literacy." *Language in Society* 10.3 (1981): 423–42.

Guidelines For the Preparation of Teachers of English/Language Arts. Urbana, Ill.: National Council of Teachers of English, 1986.

Ogbu, John U. "Cultural Discontinuities and Schooling." *Anthropology and Education Quarterly* 13.4 (1977): 290–307.

Olson, David R. "From Utterance to Text: The Bias of Language in Speech and Writing." *Harvard Educational Review* 47.3 (1977): 257–81.

Ong, Walter. *Orality and Literacy.* London: Methuen, 1982.

Pica, Theresa. "L1 Transfer and L2 Complexity as Factors in Syllabus Design." *TESOL Quarterly* 18.4 (1984): 689–704.

Pica, Theresa, Richard Young, and Catherine Doughty. "The Impact of Interaction on Comprehension." *TESOL Quarterly* 21.4 (1987): 737–58.

Reid, Joy. "The Learning Style Preferences of ESL Students." *TESOL Quarterly* 21.1 (1987): 87–112.

Richards, Jack C. "Social Factors, Interlanguage and Language Learning." *Error Analysis: Perspectives on Second Language Acquisition.* Jack C. Richards, ed. London: Longman, 1974. 65–93.

Richards, Jack, and Gloria Sampson. "The Study of Learner English." *Error Analysis: Perspectives on Second Language Acquisition.* Jack C. Richards, ed. London: Longman, 1974. 3–18.

Saville-Troike, Muriel. "What Really Matters in Second Language Learning for Academic Achievement." *TESOL Quarterly* 18.2 (1984): 199–220.

Schachter, Jacqueline, and William Rutherford. "Discourse Function and Language Transfer." *Second Language Learning.* Betty Wallace Robinett and Jacqueline Schachter, eds. Ann Arbor, Mich.: University of Michigan Press, 1983. 303–15.

Scribner, Sylvia, and Michael Cole. *The Psychology of Literacy.* Cambridge, Mass.: Harvard University Press, 1981.

Schumann, John. "Second Language Acquisition Research: Get a More Global Look at the Learner." *Papers in Second Language Acquisition.* H. Douglas Brown, ed. Special Issue No. 4. Language Learning, 1976. 15–28.

Soter, Anna. "The Second Language Learner and Cultural Transfer in Narration." *Writing Across Languages and Cultures.* Alan C. Purves, ed. San Francisco, Calif.: Sage, 1988. 177–205.

Strong, Michael. "Social Styles and the Second Language Acquisition of Spanish-Speaking Kindergarteners." *TESOL Quarterly* 17.2 (1983): 241–58.

Swain, Merrill. "Time and Timing in Bilingual Education." *Language Learning* 31.1 (1981): 1–15.

Tarone, Elaine. "Interlanguage as Chamelon." *Language Learning.* 29 (1979): 181–91.

Vygotsky, Lev S. *Mind in Society: The Development of Higher Psychological Processes.* Michael Cole, Vera John-Steiner, Sylvia Scribner, and Ellen Souberman, eds. Cambridge, Mass.: Harvard University Press, 1975.

Wells, Gordon. "Preschool Literacy-Related Activities and Success in School." *Literacy, Language and Learning.* David R. Olson, Nancy Torrance, and Angela Hildyard, eds. Cambridge, Mass.: Cambridge University Press, 1986.

About the Contributors

Dennis Baron, a specialist in the history of the English language, is Professor of English and linguistics and Director of Rhetoric at the University of Illinois at Urbana-Champaign. He taught high school English in New York City and a Boston suburb, and directed the University of Illinois Writing Outreach Workshop, offering a summer institute for secondary school English teachers. He has been a member of NCTE's Commission on the English Language, and he edits the monograph series, *Publication of the American Dialect Society.* He is also on the advisory board of University High School in Urbana. His books include *Grammar and Good Taste: Reforming the American Language* (Yale University Press, 1982), and *Grammar and Gender* (Yale University Press, 1986). He is currently preparing a book on the history of the movement to make English the official language of the United States.

Edward P. J. Corbett is Professor of English at Ohio State University where he directed Freshman English from 1966 to 1970. A Former President of the Ohio Council of Teachers of English Language Arts (OCTELA), 1971, and Chair of the Conference on College Composition and Communication (CCCC), 1971, Professor Corbett edited *College Composition and Communication* for many years. In addition, he has been Chair of the College Section of the National Council of Teachers of English (NCTE), 1984–85. Author of *Classical Rhetoric for the Modern Student* (Oxford University Press, 2nd ed., 1971), *The Little English Handbook* (Scott, Foresman, 5th ed., 1987), and *Selected Essays of Edward P. J. Corbett,* (ed. Robert J. Connors, Southern Methodist University Press, 1988), Professor Corbett was awarded the distinguished Scholar Award from Ohio State University and also the Distinguished Service Award from NCTE, both in 1986. He has recently coedited with Gary Tate, *The Writing Teacher's Sourcebook* (Oxford University Press, 2nd ed., 1988).

Sheryl L. Finkle is a doctoral candidate in rhetoric and composition at The Ohio State University. She received her M. S. at Illinois State University and taught special education as well as junior and senior high school English for ten years. Her dissertation is on the connections between reading, writing, and thinking, and she has published on the uses of literature in composition classes and the uses of writing in literature classes in the *Illinois English Bulletin.*

Ron Fortune is an Associate Professor of English at Illinois State University and teaches undergraduate writing courses and graduate courses in composition theory and practice. Much of his work focuses on integrating writing and literature instruction in high school and university English courses. In 1986, the Modern Language Association (MLA) published *School-College Collaborative Programs in English,* which he edited and to which he contributed an essay based on a school-college collaborative teaching project supported by the National Endowment for the Humanities (NEH). He is currently directing a three-year series of NEH Summer Institutes for high school teachers, concentrating on the integration of literature and writing instruction through the use of literary manuscripts. Other subjects about which he has written include learning theory and English studies, computers and composition, autobiographical writing, and the relationship between composition and literary studies.

Cheryl Glenn is Assistant Professor of English at Oregon State University. She earned the Ph. D. in English from The Ohio State University where she held a Presidential Fellowship. Her dissertation is entitled "Muted Voices: Women in Rhetoric from Antiquity through the Renaissance." She has published articles on medieval life, rhetoric, and composition. In addition to her dissertation, her current interests lie in feminist theory and historiography.

Mary Louise Gomez is Assistant Professor in the Department of Curriculum and Instruction at the University of Wisconsin-Madison and a Senior Researcher with the National Center for Research on Teacher Education at Michigan State University. She teaches courses focusing on the language arts in the elementary school, the role of technology in the K–12 curriculum, and paradigms of composing and their relation to pedagogy. Her research interests center on how preservice and inservice teachers learn to write and teach writing. She is the Associate Director of the Wisconsin Writing project and a member of the NCTE Committee on Instructional Technology.

Charles B. Harris is Professor of English at Illinois State University, where he has chaired the English Department since 1979. A specialist in contemporary American literature, he is the author of two books: *Contemporary American Novelists of the Absurd* (College and University Press, 1971) and *Passionate Virtuosity: The Fiction of John Barth* (University of Illinois Press, 1983). His articles on recent fiction and the profession have appeared in numerous journals. Professor Harris served on the Association of Departments of English (ADE) Executive Committee from 1983 to 1986 and was elected President of the ADE for 1985–86. He currently chairs the ADE Ad Hoc Committee on the English Curriculum and is a member of the steering committee for the National Coalition of English Associations. In July 1987, he was one of sixty English teachers selected to praticipate in the three-week English Coalition Conference at the Aspen Institute's Wye Plantation in Maryland.

Gail E. Hawisher is Assistant Professor of English and Education at Purdue University, where she also edits *Computers and Composition,* a professional journal for writing teachers. Before receiving the Ph. D. from the University of Illinois at Urbana-Champaign, she was head of the English Department at a large high school in Columbus, Ohio. She is also coeditor of *Critical Perspectives on Computers and Composition Instruction,* a collection of readings published by Columbia University's Teachers College Press. Currently, she chairs the NCTE Subcommittee on Instructional Technology and Teacher Education and is a member of the NCTE Commission on the Preparation of English Teacher Educators. Her articles have appeared in the *English Journal, Research in the Teaching of English, Computers and Composition,* and *Collegiate Microcomputer.*

Andrea A. Lunsford is Professor of English and Vice Chair for Rhetoric and Composition at The Ohio State University. She has coauthored *The Four Worlds of Writing* and *The Preface to Critical Reading,* and has coedited *Essays on Classical Rhetoric and Modern Discourse.* Widely published in the history of rhetoric and composition, and on basic writing, literacy, and other issues relating to composition theory and rhetoric, Dr. Lunsford has recently coauthored a handbook for St. Martin's Press and is currently preparing a book-length study of collaborative writing. She has also edited *Alexander Bain's English Composition and Rhetoric.* Professor Lunsford was the 1989 Chair of the Conference on College Composition and Communication.

Maia Pank Mertz is Professor of English and Coordinator for Holmes Programs in the College of Education at The Ohio State University. Professor Mertz's research and publications focus on reader-response, the teaching of literature, the impact of popular culture on the English curriculum, and teacher preparation for the teaching of literature. Most recently, her work has dealt with teacher education reform and the impact of teacher testing on the teaching profession. In 1987 she chaired the NCTE Task force on Teacher Competency Issues, which examined the effects of standardized teacher examinations on retaining teachers, particularly minority teachers. Dr. Mertz has served on the NCTE Standing Committee on Research, the Conference on English Education Executive Committee, the NCTE Response to Literature Committee, and is the Current Chair of the NCTE Standing Committee on Teacher Preparation and Certification. Her articles have appeared in journals such as *Research in the Teaching of English, English Journal, English Education, Phi Delta Kappan,* and *Theory into Practice,* among others.

George E. Newell was a secondary school English teacher and is now Assistant Professor in the Department of Educational Studies at The Ohio State University. Formerly he directed the English Education Program and the Blue Grass Writing

Project at the University of Kentucky. His research interests include investigating the cognitive and linguistic demands of school tasks, especially writing; examining the kinds of instructional support provided for those tasks; and the assessing of skills and knowledge that result. He has had articles appearing in *Research in the Teaching of English,* the *Journal of Reading Behavior* and *Written Communication.* He holds the Ph. D. from Stanford University.

Martin Nystrand is Professor of English at the University of Wisconsin-Madison and Faculty Associate of the Wisconsin Center for Education, where he is a principal investigator at the National Center on Effective Secondary Schools. He is author of *The Structure of Written Communication: Studies in Reciprocity between Writers and Readers* (Academic Press, 1986) and editor of *What Writers Know: The Language, Process, and Structure of Written Discourse* (Academic Press, 1982) and *Language as a Way of Knowing* (The Ontario Institute for Studies in Education, 1977). Together with Adam Gamoran, he currently has a five-year grant from the U. S. Office of Educational Research and Improvement to study the effects of ability grouping on the quality of writing, reading, and discussion in eighth and ninth grade English and social studies.

Robert E. Probst is Professor of English Education at Georgia State University in Atlanta. He was before that an English teacher, both junior and senior high school, in Maryland, and Supervisor of English for the Norfolk, Virginia, public schools. Interested in the teaching of both writing and literature, he has written *Response and Analysis: Teaching Literature in Junior and Senior High School* (Boynton Cook, 1988 [originally published under another title by Merrill]) and was part of the team that prepared *New Voices,* a high school English textbook series published by Ginn. He has had articles appearing in *English Journal, Journal of Reading, Educational Leadership, The Clearing House,* and elsewhere.

He is a member of the NCTE where he has worked on the Committee on Research and the Commission on Reading, and is currently on the Board of Directors of the Adolescent Literature Assembly. He is also a Colleague and faculty member of the Creative Education Foundation.

Alan C. Purves, Director of the Center for Writing and Literacy and Professor of Education and Humanities at The University at Albany, State University of New York, received his A. B. from Harvard College and his M. A. and Ph. D. in English from Columbia University. He has taught at Columbia and Barnard Colleges, the University of Illinois, and Indiana University before coming to Albany. He has served in many professional organizations and has held office in the National Council of Teachers of English and The International Association for the Evaluation of Educational Achievement (IEA), of which he is currently chairman. He has written or edited some twenty-five books and seventy articles dealing with literature, written composition, reading, and measurement. Among his titles are *The Selected Essays of*

Theodore Spencer, Literature Education in Ten Countries, Evaluation of Learning in Literature, Achievement in Reading and Literature: The United States in International Perspective, Becoming Readers in a Complex Society, The Idea of Culture and General Education, and *Writing Across Cultures.*

Cynthia L. Selfe lives in Houghton, America, a tiny town in Michigan's remote Upper Peninsula. There Selfe serves as Associate Professor and Assistant Head of the Humanities Department at Michigan Technological University. In this strange and wonderful place, which receives between 200 and 400 inches of snow a year and is more than 100 miles from the nearest stoplight, Selfe studies the effects of computers on writers, writing processes, texts, and the communities that form among working communicators. She is author of *Computer-Assisted Instruction in Composition: Create Your Own,* a 1986 NCTE publication, and coeditor of *Critical Perspectives on Computers and Composition Instruction* published by Teachers College Press in 1989. In addition to being Chair of NCTE's Instructional Technology Committee, she co-edits *Computers and Composition,* a journal for writing teachers. She received the Ph. D. from The University of Texas at Austin.

R. Baird Shuman is Professor of English at the University of Illinois at Urbana-Champaign, where he has served as Director of Freshman Rhetoric and as Director of English Education. He has also taught at Duke University, San Jose State University, Drexel University, and the University of Pennsylvania, before which he was a secondary school English teacher. The author or editor of sixteen books, Shuman is now completing a critical biography of playwright William Inge. Among his other books are volumes on Clifford Odets and Robert Sherwood. He has also written *The First R: Fundamentals of Initial Reading Instruction* (1987), *Elements of Early Reading Instruction* (1979), (with Robert Krajewski) *The First Year Teacher: A Practical Guide to Problem Solving* (1979), and *Strategies for Teaching Reading: Secondary* (1978). Among the books he has edited are *Creative Approaches to the Teaching of English: Secondary* (1974), *Questions English Teachers Ask* (1977), *Educational Drama for Today's Schools* (1978), *Education in the 80's: English* (1981), and *The Clearing House: A Closer Look* (1984).

Anna O. Soter is Assistant Professor in English education at The Ohio State University. A Rotary International Foundation Fellow and a Connell Scholar while at the College of Education, University of Illinois, she has worked extensively with schools both in the United States and Australia on reading and writing related projects. She also participated in assessment of writing projects with Professor Alan C. Purves in the IEA study of written language assessment. Prior to her university work, she taught for fifteen years and chaired English Departments for ten years in Australia.

Connie Swartz Zitlow serves as Assistant Professor in English education at Ohio Wesleyan University where she teaches courses in language and literature materials, reading and writing methods, and young adult literature. She was named a NCTE

Promising Researcher Award Finalist for her dissertation, "A Search For Images: Inquiry With Preservice English Teachers." Her supervision work with student teachers and participation as a researcher in a project designed to promote faculty use of practice-centered inquiry have led to her current interest in teacher education reform and research efforts in teacher thinking.

Index